Liberal Order
and
Imperial Ambition

for Lidia

Liberal Order and Imperial Ambition

Essays on American Power and World Politics

G. John Ikenberry

polity

First published in 2006 by Polity Press

Polity Press
65 Bridge Street
Cambridge CB2 1UR, UK.

Polity Press
350 Main Street
Malden, MA 02148, USA

ISBN-10: 0-7456-3649-7
ISBN-13: 978-07456-3649-8
ISBN-10: 0-7456-3650-0 (pb)
ISBN-13: 978-07456-3650-4 (pb)

A catalogue record for this book is available from the British Library.

Typeset in 10.5 on 12 pt Times
by SNP Best-set Typesetter Ltd, Hong Kong
Printed and bound in Great Britain by the Maple-Vail Book Manufacturing Group

For further information on Polity, visit our website: www.polity.co.uk

Contents

Acknowledgments

The author and publisher gratefully acknowledge the permission granted to reproduce the copyright material in this book:

Chapter 1, originally published as "Rethinking the Origins of American Hegemony," *Political Science Quarterly*, vol. 104, no. 3 (Fall 1989): 375–400. Reproduced with the permission of the editors.

Chapter 2, originally published as "Socialization and Hegemonic Power" with Charles A. Kupchan, *International Organization*, vol. 44, no. 3 (Summer 1990): 283–315. Reproduced with the permission of the editors and Charles A. Kupchan.

Chapter 3, originally published as "The Nature and Sources of Liberal International Order" with Daniel Deudney, *Review of International Studies*, vol. 25 (April 1999): 179–96. Reproduced with the permission of the editors and Daniel Deudney.

Chapter 4, originally published as "Constitutional Politics in International Relations," *European Journal of International Relations*, vol. 4, no. 2 (June 1998): 147–77. Reproduced with the permission of Sage Publications Limited, © SAGE Publications and ECPR-European Consortium for Political Research, 1998.

Chapter 5, originally published as "American Power and the Empire of Capitalist Democracy," *Review of International Studies*, vol. 27 (December/January 2001–2): 191–212. Reproduced with the permission of the editors.

Chapter 6, originally published as "The Myth of Postwar Chaos," *Foreign Affairs*, vol. 75, no. 1 (March/April 1996): 79–91. Reproduced by permission of Foreign Affairs, © 1996 by the Council on Foreign Relations, Inc.

Chapter 7, originally published as "Getting Hegemony Right," *The National Interest* (Spring 2001): 17–24. Reproduced with the permission of the editors.

Chapter 8, originally published as "American Grand Strategy in the Age of Terror," *Survival* (Spring 2002): 19–34. Reproduced with the permission of the editors.

Chapter 9, originally published as "America's Imperial Ambition," *Foreign Affairs*, vol. 84, no. 5 (September/October 2002): 44–60. Reproduced by permission of Foreign Affairs, © 2002 by the Council on Foreign Relations, Inc.

Chapter 10, originally published as "The End of the Neo-Conservative Moment," *Survival* (Spring 2004): 7–22. Reproduced with the permission of the editors.

Chapter 11, originally published as "Is American Multilateralism in Decline?" *Perspectives on Politics*, vol. 1, no. 3 (Fall 2003): 533–50. Reproduced with the permission of the editors, © Cambridge University Press, 2003.

Introduction

The United States dominates the world as no state has done before. It emerged from the Cold War as the world's only superpower and no geopolitical or ideological contenders are in view. Europe is drawn inward and Japan is stagnant. US military bases and carrier battle groups ring the world. Russia is in a quasi-formal security partnership with the United States, and China has accommodated itself to US dominance, at least for the moment. For the first time in the modern era, the world's most powerful state can operate on the global stage without the counter-balancing constraints of other great powers. We have entered the American unipolar age.

But America has long been the world's most powerful country. Sixty years ago, the United States stepped forward after World War II to organize and lead a global Cold War alliance. It opened up the world economy and sponsored the creation of an array of multilateral institutions. This American-led order spanned Europe and Asia and established a thriving system of integrated markets and political partnerships.

Indeed, for over half a century the United States has not just been a superpower pursuing its interests; it has been a producer of world order. Over the decades, and with more support than resistance from other states, it has fashioned a distinctively open and rule-based international order. Its dynamic bundle of oversized capacities, interests, and ideals together constitute an "American project" with an unprecedented global reach. For better or worse, states today must operate in, comes to terms with, or work around this protean order.

This book of essays explores the theoretical, historical, and foreign policy dimensions of American power and postwar order. Written over the last decade and a half, these scholarly articles and policy essays form a sort of "intellectual arc" of inquiry. The early articles focus on the origins and foundational logic of America's postwar order-building project. The later articles reflect on its evolving character and fate in the aftermath of the Cold War, the rise of unipolarity, and the post-9/11 threat of global terrorism. The early essays – two of which are co-authored – provided preliminary thinking and arguments that eventually informed my book, *After Victory.*[1] The later essays are my attempt to make sense of the upheavals in the global system – and the Bush administration's controversial foreign policy – in light of my earlier theoretical arguments and policy convictions.

Taken together, the chapters explore four themes. The first theme concerns the sources and character of America's postwar liberal international system. Here I am interested in how the United States turned power into order and domination into legitimate authority. This is the classic question of how international orders get established. A second theme focuses on the role of institutions and political bargains within this order. This is the equally classic question of how international orders operate – and the way in which institutions play a role as tools to help states overcome uncertainty and insecurity. The third theme focuses on how the American postwar order has coped with dramatic changes in the wider global system. Here I am interested in the relevance and viability of America's liberal international orientation in the wake of shifts in the underlying distribution of power, interests, and threats – and the foreign policy "new thinking" of the Bush administration. The fourth theme concerns the future of multilateralism. The question here is as old as the study of international relations itself: namely, can state power – and in this instance, American unipolar power – coexist with an international order built on rules and law? The answer to this question will tell us a great deal about the likely character of world politics in the twenty-first century.

Lurking in the background of these essays is a general argument. The United States, together with allied European and East Asian partners, created a distinctive type of international order – organized around open markets, social bargains, intergovernmental institutions, and cooperative security. This political order was cemented by both the hegemonic power of the United States and the unusual bonds of cooperation that are possible among democracies. Today this order is in jeopardy. The United States is deeply ambivalent about making institutional commitments and binding itself to other states – ambivalence and hesitation that has been exacerbated by the end of the Cold War, American unipolarity, and new security threats. But the United States still possesses profound incentives to build and operate within a liberal rule-based order. Just as importantly, that order is now not simply an extension of American power and interests – it has taken on a life of its own. American power may rise or fall and its foreign policy ideology may wax and wane between multilateral and imperial impulses – but the wider and deeper liberal global order is now a reality to which America itself must accommodate.

Power and Hegemonic Order

International orders rise and fall and come and go. America had an extraordinary opportunity in the 1940s to build a global system. So what did it do and how did it do it? The first two essays in this volume – written at the very end of the Cold War – focus on these questions. In the late 1980s, one of the great debates in international relations concerned American hegemonic decline. Robert Gilpin, Stephen Krasner, and Charles Kindleberger pioneered thinking about how powerful states might act to order and stabilize economic and security relations.[2] The question soon became: how would the international system cope with what appeared to be the coming decline of American power? This was a grand question, but I became more interested in the prior issue: how was order created in the first place?

I was dissatisfied with the realist notion that drew straightforward lines between the rise of powerful states and the organization of the international system. Lots of questions loomed. How were America's material capabilities used in the process of creating rules and agreements? To what extent was the postwar system a product of American coercion and to what extent was it organized in a consensual manner by the participating states? Power realities dictated which states have the most to say about the organization of interstate relations after the war – but what accounted for the ideas that informed the exercise of state power?

My first answer to these questions – and the first essay in this volume, "Rethinking the Origins of American Hegemony" – essentially argues, in an echo of Karl Marx, that powerful states make international order but not entirely as they wish. In its efforts to work with Europe to organize the peace after World War II, the United States "got less than it wanted and more than it bargained for." America had formidable material capabilities but the process of translating this power into institutions and agreements took the US on a long journey into a negotiated peace settlement. The British were able to blunt and redirect some of the initial American proposals – but they were also able to pull the United States into a more direct and ongoing security relationship. The American desire for a legitimate and mutually satisfactory Atlantic partnership meant that power disparities would not determine more than the broad outlines of the peace.

My second answer to these questions – and the essay "Socialization and Hegemonic Power," which is co-authored by Charles Kupchan – follows the same logic but makes the argument in a more systematic and historically expansive way. Again the question was posed: how do hegemonic states assert control over weaker states? Or as the question is sometimes asked: what do hegemonic states do when they are being hegemonic? In this essay, Charles Kupchan and I want to know whether American hegemonic order is established primarily by the leading state's manipulation of material incentives or through the acceptance by elites in weaker and secondary states of the norms and purposes of the order. This process of the evolution in the substantive beliefs of elites in the desirability of the hegemonic order amounts to a process of socialization. We develop a set of hypotheses that allow us to distinguish between power as coercion and power as socialization in the order-building process – and we explore these hypotheses in historical cases of American diplomacy after World Wars I and II and in the British colonial experience in India and Egypt. In working through the empirical record, we came to argue that hegemonic orders do rely on the wielding of material incentives – but not entirely. The hegemonic state has incentives of its own to get elites in weaker and secondary states to "buy into" the order. This search for legitimacy helps explain what hegemonic states do with their power – and it helps account for the quality and durability of compliance in the wider political order.

This conceptualization of hegemony and socialization has been taken up by others who have also sought to probe the exercise of power and the diffusion of norms. It is a line of work that has become part of the so-called constructivist research agenda.[3] When these essays were written, the dominant image of international relations was defined by realist theory. The profession itself was seized by the structural realist vision of anarchy and order put forth by Kenneth Waltz.[4] Robert Gilpin offered an alternative realist vision of international order organized around the rise and decline of hegemonic orders.[5] My initial inquiry into the origins of the American postwar system revealed a more complex and reciprocal process of order formation. The pre-eminence of American power insured that the organization of relations after World War II would be decisively shaped by Washington. But power needs ideas and legitimacy – and these practical necessities opened the door to negotiation, compromise, and intellectual innovation.

Institutions and Political Bargains

If the American hegemonic order is held together by more than coercion, it is because that order is infused with institutions and political bargains. Indeed, two puzzles – situated historically before and after the Cold War – lead us to a direct focus on the institutional dimensions of the postwar order. The first puzzle is why the United States engaged in so much institution building after World War II. This is remarkable and unprecedented. Between 1944 and 1952 the United States engaged in an almost hyperactive effort at institution building – regional, global, economic, political, and security. The Bretton Woods institutions, the United Nations, the General Agreements on Tariffs and Trade (GATT), the North Atlantic Treaty Organization (NATO), and the US–Japan security pact were all established and served as cornerstones of the American-led order. The puzzle is why the United States decided – unlike past great powers – to build order around this array of institutions. Why did the US at the zenith of its power decide to embed itself in such a complex of rules, institutions, and partnerships? And why did other states agree to participate in this institutionalized order?

The other puzzle lies on the other side of the Cold War. Why did these institutions remain in place after the Cold War? The structural realist view is that the extraordinary degree of cooperation and partnership that flourished between the United States and its European and East Asian allies after World War II was a result of bipolarity and Cold War threats. The external threat of Soviet power was the critical ingredient for Western solidarity. The expectation follows immediately that with the end of the Cold War, the American-centered partnerships will unravel. The puzzle is that at least throughout the 1990s – and even today despite the crisis between Europe and the United States over Iraq – the dense web of cooperation between the Western democracies and the wider "free world" has remained in place. Indeed, the broad architecture of order that was put in place in the 1940s still provides the organizing logic of the core global order. Not only are Western Europe and Japan still tied to the United States in a multitude of ways, so too are Russia and China. This is a puzzle that the realist balance of power theory presents us. To unravel it, I suggest that we need to look more closely at the bargains and institutions inside this postwar order.

The third essay in this volume – "The Nature and Sources of Liberal International Order," co-authored with Daniel Deudney – is an attempt to sketch the contours of the liberal international order. It explicitly invokes realist theories of order as a foil for the elucidation of the "structural

liberal" logic of Western order. We argue that the post-Cold War international order does not seem to function in the way anticipated by classic
realist theory. Neither anarchy nor realist-style hegemony seems to be
generating the expected patterns of state behavior. In offering an alternative formulation of Western liberal order, we do not advance a specific
theory. We offer a series of basic characteristics or dimensions of
this order.

The first characteristic is the special "security binding" logic of relations
within the order. The United States and the other postwar democratic
powers – Britain, France, Germany, and Japan – tied themselves together
in alliance partnerships in ways that reduced the strategic insecurity and
uncertainty among them – thereby dampening or eliminating the anarchy-
driven sources of conflict and strategic rivalry that realist theory expects.
The second characteristic is the penetrated and reciprocal aspects of
American hegemony. The US is an open democratic polity with multiple
pathways leading from the outside into the center of the national government, thereby allowing weaker states to engage and influence the
American exercise of power. These institutional features of the American
system – both its domestic democratic system and the wider international
system it leads – provide access points that reduce the coercive domination
of the United States. American hegemony, in effect, takes on liberal characteristics. Together, security co-binding and penetrated hegemony create
incentives for other states to "bandwagon" rather than "balance" against
the United States.

This essay identifies additional dimensions of liberal order. The semi-
sovereign character of Germany and Japan is explicable in terms of the
binding security ties that allow these states to make a virtue out of a
postwar necessity – that is, to not acquire nuclear weapons but rather to
embed their security into a multilateral (Germany within NATO and the
EU) or bilateral (Japan within the US–Japan security pact) framework.
The open system of trade and investment is another dimension of liberal
order. Remarkably, the 1930s-style notions of zero-sum and relative gains
trade relations has given way to a system of open markets that has increasingly integrated the United States and its East Asian and European partners
into a single global complex. The "embedded liberal" compromise of the
early postwar era, noted by John Ruggie and others, has provided additional political cement for the wider liberal system.[6] Finally, the "civic
nationalism" of the United States and Europe has facilitated forms of
political identity that go beyond old-style nationalism. The complexity of
political identities is what is distinctive about the postwar liberal order.
Ethnic, racial, and religious identities are semi-privatized in the advanced

democratic societies which, in turn, allows for immigration, exchange, and transnational allegiances that tie these countries together. These aspects of liberal order are not definitive and they do coexist with more traditional – and realist-oriented – patterns of order.

Chapter 4, "Constitutional Politics in International Relations," provides a more elaborate and definitive theoretical argument about the institutional logic of the American-led postwar system. This is where I look more specifically at the institutional bargain that lay behind the settlements after wars between victors and weaker and defeated states – and where I sketch a theory of when, why, and how a political order with "constitutional characteristics" might emerge between sovereign states. In my view, the general problem of creating order in the aftermath of war is one of creating credible institutionalized restraints and commitments regarding the exercise of power. This is a problem that unfolds between a powerful state that wants to gain the advantages of winning the war and organizing the peace, and weaker and secondary states that worry about domination and exploitation by the strong. The argument I advance is that the character of the order that emerges after war hinges on the willingness and ability of the leading state to engage in strategic restraint. If the leading state is unwilling or unable to restrain its power and thereby negotiate mutually agreeable and legitimate rules and institutions between postwar states, the order will take on characteristics of either a balance of power or coercive hegemonic order. However, where leading states are able to credibly restrain and commit power and offer these restraints and commitments as political concessions within a negotiated settlement, a more complex and constitutional-like order is possible.

Seen in this light, the core of a liberal constitutional order is a set of fixed arrangements that reduce "the returns to power." That is, rules and institutions – credibly established – operate to make domination and exploitation by powerful states of weaker and secondary states less likely. Winning and losing in such an interstate political order starts to look more like winning and losing within domestic constitutional polities. Winners win and losers lose, but the stakes are not ultimate or existential – and the fortunes of specific states change and rotate. Under these circumstances, the old catastrophic dangers posed by anarchy, power, and domination are weakened, and possibilities emerge for more domesticated politics among nations.

This essay sketches the logic of this constitutional bargain between strong and weak states. The leading state has an incentive to offer institutionalized restraints and commitments. These restraints and commitments reduce its freedom of action but the institutionalized order that results serves to lock in its leading position for the long term. The limitations that are imposed on its exercise of power also pave the way for agreement by weaker and secondary states to participate willingly within the order. This reduces the costs that would otherwise be incurred by the leading state in enforcing compliance. Weaker and secondary states are obliged to operate according to established rules and institutions, but this buys them a more predictable order. They give up the option of balancing against or at least resisting the leadership of the most powerful state, but they receive assurances that their weaker position will not be exploited or entail threats to their existence. These are the elements of the institutional bargain that lie behind constitutional orders. This essay argues that while the post-1945 Western system manifests various logics of order, its patterns and character cannot be fully appreciated without some reliance on insights about constitutionalism.

In the essay "American Power and the Empire of Capitalist Democracy," I take my argument about the distinctive character of American-led order one step further. The first observation is simply that the United States emerged from the Cold War as the only superpower – the world has entered a unipolar era. My claim is that this American unipolar political formation is unusually durable because it is not based on the same simple exertion of power that allowed past hegemonic states to organize the geopolitical landscape. In effect, the order itself – built on the complex fusion of capitalist and democratic systems that cut across the advanced industrial world – is no longer supported by American power and leadership. The order has taken on a life of its own. If we live in an era of a "global empire," it is not essentially an American empire but rather an empire of capitalist democracy.

This is a very American-style, optimist essay. It contends that the United States has pulled something off that no other great power has accomplished: to preside over the emergence of a one-world order where all the parts of the globe are loosely integrated into a single governance system. Hence my claim: that American unipolarity is an expansive and highly durable political order. It is not a transitional phase in international relations but is a political formation with its own character and logic. Nor is it a political formation that falls easily into a particular historical category – empire, superpower, hegemonic order. American power is still at the core of this order, but it is an order with "deep foundations" that is sustained by more than material power capabilities. As a result, its political dynamics – and historical trajectory – are not intelligible simply by looking at the rise and decline of state power. The argument of this essay – written before September 11, 2001 – has certainly been put to the test in the years that followed.

Unipolarity and Bush Grand Strategy

Solidarity among the Western countries during the Cold War was not surprising. Explanations for the unprecedented political cooperation among these democratic states are – to use a term of art – overdetermined. Realists point to the unrelenting global Soviet threat which generated incentives for security cooperation. Liberals point to the economic and political incentives that brought America and Europe together to overcome the problems of the 1930s and build a stable order. But with the collapse of the Soviet Union and the end of bipolarity, debates ensued and theoretical expectations diverged about the coming shape of the post-Cold War world. Over the last decade a series of "shocks" to the postwar international system – Soviet collapse, the rise of American unipolarity, and 9/11 terrorism – have raised again and again these basic questions and sparked theoretical and policy controversies.

In "The Myth of Post-Cold War Chaos," I argue that expectations of conflict and breakdown in relations between the United States and Europe and Japan were wrong. The world that these countries had built over 50 years would not unravel even though the great existential threat of Soviet communism was gone. What was missing in the visions of conflict and breakdown in the West was a simple observation: that these countries had labored in the shadow of the Cold War to construct a democratic political order that was, at the very least, semi-independent in purpose and scope from their joint project of resisting Soviet power. The West had been constructed *for* something and not just *against* something. Indeed, there have been two postwar settlements. One was the famous settlement that created the Cold War containment order. This was an order built around deterrence, alliance cooperation, bipolarity, and containment of Soviet power. This is the order that ended with the fall of the Berlin Wall and the death of Soviet communism. The other settlement – less noticed or appreciated – was the settlement among the Western democracies. This entailed the creation of a new set of relations among these advanced postwar countries – constructing trade and political linkages and intergovernmental institutions for management of joint problems. Those that forecast breakdown and disarray missed the political *gravitas* of this intercontinental democratic capitalist community.

By the end of the 1990s, the debate was no longer about a post-Cold War return to a multipolar balance of power system. The new reality was American unipolarity. The United States had started the 1990s as the world's only superpower and it had a more prosperous decade than the other great powers. In the last years of the Clinton administration the question began to arise: how would the United States exercise its power in an historical moment when it had no serious geopolitical rivals? It is useful to remember that worries began to emerge even before the George W. Bush administration came to power about America's wavering commitment to global rules and institutions.[7] Clinton's Secretary of State Madeleine Albright famously proclaimed that the United States was the world's "indispensable power," which underscored the Clinton administration's determination to operate above the fray of great power politics. It is also worth remembering that then French Foreign Minister Hubert Vedrine made his comments about America as a "hyperpower" in early 1999. Indeed, it was candidate George W. Bush who argued in the presidential debates of 2000 that the United States needed to be a humble superpower.

The essay "Getting Hegemony Right" was written to remind others that American hegemony could either be a force for stability and cooperation – or the opposite. If American hegemony manifests "liberal" characteristics – openness, reciprocity, shared decision-making, voice opportunities, security binding – it would be accepted by most of the world as an attractive vehicle for organizing international relations. If the United States turns its back on this liberal mode of organization, the world will resist. The theme of this essay is the importance of integrating America's European and East Asian partners into Washington's strategic decision-making. It is when there is "stake-holder" hegemony that the system functions effectively for the United States. Without self-conscious American efforts to restrain its power, a dangerous political backlash from countries around the world might well ensue.

It was at this juncture that America experienced the September 11, 2001, terrorist attacks. This surprise attack triggered the most far-reaching rethinking of American foreign policy since the early Cold War. To the Bush administration and many policy intellectuals this signaled the end of the postwar era. A dangerous and darkly lurking new world of terrorism meant that the old American national security precepts and partnerships had to be transformed. Out with the old, in with the new. The essay "American Grand Strategy in the Age of Terror" argues: not so fast. My central thesis is that the world has actually arrived at an extraordinarily opportunistic moment. The great powers that had fought the Cold War – America, Germany, France, Great Britain, and Japan – were all tightly connected in economic, political, and security partnerships. Even more remarkably, China and Russia were seeking grand strategic pathways into this American-centered order. The rise of global terrorism – if this is the new global threat – actually can reinforce this post-Cold War nascent "concert of great powers." After all, the terrorists who threaten the United

States do not represent an ideology that any of the traditional great powers embrace. It is a transnational threat that lies outside the old geopolitical battlefields. After September 11, the United States began to mobilize its power – and soon it invaded Afghanistan – but this was the first time in American history when the mobilization of national power was not aimed at another great power.

The other theme of this essay is one that appears repeatedly in my later writing on American power and the war on terrorism, namely that a serious response to terrorism must lead the US back to the embrace – rather than rejection – of its postwar alliance partnerships and institutions of cooperation. The war on terrorism means more than the employment of American military power. It entails intelligence, sanctions, diplomacy, financial regulation, development aid, and a multitude of other ongoing efforts – all of which require extensive multilateral cooperation. This argument reinforces the general point that September 11 revealed a new type of threat to America and the world, but it did not undermine the virtues and importance of the American system of multilateralism and security cooperation. Quite the contrary.

The Bush administration did not share this view of the opportunities and necessities of a modern-day American-led concert of great power. In fact, September 11 brought to prominence within the American government a very different sort of grand strategic view. The essay "America's Imperial Ambition" is an effort to identify the ideas and policies of this radically different orientation. This orientation, often dubbed "neo-conservative," offers a vision of America as a unipolar state that operates above the old rules and institutions of the international system. In my view, this neo-imperial grand strategy is one in which the US arrogates to itself the global role of setting standards, determining threats, using force, and meting out justice. It is a vision in which sovereignty becomes more absolute for America even as it becomes more conditional for countries that challenge Washington's standards of internal and external behavior.

The essence of Bush's post-9/11 war on terrorism entailed two propositions: we need to kill the terrorists before they kill us, and you are either with us or against us. As President Bush announced in a joint session of Congress soon after the terrorist attacks: "Every nation, in every region, now has a decision to make. Either you are with us, or you are with the terrorists." Needless to say, there is not much in these exhortations to rally international support. In effect, the administration was telling countries large and small that their treatment by the world's most powerful state would hinge on their fidelity to Washington's campaign against terrorism. There was no positive vision of international order that other states could buy into. The Bush administration's more general impulse toward unilateralism and resistance to international rules, institutions, treaties, and commitments made it worse. In effect, Bush's war on terrorism released the United States from the discipline of international law and obligations but simultaneously put other countries under Washington's thumb, to be held to standards imposed by America.

These circumstances have created a deep crisis in America's global position – a crisis that has not yet abated. If American power is measured not only in terms of hard military power but also as a bundle of assets which include prestige, credibility, respect, and the ready support of allies, the United States has just witnessed a massive collapse of national power, perhaps the worst in the country's history. It is a crisis of legitimacy in which governments and people around the world have lost confidence in the leadership and moral authority of America.

The next essay – "The End of the Neo-Conservative Moment" – takes this argument one step further and argues that the grand strategic vision behind the Iraq war and the unilateral turn in Bush foreign policy failed. My argument is that the key ideas behind the neo-conservative vision – the assumptions, claims, and expectations – are incorrect and untenable. One mistaken view is the assumption that the "costs of unilateralism" are insignificant or that – despite their costs – they are worth incurring to achieve desired goals. In fact, one of the lessons that can already be drawn from the Iraq war and the more general disregard of the Bush administration for postwar multilateral rules and institutions is that the costs have been surprisingly high. Another mistaken view is the neo-conservative reading of the Reagan administration and the end of the Cold War. Their view is that the Soviet Union collapsed under the pressure of a Reagan-era defense build-up and heightened ideological warfare. Reagan succeeded because of his toughness. But the dramatic shifts in Soviet foreign policy and the end of the Cold War actually reveal how the liberal character, unity, and ultimate defensiveness of the West provided an array of "pulls and pushes" that helped guide the flow of change.[8] Finally, the neo-conservative assessment of American power – and its ability to alter the outside world through the use of force – is radically inflated. These and other flawed assumptions and claims are being painfully revealed today as the Bush administration foreign policy plays itself out. The Bush administration has launched the United States on a bold experiment – offering a new doctrine for running the world – but it has failed.

Future of Multilateralism

In the background of these debates about post-September 11 Bush foreign policy are ongoing scholarly and policy questions about unipolarity and the future of multilateralism. One question that looms is whether the unilateral turn in foreign policy is a momentary aberration in a deeply rooted and progressive American commitment to multilateralism and rule-based order, or if it is actually an epochal shift that will outlast the Bush administration and the Iraq debacle. In effect, the question is: does unipolarity select for unilateralism? This raises a more general set of research questions that focuses on the patterns of state behavior unleashed by American unipolarity. Unipolarity is a profoundly new type of international distribution of power, so it is not surprising that the debate is so intense regarding the political formation that is crystallizing around it.

The rise of unipolarity does alter America's position with other states. Increased power advantages give the United States more freedom of action. It is easier for Washington to say no to other countries or to go it alone. Growing power – military, economic, and technological – also gives the US more opportunities to control outcomes around the world, or at least attempt to do so. But unipolarity also creates problems of governance. Without bipolar or multipolar competition, it is not clear what disciplines or renders predictable American power. Other countries worry more than in the past about domination, exploitation, and abandonment. They may not be able to organize a counter-balancing alliance but they can resist and undermine American policies. Moreover, when countries confronting the US are democracies, their leaders may have electoral incentives not to bend to American pressure.[9]

The essay "Is American Multilateralism in Decline?" explores these emerging patterns of cooperation and unilateralism under conditions of unipolarity. I argue that the shift from bipolarity to unipolarity does have consequences for American foreign policy but that incentives still endure for the United States to support and operate within a loose rule-based system.

There are several aspects to American unipolar dilemmas. First, a unipolar distribution of power creates "legitimacy problems" for the lead state in a way that great powers operating in other power configurations – such as bipolar and multipolar orders – do not experience. And indeed, American unipolar power today is experiencing a legitimacy problem. In a bipolar or multipolar world, the legitimacy of state power is easier to achieve. During the bipolar Cold War struggle, American power was seen as legitimate by other states within its orbit because that power was embedded in mutual security pacts and put at the service of the common defense against Soviet communism. America was *primus inter pares* within a Free World partnership.

But power under conditions of unipolarity is more difficult to legitimate. It is easier for other states and peoples to ask basic questions about the rectitude and legitimacy of American power: why should the United States rule the system? What gives it the right to decide right and wrong, good and evil, or make and enforce rules? After the Cold War, the Clinton administration legitimated American power by championing globalization and open markets – engagement and enlargement were the watchwords. United States power was aligned with the progressive forces of capitalism and democracy. The Asian financial crisis and the anti-globalization movement have tarnished this legitimating cover for American power. The Bush administration has elevated the war on terrorism as the cutting edge of American foreign and master principle of international order. But fear of terrorism is not a sufficient legitimating cover for American power.[10]

Second, unipolarity also appears to have created problems in how the world sees the American provision of public goods. In the past, the United States provided global "services" – such as security protection and support for open markets – which made other states willing to work with rather than resist American pre-eminence. The public goods provision tended to make it worth while for these states to endure the day-to-day irritations of American foreign policy. But the trade-off seems to be shifting. Today, the United States appears to be providing fewer global public goods while at the same time the irritations associate with American dominance appear to be are growing.

It might be useful to think of this dynamic in this way: the United States is unique in that it is simultaneously both the provider of "global governance" – through what has tended in the past to be the exercise of "liberal" hegemony – and it is a great power that pursues its own national interest. America's liberal hegemonic role is manifest when it champions the World Trade Organization, engages in international rule or regime creation, or reaffirms its commitment to cooperative security in East Asia and Europe. Its great power role is manifest, for example, when it seeks to protect its domestic steel or textile industry – or when President Bush proclaims, as he did in the 2004 State of the Union message, that "the United States doesn't need a permission slip" to use force to protect its citizens. When it acts as a liberal hegemon, it is seeking to lead or manage the global system of rules and institutions; when it is acting as a nationalist great power, it is seeking to advance domestic interests and its relative power position.[11] Today, these two roles – liberal hegemon and nationalist great power – are increasingly in conflict.

In the end, I argue that there are three incentives for the United States to continue to operate within a loose multilateral order rather than simply disentangle itself from rules and institutions. The first incentive is functional demands for cooperation. American support for multilateralism is likely to be sustained – even in the face of resistance and ideological challenges to multilateralism within the Bush administration – in part because of a simple logic: as global economic interdependence grows, the need for multilateral coordination of policies also grows. The more economically connected that states become, the more dependent they are for the realization of their objectives on the actions of other states. A second incentive for American commitment to multilateralism stems from a grand strategic interest in preserving power and creating a stable and legitimate international order. This is the incentive that earlier essays in this volume explore in depth. The rise of unipolarity does not extinguish this overriding hegemonic incentive in legitimacy and stability. A final source of American multilateralism emerges from the policy itself. The United States has a distinctive understanding of the nature of political order. Its enlightenment and republican democratic tradition enshrines the rule of law as an essential aspect of the polity. The country's tradition of civic nationalism also reinforces this notion that the rule of law is the source of legitimacy and political inclusion. This tradition provides a background support for a multilateral-oriented foreign policy. America's past – its ideals and accomplishments – still weigh heavy on its future.

Conclusion

Since 2004, the Bush administration has implicitly acknowledged that its attempt to break out of the American postwar order has failed. It is attempting to recast its vision in the imagery of past liberal internationalist presidents – Wilson, FDR, Truman, and Kennedy. In his second inaugural address, Bush proclaimed that "America's national interests and our deepest beliefs are now one" – and he articulated a Truman-doctrine-like American commitment: "It is the policy of the United States to seek and support the growth of democratic movements and institutions in every nation and culture, with the ultimate goal of ending tyranny in our world."

But the big difference between Bush and the great liberal internationalist presidents is that Bush wants to promote democracy and freedom, while Wilson, FDR, Truman, Kennedy, and Clinton wanted to build liberal order. More precisely, they believed that you cannot really have one without the other – to spread democracy you must also deepen the liberal democratic order.

The Bush – and neo-conservative – view seems to be that you can do democratic engagement without building liberal order. One reason seems to be that, in their view, the character of regimes matters more than the institutions, treaties, and other aspects of international community that sit atop and bind together democratic states. If all the states of the world are democratic, you don't need a lot of international rules and institutions – you will get peace without a lot of international superstructure. This view is reinforced by the companion conservative view that resists compromising American sovereignty and national autonomy. In effect, democracy promotion is a goal partly because it will create an international environment that will free the US from the need to build and commit to multilateralism. Another argument the Bush administration and the neo-conservatives make is that democratic enlargement is in fact undermined by commitments to the current liberal order. The current liberal order, in their view, acts as a constraint on the use of US power which is needed to facilitate democratic enlargement.

Woodrow Wilson's view and that of the more "realist" liberal internationalist presidents – FDR, Truman, Kennedy, and Clinton – has been that democratic enlargement and liberal order must go together. One reason is that democracies share values and aspirations that can only be fully realized through a thriving liberal international order. Democratic "man" is a free individual and a citizen with civic sensibilities and responsibilities that cut across national borders. Secondly, and perhaps more importantly, liberal order is needed so as to generate the collective resources and cooperative efforts to sustain the long-term democratic enlargement agenda. Indeed, this is increasingly true: The "easy" cases of democratization have been achieved. After each wave of democratic enlargement, the remaining laggard states are increasingly tough cases – requiring the democratic world to concert their efforts. Democratic enlargement requires a "democratic village." Thirdly, the absence of an American commitment to liberal order – i.e. a commitment to multilateralism and rules-based relations – imposes too high a cost on the US in terms of encouraging balancing, resistance, and free riding by other democracies – and it undermines the legitimacy of the broader commitments to international and domestic liberalism.

In the end, the Bush administration's championing of liberal democratic values is incomplete. Bush gives voice to the spread of democracy but little to the values, institutions, and mutual responsibilities of the wider democratic community. Bush wants to "extend the benefits of freedom across the globe" and "actively work to bring the hope of democracy" to "every corner of the globe" – but does he want to strengthen and operate within the liberal international order that is brought to life by the spread of democracy? What separates Bush from Wilson, Roosevelt, Truman, Kennedy, and Clinton – and Reagan and Bush Sr. for that matter – is his administration's inattention to the obligations, commitments, and restraints that come with a thriving international democratic community.

These essays seek to show that America has accomplished something extraordinarily special in the 60 years since the end of World War II. It is an international order more durable and complex than realist theory can explain and more successful than neo-conservatives can appreciate. American power and liberal order share an historical moment; they are tied together and rely each other. America's post-September 11 foreign policy has sought to deny this reality, but the global politics of recent years has demonstrated otherwise – power and liberal order are of one piece.

Notes

1 G. John Ikenberry, *After Victory: Institutions, Strategic Restraint and the Rebuilding of Order after Major War* (Princeton: Princeton University Press, 2001).

2 Robert Gilpin, *War and Change in World Politics* (New York: Cambridge University Press, 1981); Stephen D. Krasner, "State Power and the Structure of International Trade," *World Politics* 28 (1976): 317–47; and Charles P. Kindleberger, *The World in Depression: 1929–1939* (Berkeley: University of California Press, 1973).

3 See Alastair Iain Johnston, "Treating International Institutions as Social Environments," *International Studies Quarterly* 45: 4 (December 2001): 487–516. On the constructivist tradition, see John Ruggie, *Constructing the World Polity: Essays on International Institutionalization* (New York: Routledge, 1998); Martha Finnemore, *National Interests in International Society* (Ithaca: Cornell University Press, 1996); and Alex Wendt, *Social Theory of International Politics* (New York: Cambridge University Press, 1999).

4 Kenneth Waltz, *Theory of International Politics* (Reading, Mass.: Addison-Wesley, 1979).

5 Gilpin, *War and Change.*

6 John Gerard Ruggie, "International Regimes, Transactions, and Change: Embedded Liberalism in the Postwar Economic Order," *International Organization* 36 (1982): 379–415. See also G. John Ikenberry, "Creating Yesterday's New World Order: Keynesian 'New Thinking' and the Anglo-Postwar Settlement," in Judith Goldstein and Robert O. Keohane, eds., *Ideas and Foreign Policy: Beliefs, Institutions, and Political Change* (Ithaca: Cornell University Press, 1993), pp. 57–86.

7 See Stewart Patrick and Shepard Forman, eds., *Multilateralism and US Foreign Policy: Ambivalent Engagement* (New York: Lynne Rienner Publishers, 2002).

8 See Daniel Deudney and G. John Ikenberry, "The International Sources of Soviet Change," *International Security* 16: 3 (Winter 1991/2): 74–118; Deudney and Ikenberry, "Soviet Reform and the End of the Cold War: Explaining Large-Scale Historical Change," *Review of International Studies* 17 (Summer 1991): 225–50; and Deudney and Ikenberry, "Who Won the Cold War?" *Foreign Policy* 87 (Summer 1992): 123–38.

9   Efforts to sketch the emerging politics of unipolarity include: Ethan Kapstein and Michael Mastanduno, eds., *Unipolar Politics: Realism and State Strategies after the Cold War* (New York: Columbia University Press, 1999); and G. John Ikenberry, ed., *America Unrivaled: The Future of the Balance of Power* (Ithaca: Cornell University Press, 2002).

10 Commentators on the left, right, and center have identified a legitimacy crisis. See Perry Anderson, "Force and Consent," *New Left Review*, 17 (September–October 2002); Robert Kagan, "A Tougher War for the US is One of Legitimacy," *New York Times*, January 25, 2004; and Zbigniew Brzezinski, *The Choice: Domination or Leadership* (New York: Basic Books, 2004).

11 For a useful discussion, see Bruce Cronin, "The Paradox of Hegemony: America's Ambiguous Relationship with the United Nations," *European Journal of International Relations* 7: 1 (2001): 103–30.

Part I

Constitutionalism and Liberal Hegemony

1

Rethinking the Origins of American Hegemony

In recent years no topic has occupied the attention of scholars of international relations more than that of American hegemonic decline. The erosion of American economic, political, and military power is unmistakable. The historically unprecedented resources and capabilities that stood behind United States early postwar diplomacy, and that led Henry Luce in the 1940s to herald an "American century," have given way to an equally remarkable and rapid redistribution of international power and wealth. In the guise of theories of "hegemonic stability," scholars have been debating the extent of hegemonic decline and its consequences.[1]

Although scholars of international political economy have analyzed the consequences of American hegemonic decline, less effort has been directed at examining the earlier period of hegemonic ascendancy. Theorists of hegemonic power and decline pass rather quickly over the early postwar period. In rather superficial fashion, it is assumed that the United States used its power to organize the operation of the non-communist international system – to "make and enforce the rules for the world political economy" as one scholar put it.[2] While the rest of the industrialized world lay in economic and political ruin, American resources and capabilities were at their peak. Out of these historical circumstances, the conventional view suggests, the United States got its way and created a postwar order of its choosing.

This conventional view, wielded by those scholars more interested in hegemonic decline, requires closer attention; and so it is useful to re-examine the origins and character of American power in the early postwar era. The questions are several: How was US hegemonic power used after World War II in constructing the postwar world order? How successful was the United States in creating a postwar order of its choosing? What did the United States want and what did it get in the early postwar years? Most importantly, what does a hegemonic state, such as the United States, do when it is being hegemonic?

The answers to these questions require us to rethink the nature of American hegemonic power. I argue that the United States got both less than it wanted and more than it bargained for in the early postwar period. In terms of the ideals and plans it originally articulated, the United States got much less than it wanted; in terms of direct involvement in leading the postwar Western system, it got much more involved than it wanted. The United States was clearly hegemonic and used its economic and military position to construct a postwar order. But that order was not really of its own making. There was less exercise of coercion than is commonly assumed in the literature on hegemonic power, and where it was used, it was less successful than often thought.

I want to make three general points. First, the early efforts by the United States to build a postwar liberal multilateral system largely failed. Those efforts, in part attractive to the United States because they did not require a direct political or military presence in Europe, failed because of the rise of the East–West struggle and the underestimated problems of postwar economic and political reconstruction in Europe. Second, at each step along the way, the United States sought to minimize its direct (that is, formal, hierarchical) role in Europe. It was the European governments that sought to elicit and influence the projection of US power into Europe – and they did so primarily for security and resource reasons. In short, US hegemony in Europe was largely an empire by invitation. Third, while European nations sought to promote US involvement in Europe, they also acted to rework the liberal, multilateral ideas that initially propelled the United States during and after World War II. In effect, the European nations successfully modified liberal multilateralism into a welfare state liberalism (or embedded liberalism). The United States tried to use its power to create a system that would allow it to stay out of Europe – a sort of self-regulating and automatic international political economy. This failed, and the United States was drawn into a more direct role in Europe, defending a system that the Europeans themselves effectively redefined.

This essay traces the evolution of US policy as it reveals the mechanisms and limits of hegemonic power. US policy traveled through different phases: the one world ideals of liberal multilateralism (1941–7); the shift to a two worlds concept and the attempt to build a United Europe (1947–50); and the subsequent emergence of an ongoing and direct American political and security presence in Europe – an empire by invitation. A close historical reading of policy change suggests the need to rethink the nature and limits of US hegemonic power.

Theories of Hegemonic Power

The central claim of hegemonic stability theory is that a single Great Power is necessary to create and sustain order and openness in the international political economy. Accordingly, *Pax Britannica* and *Pax Americana* both represent historical eras when a hegemonic power held sway and used its dominant position to ensure an orderly and peaceful international system. Reflecting this position, Robert Gilpin argues that "Great Britain and the United States created and enforced the rules of a liberal international economic order."[3] Likewise, as the power of these hegemonic nations declines, so also does the openness and stability of the international economic system. The decline of Britain's nineteenth-century order foreshadowed the decline of America's postwar system. In each era it was the dominant role of the hegemonic nation that ensured order and liberal relations among nations.

This thesis draws powerful conceptual links between the rise and decline of nations and the structure of international relations. Scholarly interest in this type of argument was stimulated by the writings of Charles Kindleberger and Robert Gilpin. In a study of the sources of the Great Depression, Kindleberger argued that the stability of the pre-World War I international political economy rested on the leadership of Britain.[4] This leadership role involved the provision of a variety of collective goods, in particular the willingness of Britain to extend credit abroad and to maintain open markets at home. In the midst of falling commodity prices beginning in 1927 and the emerging shortage of international credit, the United States failed to act in a counter-cyclical manner to reverse the flow of funds and raised protectionist barriers. The collapse of the system in the interwar period was due to the absence of a hegemonic leader able and willing to maintain open markets for surplus goods and capable of maintaining the flow of capital. Kindleberger argues that the return to mercantilist relations in the interwar period was largely due to the inability of a weakened Britain to continue to play this leadership role and the unwillingness of the United States to take up these international responsibilities.

Similarly, Robert Gilpin developed a theory of global leadership emphasizing the active role of the hegemonic nation in creating and sustaining international economic and political order.[5] The rise of a hegemonic nation, Gilpin argues, "resolves the question of which state will govern the system, as well as what ideas and values will predominate, thereby determining the ethos of succeeding ages."[6] In this formulation, the hegemonic nation dominates the creation of the rules and institutions that govern international relations in a particular age. Gilpin's argument was that Britain undermined its own economic base of hegemonic power by investing heavily in overseas production at the expense of its own economy.[7] In the twentieth century, moreover, the United States was in danger of repeating the cycle of hegemonic decline and instability.[8]

In these studies and in the literature on hegemonic stability that they continue to inspire, attempts are made to find systematic links between the prevailing distribution of power (that is, military capabilities, control over trade, capital, and raw materials) and the organization of international political and economic processes. In doing so, these theories share several assumptions. First, they tend to conceive of power in traditional resource terms. Reflecting this position, Robert Keohane defines hegemony as "preponderance of material resources."[9] Thus, the constitutive elements of hegemonic power, as it relates to the world political economy, include control over raw materials, markets, and capital as well as competitive advantages in highly valued goods. Second, according to this perspective, these material resources provide the means for the hegemon to "make and enforce the rules for the world political economy."[10] Power is exercised by the hegemon primarily through the use of coercion, inducements, or sanctions. In effect, power is manifest as arm twisting.

While sharing these basic assumptions, scholars working in this tradition disagree over the manner in which hegemonic power is exercised.[11] Some writers, such as Kindleberger, see that power as basically benign, centering around the provision of public goods and leadership.[12] The image of the hegemon in this formulation is that of an enlightened leader, submerging narrow and short-term national interests to the preservation of a well-ordered and mutually beneficial international system. Others stress the importance of self-regarding actions by the hegemon directed at the creation and enforcement of the essential rules of the system.[13] Here the image is of a much more coercive hegemon, structuring the system to strengthen its own international economic position.

The debate within this literature tends to focus on the implications of the loss of American hegemonic power. The questions at this level are twofold. One concerns the manner and extent to which the loss of hegemonic power has impacts on international regimes. The debate here is about how autonomous and powerful regimes may be as an independent force for order and openness, even with the declining hegemon playing a less constructive role.[14] A second debate asks the prior question of the extent to which the United States has in fact lost its hegemonic capabilities.[15]

This literature provides fertile ground for research on American power in the postwar period by drawing bold lines between the rise and decline of nations and the international political economy. Its power is in its simplicity, and the images it presents are evocative. Nonetheless, it suffers from at least two problems – one theoretical and the other historical. Theoretically, the literature suffers from the absence of a clear theoretical understanding of the manner in which hegemonic power is manifest as it promotes international order and openness. The mechanisms and the texture of hegemonic power have not been captured in the literature. Susan Strange notes that "we have not clearly understood the alternative ways hegemons exercise power and the alternative uses to which their power may be put."[16] What factors determine when and how the rich and militarily strong nations are able to convert their power into hegemonic domination? Through what mechanisms and processes does power manifest itself? Why do some states come to accept, even invite, the rule of the hegemon, while others resist? And how do the goals of the hegemon change in the process of building international order? These questions remain unanswered because the focus of hegemonic stability theory remains fixed on the material resources of power and fails to explore the larger dimensions of power.

The second problem is historical. As noted above, the literature on hegemonic stability passes very briefly over the early phases of the cycle of rise and decline. In particular, it is assumed that the rules and institutions that emerged in the early postwar period are essentially the creations of the United States. The unprecedented position of the United States gave it a unique historical license to create international order on its own terms, or so it is thought. We are left only to trace the course of that power and analyze the fate of the rules and institutions it fathered. This image is a distortion: it is, to borrow Dean Acheson's memorable phrase, a view that is "clearer than the truth." And it serves to mislead the subsequent inquiry into the processes of hegemonic decline. If the capabilities of the United States in the early postwar period were less overpowering than commonly assumed, and if that power was exercised in less direct ways, this is important for the way we are to judge the current period of decline.

The limits of American postwar power

Viewed in terms of material capabilities, the United States did occupy an overwhelmingly powerful position at the close of the war. The disparity in resources and capabilities was huge, not only in general aggregate economic and military terms, but also in the wide assortment of resources the United States had at its disposal. As early as 1900 the United States was already the world's largest industrial producer; on the eve of World War I the United States had twice the share of world industrial production as Britain and Germany, its nearest industrial rivals. This trend toward economic dominance was rendered more pronounced by the war itself, which destroyed the industrial base of the European economies and further expanded the American counterpart.[17]

The unprecedented nature of the American position is reflected in comparisons with British economic strength in the nineteenth century. While the British in 1870, at the zenith of their power, possessed 32 percent of the global distribution of industrial production, the United States held 48 percent of the global share in 1948. The scope of British and American power, in their respective eras, is often found to be similar; yet in terms of the preponderance of material resources, American power was much greater.

As the hegemonic account of the early postwar period suggests, the United States did employ its resources to help shape the global political and economic order. American oil reserves were used in the 1950s and 1960s to make up for global shortfalls triggered by a series of crises and embargoes in the Middle East. Lend-lease arrangements and loans were used to influence British commercial policy immediately after the war. Foreign aid was used to influence European monetary policy in the 1950s.[18] An entire range of postwar rule-making and institution-building exercises were influenced and supported by the American resort to inducements and coercion, all backed by US resource capabilities.

Closer historical scrutiny of the period suggests that the absence of success by the United States in implementing its liberal designs for order was more pervasive than the hegemonic account allows. American officials consistently were forced to modify their plans for a liberal, multilateral order; and they often found themselves at a loss in attempting to draw others into such a system.

In the various commercial negotiations after the war, the United States was unable or unwilling to pursue consistent liberal policies. The most ambitious efforts at trade liberalization, embodied in the International Trade Organization proposal, were blocked by the United States Congress.[19] The General Agreement on Tariffs and Trade (GATT) that did survive was less extensive, contained escape clauses and exemptions, and left agriculture trade outside the multilateral framework. In areas such as maritime rights and shipping, as Susan Strange notes, the United States also pursued less than liberal policies.[20] Moreover, despite the unprecedented power position of the United States, holding the dollars and relief funds desperately needed in Britain and on the continent, American officials were less than successful in persuading Europe to embrace US policies. In a recent study, Michael Mastanduno finds that the United States was surprisingly ineffective in convincing Europe to adopt its hardline East–West trade strategies.[21] Moreover, the US was unable to push the European governments toward full-scale economic integration, despite its continued efforts and the massive aid of the Marshall Plan.

From Liberal Multilateralism to a United Europe

The unprecedented opportunity for United States to construct a postwar international order congenial with its interests and ideals was not wasted. The order that took shape in the late 1940s, however, was not what wartime planners had envisaged or sought to implement during and immediately after the war. The one world of American wartime planning gave way to efforts to build Europe into an independent center of global power; these revised plans, signaled by the Marshall Plan, in turn gave way to a bipolar system and the active courtship by Europe of American hegemonic leadership.

The chief focus of wartime planners was the construction of a postwar economy based on liberal, multilateral designs. The primacy of economic planning reflected both principle and prudence. It was part of the liberal faith that if the economic foundation were properly laid, the politics would follow. "If goods can't cross borders, soldiers will" was the slogan of the time, capturing the liberal faith.

The absence of postwar political and military planning also followed from more explicit wartime constraints. Franklin D. Roosevelt's vision of Great Power postwar cooperation held sway, an approach difficult to break with as long as the war persisted. Well into 1947 the idea that postwar order would be one world, with collective security and a liberal international economy, continued to drive policy in the Roosevelt and Truman administrations.

Domestic considerations, moreover, made a large-scale peacetime military commitment to Europe and a spheres-of-influence policy difficult to sustain.[22] A liberal, multilateral system would allow the United States to project its own ideals onto a world where depression and war had clearly demonstrated the bankruptcy of European ideas of spheres of influence and economic nationalism. If the United States could no longer isolate itself from the affairs of Europe, it would need to alter the terms of international politics. Only on this basis would congressional and public opinion allow the United States to play an internationalist role. A liberal, multilateral system, once established, would be self-regulating and would not require direct American involvement in Europe. For an American public eager to see its troops return home, ideals and prudence reinforced the initial American designs for postwar order.

The failure of liberal multilateralism

The tenets of liberal multilateralism were several: trade and financial relations are best built around multilateral rather than bilateral or other partial arrangements; commercial relations are to be conducted primarily by private actors in markets; and states are to become involved in setting the domestic and international institutional framework for trade and financial relations, both participating in liberalizing international negotiations and facilitating domestic adjustment to international economic change.[23]

American officials involved in economic planning in the Departments of State and Treasury were strikingly in accord on the need for the creation of international institutions to support liberal, multilateral economic relations. All were influenced by the failures after World War I: the lack of preparations, the failure of American participation in the League of Nations, the inadequacy of attention to economic problems.[24] "The postwar planners were united in their determination to break with the legacy of economic nationalism. . . . They recognized that the United States, despite its comparative self-sufficiency, had a very great stake in the economic well-being of the rest of the world, not only because it needed foreign markets for the produce of its factories and farms, but because it needed a healthy environment on which to base its efforts at world peace."[25]

Most of the American wartime efforts to insure a liberal, multilateral system were directed at Britain. British economic planners were generally sympathetic to American liberal, multilateral ideas; but outside the government, political groups and individuals were profoundly divided. On the Left, free markets were associated with unemployment and social injustice. Segments of British industry feared competition with American industry. On the Right, liberal multilateralism was a threat to the Imperial Preference system (providing privileged trade relations among commonwealth nations) and the remains of the British Empire.[26] In various ways these groups favored national, bilateral, or regional economic relations.

Directed primarily at dismantling British Imperial Preferences, American officials resorted to several bargaining tools and advantages. In 1941 Lend-Lease negotiations, the United States sought to tie aid to the removal of discriminatory British trade practices.[27] Compromises were achieved, and the British were able to resist a firm commitment to multilateral principles.[28]

The most far-reaching discussions between the United States and Britain over the principles and mechanisms of postwar economic order were agreed upon at the 1944 Bretton Woods conference in New Hampshire.[29] In these monetary negotiations, the British-American differences were considerable in regard to the provision for liquidity and the allocation of responsibility for adjustment between creditor and debtor countries. The British emphasized the primacy of national control over fiscal and monetary policy, the importance of biasing the arrangements toward economic expansion, and the need for a large international reserve and relatively easy terms of access to adjustment funds.

In the compromise agreement that created the charters of the International Monetary Fund and the International Bank for Reconstruction and Development (World Bank), major differences of perception remained between the British and the Americans. In the American Senate debate, administration officials gave the impression that the institutional foundations had been laid for a liberal, multilateral system. Further funds would not be necessary for British economic reconstruction, and a British commitment to nondiscrimination had been achieved. The British, for their part, understood that the United States had committed itself to helping Britain in what would be a lengthy economic transition period, and that the American government would make the sacrifices necessary to insure postwar economic expansion.[30]

At the same time that British–American negotiations dealt with monetary arrangements, the framework for international trade was also debated. In 1945 a set of proposals were worked out between the two countries on commercial policy. British reluctance to endorse the full array of American proposals for nondiscriminatory trade and multilateral tariff reductions was similar to that in the monetary area. The British were not prepared to eliminate the Imperial Preference arrangement. Concerns about employment and economic stability made the British cautious of a full-blown, liberal trading system.[31]

Further efforts by the United States to use its economic pre-eminence to alter British commercial and monetary practices came during consideration of the British loan in 1945–6. The core of this effort was to gain a British pledge to lift discriminatory controls earlier than mandated by the Bretton Woods agreement. Negotiations over the British loan provided the most coercive use of American power for liberal, multilateral purposes during this period. Reflecting the attitude of Congress on this issue, a congressional report argued that "the advantages afforded by the United States loans and other settlements are our best bargaining asset in securing political and economic concessions in the interest of world stability."[32] The British found little room to reject the conditions of the loan.[33]

Under the terms of the Anglo-American Financial Agreement, the British were obliged to make sterling externally convertible. Yet this action led in only six weeks to a massive drain on British reserves, forcing the suspension of convertibility. Despite its commanding bargaining position, the United States was unable to bring Britain into a multilateral order.

Moreover, the chief political strength of the British (and the Europeans generally) in resisting American designs was their economic weakness. The early move toward multilateralism would not be possible.

Throughout the 1944–7 period, the United States attempted to build a framework for international economic relations with the reconstruction of multilateral trade as its centerpiece. This objective largely failed. The most basic obstacle in the way of American policy was the economic and political dislocation of the war itself. The American proposals required, as Richard Gardner maintains, a reasonable state of economic and political equilibrium:

> The multilateral system could not be achieved unless individual nations were in approximate balance with the world as a whole. Unfortunately the post-war planners did not foresee the full extent of the measures necessary to achieve such balances after the destruction and dislocation of the Second World War. . . . The institutions they built for the achievement of multi-lateralism were not designed to withstand the unfavorable pressures of the post-war transition period.[34]

The objectives of the hegemonic power were not in balance with the power and influence at its disposal.

Moreover, in the rush to international economic rule-making, important differences were masked concerning the proper role of governments in promoting full employment, price stability, and social welfare. These differences would reappear as the transition period of reconstruction and alliance building ended in the late 1940s.

Finally, there was the problem of the emergence of US–Soviet hostilities. Ernst H. Van Der Beugel notes: "The political hopes of the United States were shattered by the nature of Soviet policy. The total ruin of Europe destroyed the hope of economic stability."[35] Taken together, the early efforts to usher in a period of liberal multilateralism were thwarted by the same forces that destroyed the wartime vision of one world. American officials were determined not to repeat the errors of World War I, but the plans themselves would need revision. In the end, as Richard Gardner notes, the assumptions of an early return to political and economic equilibrium were unfounded.[36] In political terms, the postwar world was moving toward two worlds, not one. In economic terms, the Europeans suffered from a severe dollar shortage, importing as much as seven times the value of goods they were exporting to the United States.

The Marshall Plan and a European third force

As the difficulties of implementing the liberal, multilateral proposals became evident, American policy began to involve efforts to bolster the political and economic foundations of Europe – to create in effect a third force. Burton Berry, a career Foreign Service officer, noted in July 1947 that it was time to "drop the pretense of one world."[37] The need to search for a new approach to Europe was underscored by State Department official Charles Bohlen:

> The United States is confronted with a condition in the world which is at direct variance with the assumptions upon which, during and directly after the war, major United States policies were predicated. Instead of unity among the great powers – both political and economic – after the war, there is complete disunity between the Soviet Union and the satellites on one side and the rest of the world on the other. There are, in short, two worlds instead of one. Faced with this disagreeable fact, however much we may deplore it, the United States in the interest of its own well-being and security and those of the free non-Soviet world must reexamine its major policy objectives.[38]

American officials were forced to attend to the balance of power in Europe. Accordingly, the new policy emphasis – embodied in the proposals for a European Recovery Program (what became known as the Marshall Plan) – was to establish a strong and economically integrated Europe.[39] Importantly, the policy shift was not to a sphere-of-influence approach with a direct and ongoing American military and political presence in Europe. Rather, the aim was to build Europe into an *independent* center of military and economic power, a third force.

This new policy was advanced by several groups within the State Department.[40] The new emphasis on building centers of power in Europe was a view George Kennan had already held, and it was articulated with some vigor by Kennan's Policy Planning staff, newly organized in May 1947. "It should be a cardinal point of our policy," Kennan argued in October 1947, "to see to it that other elements of independent power are developed on the Eurasian land mass as rapidly as possible in order to take off our shoulders some of the burden of 'bi-polarity.' "[41]

Kennan's Policy Planning staff presented its first recommendations to Secretary of State George Marshall on May 23, 1947. Their emphasis was not on the direct threat of Soviet activities in Western Europe, but on the war-ravaged economic, political, and social institutions of Europe that made communist inroads possible. An American effort to aid Europe "should be directed not to combating communism as such, but to the restoration of the economic health and vigor of European society."[42] In a later memorandum the Policy Planning staff argued that the program should take the form of a multilateral clearing system to lead to the reduction of tariffs and trade barriers and eventually to take the form of a European Customs Union.[43] Moreover, the Policy Planning staff argued that the initiative and responsibility for the program should come from the Europeans themselves. This group clearly envisaged a united and economically integrated Europe standing on it own apart from both the Soviet sphere and the United States.[44] "By insisting on a joint approach," Kennan later wrote, "we hoped to force the Europeans to think like Europeans, and not like nationalists, in this approach to the economic problems of the continent."[45]

Another group of State Department officials working on European recovery prepared a memorandum of major importance in May 1947 that outlined objectives of American foreign aid.[46] The chief objective of US policy, they argued, should be to strengthen the political and economic countries of Europe and by so doing create the conditions in Europe to induce the Soviets to negotiate with the West rather than continue a policy of unilateral expansion. The objective was to foster a strong and economically integrated Europe. Moreover, the memorandum argued that US policy should be directed at increasing the Western orientation of European leaders. In France, Italy, and Germany, in particular, policy should be directed at preventing leaders from drifting to the extreme Left or Right. A European recovery program, these officials argued, would need to stress political and ideological as well as economic objectives. In summarizing the document, Beugel notes that in meeting these objectives a "purely economic program would be insufficient. Non-communist Europe should also be provided with possible goals to help fill the present ideological and moral vacuum. The only possible ideological content of such a program was European unity."[47] The idea of a united Europe was to provide the ideological bulwark for European political and economic reconstruction.

Other State Department voices echoed the call for a shift in policy. Under-Secretary of State William Clayton returned from Europe on May 19 alarmed by the economic distress of Europe. In a memorandum to Acheson and Marshall, Clayton argued that the United States had underestimated the destruction of Europe's economy and stressed the need for immediate and large-scale action.[48] On May 8 Under-Secretary Acheson took the occasion of a public speech to outline the imperatives of European recovery and foreshadowed the Marshall Plan.[49]

The public turning point in US policy came on June 5, 1947, with Marshall's speech at Harvard University. The American government was now ready to play a much more direct and systematic role in European reconstruction. Yet State Department officials, in a theme echoed throughout this period, were insistent that European leaders themselves take responsibility for organizing the program. At a State Department meeting on May 29, 1947, for example, Kennan "pointed out the necessity of European acknowledgement of responsibility and parentage in the plan to prevent the certain attempts of powerful elements to place the entire burden on the United States and to discredit it and us by blaming the United States for all failures." Similarly, Bohlen noted that the United States had to balance the "danger of appearing to force 'the American way' on Europe and the danger of failure if the major responsibility is left to Europe." The United States would need to make it clear to the Europeans, Bohlen argued, that "the only politically feasible basis on which the United States would be willing to make the aid available is substantial evidence of a developing overall plan for economic cooperation by the Europeans themselves, perhaps an economic federation to be worked out over 3 or 4 years."[50]

A policy of fostering European independence rather than a spheres-of-influence policy had both practical and ideological considerations. Within the Truman administration some officials stressed the policy's importance in strengthening European democracies against communist subversion. Others focused on its usefulness in rebuilding Franco-German relations. Still others found the policy important in promoting expanded production and stability of the European economy.

There were also domestic political reasons for administration support for a united Europe. Congress and American public opinion were in 1947 still wary of permanent political and military commitments to Europe. Such domestic considerations are evident in discussions by Truman administration officials as they prepared to sell the Marshall Plan aid program to Congress. In the foreign assistance legislation that funded the European Recovery Program, Congress made greater European unification a condition for aid.[51]

The idea of a united Europe also fit well with American ideals. "The vague uneasiness and even irritation about the fragmentation of the old world and the genuine desire to transplant the American image to the shattered European countries were translated into a plan and subsequent action." Moreover, State Department officials felt that by encouraging independence and self-determination in Europe, the emergence of democratic institutions would be more likely to succeed. John Gaddis summarizes this notion: "the view in Washington persisted throughout the late 1940s that the viability of political systems depended in large part upon their autonomy, even spontaneity. For this reason, Americans were willing to tolerate a surprising amount of diversity within the anti-Soviet coalition."[52]

The European Recovery Program put the economic and political reconstruction of Europe into a security framework. It was at this juncture that Kennan's ideas most resonated with official US policy. The crisis of Europe, according to these officials, was not due to the pressure of communist activities. Policy Planning and the others believed that "the present crisis resulted in large part from the disruptive effects of the war on the economic, political and social structure of Europe."[53]

European responses to American efforts to assist in economic and political reconstruction were initially quite enthusiastic. British Foreign Minister Ernest Bevin, listening to Marshall's speech on the BBC, accepted the offer of assistance immediately; and he quickly traveled to Paris to begin consultations with the French. The new attitude toward European unity was later reaffirmed by Bevin on January 22, 1948. Announcing that the time had arrived for a new consolidation of Western Europe, Bevin argued for an association of the "historic members of European civilization." United States officials welcomed Bevin's speech as a signal of European initiative.[54]

The major product of the early negotiations among European officials was the Organization for European Economic Cooperation (OEEC), which came into being on June 5, 1948. At each step along the way, the United States used its economic strength, primarily in the form of dollar aid, to promote European unity, while at the same time attempting to remain outside the negotiations. In addition to organizations devoted to the administration of US aid, monetary and trade liberalization agreements were also forged.

Yet the building of a third force, the central objective of American policy between 1947 and 1950, fell short of American hopes. Disagreements between the British and the French over the extensiveness of supranational political authority and economic integration left the early proposals for unity unfulfilled. W. W. Rostow notes: "[B]ecause the British opposed it, because the economic requirements of unity did not converge with requirements for prompt recovery, and because the United States was unclear as to how its influence should be applied – the Marshall Plan did not succeed in moving Western Europe radically towards unity."[55]

In late 1949 a tone of urgency was heard in State Department discussions of European integration. In a memorandum written by Secretary of State Acheson, shifts in administration thinking were evident. With British reluctance to lead a movement toward European integration, Acheson noted that "[t]he key to progress towards integration is in French hands." Moreover, Acheson was willing to settle for integration on the continent itself and introduced the possibility of American participation in the Organization of European Economic Cooperation. Yet on these revised terms the United States continued to push for integration that would involve "some merger of sovereignty."[56]

The United States wanted to encourage an independent Europe – a third force – and not to establish an American sphere of influence. Yet the

Europeans could not agree among themselves to organize such a center of global power; the United States, despite its hegemonic power, could not see to its implementation. Just as in the earlier phase, when the goal of US policy was that of global, liberal multilateralism, severe limits of US power were experienced. Beugel makes this point:

> In dealing with sovereign states, even if these states are impoverished and politically and economically impotent, as was the case in Europe during the first years of the Marshall Plan, there is a limit beyond which even a country of the unique power of the United States cannot go in imposing far-reaching measures such as those leading to European integration.[57]

The irony is that while the United States was unwilling and probably unable to use more direct coercive power to encourage European unity, European resistance was not to the use of American power but to the ends toward which it was to be put. The United States wanted to avoid a direct, ongoing security commitment to Western Europe and the emergence of a sphere of influence that such a policy would entail. Yet as East–West tensions increased and as British and continental governments frustrated plans for a geopolitical third force, a new phase of American policy unfolded. Europe actively courted the extension of American power and, in the guise of NATO, a subordinate position in an American sphere of influence.

The "Pull" of Europe: Empire by Invitation

In 1947 and the following years, the United States appeared to hold the military and economic power needed to shape the terms of European reconstruction. With a monopoly on the atomic bomb, a massive (although demobilizing) standing army, and an industrial economy enlarged by the war, the United States appeared to have all the elements of hegemonic power. Moreover, the United States had what Europeans needed most: American dollars. "More and more as week succeeds week," *The Economist* noted in May 1947, "the whole of European life is being overshadowed by the great dollar shortage. The margin between recovery and collapse throughout Western Europe is dependent at this moment upon massive imports from the US."[58]

It is all the more striking, therefore, how successful the European governments were at blunting and redirecting American policy toward Europe. This resistance by Europe to the construction of a third force had several sources and differed from country to country. Each sought to use

American hegemonic power for its own national purposes. At the same time, the same considerations that led to the rejection of a full-blown united Europe prompted these same governments to encourage a direct American political and security presence in Europe.

The British were the most resistant to a united Europe. Britain initially reacted positively to the larger political objectives of Marshall Plan aid. A secret Cabinet session in March 1948 concluded that Britain "should use United States aid to gain time, but our ultimate aim should be to attain a position in which the countries of western Europe could be independent both of the United States and of the Soviet Union."[59] Yet as a practical matter, the British resisted significant steps in that direction. In a meeting of American ambassadors in Europe in October 1949, David Bruce argued: "We have been too tender with Britain since the war: she has been the constant stumbling block in the economic organization of Europe."[60]

The British were eager to maintain their special relationship with the United States, but feared it would be undermined by the emergence of a confederation with European countries. Moreover, the political and economic burdens of sustaining a European center of power would only further strain the British Commonwealth system. As with several of the other European countries, the British also feared the eventual dominance of Germany or even Russia in a unified Europe. These considerations implied the need for more, not less, American involvement in postwar Europe, particularly in the form of the NATO security relationship. As David Calleo has recently noted: "NATO seemed an ideal solution. With American commanders and forces taking primary responsibility for European ground defense, no question would remain about America's willingness to come to Europe's aid. Britain could reserve for itself those military and naval commands needed to retain control over its own national defense."[61] Indeed, in 1952 the British sought to reduce the role of the OEEC and transfer its functions to NATO – an attempt to build the Atlantic relationship at the expense of European unity.[62]

British officials were more concerned with preventing a return by the United States to an isolationist position than with an overbearing American hegemonic presence in Europe. "The fear was not of American expansionism," Gaddis notes, "but of American isolationism, and much time was spent considering how such expansionist tendencies could be reinforced."[63] It is no surprise, therefore, that in encouraging the United States to lead a security protectorate of Europe, the British began to stress the seriousness of the Soviet threat in Europe. In January 1948, British Foreign Minister Ernest Bevin warned Washington of "the further encroachment of the Soviet tide" and the need to "reinforce the physical barriers which still guard Western civilization."[64]

The French also sought to put American resources to their own national purposes and encourage an Atlantic security relationship. To be sure, France was more sympathetic to American ideas of European integration. Integration was useful in fostering French-dominated coalitions of governments in Western Europe. A political and economic union would also allow France to have some influence over the re-emergence of the German economy as well as tie Germany to a larger regional framework.[65] At the same time, however, the French also had an interest in encouraging a larger American security relationship with Europe. NATO, even more than a European community, would serve to contain Germany and the Soviets. Moreover, as with Britain, an American presence would free French resources, otherwise tied up in European defense, for purposes of preserving the remains of its colonial empire.[66]

Germany also supported American leadership of NATO. For West Germany's Chancellor Konrad Adenauer, the Atlantic security relationship was a means of rebuilding German sovereignty and equality on the continent. Germany had less room for maneuver than Britain or France. But participation in regional integration and NATO served the goals of political and economic reconstruction.[67]

In late 1947, efforts intensified by Europeans to draw the United States into a security relationship. British Foreign Minister Bevin outlined his ideas on military cooperation to Secretary of State Marshall on December 15, 1947. A regional European organization centered around Britain, France, and the Benelux countries would be linked to the other Western European countries and to the United States. Marshall signaled his interest in the plan but later indicated that the United States could not presently make any commitments.[68] Other European officials, such as Belgian Prime Minister (and Foreign Minister) Paul-Henri Spaak, were also calling for American military cooperation.[69]

Bevin's urgings were given prominence in his January 22, 1948 speech in the House of Commons. Later Bevin argued that European defense efforts would not be possible without American assistance. "The treaties that are being proposed cannot be fully effective nor be relied upon when a crisis arises unless there is assurance of American support for the defense of Western Europe."[70]

The French also sought to draw the United States into playing a military role in Western Europe. Foreign Minister Georges Bidault called upon the United States "to strengthen in the political field, and as soon as possible in the military one, the collaboration between the old and the new worlds, both so jointly responsible for the preservation of the only valuable civilization."[71]

Some officials in the Truman administration, such as Director of the Office of European Affairs John D. Hickerson, were urging military cooperation with Western Europe.[72] Others, most notably George Kennan, resisted the idea of a military union, arguing that it would be destructive of the administration's goal of European unity.[73] The official position of the Truman administration during this period was ambiguous: it was sympathetic to European concerns but reluctant to make a commitment. After repeated British attempts to obtain an American pledge of support, Under-Secretary Robert Lovett informed the British ambassador that the Europeans themselves must proceed with discussions on European military cooperation. Only afterward would the United States consider its relationship to these initiatives.[74] The British, undeterred, continued to insist on American participation in plans for Western European defense.

It was not until March 12, after the coup in Czechoslovakia, which demonstrated the Soviet hold on East Europe, and the further deterioration of East–West relations, that the United States agreed to engage in joint talks with the West Europeans on an "Atlantic security system."[75] In the months that followed, American and European differences narrowed, largely with the United States coming to agree on an integrated security system with itself at the center.

Taken together, the United States and State Department officials such as George Kennan were much more eager to see an independent Europe than the Europeans themselves. In the end, the European governments were not willing to take the risks, expend the resources, or resolve the national differences that would necessarily be a part of an independent, third force. Political life within an American hegemonic system and a bipolar world was the more acceptable alternative.

Part of the reason for this "craving for dependence,"[76] as David Calleo has recently put it, is that the European nations, except perhaps for Germany, were able to develop the means for maneuver within that American hegemonic system. Such was the case for Britain, as it is noted by Charles Maier:

> Within the American "hegemony" Britain preserved as much of her Commonwealth position, her shielding of her balance of payments, as possible. She also played what might be termed the "Polybian" strategy, attempting to become the Greeks in American's Roman empire, wagering on the "special relationship" to prolong their influence and status.[77]

The more general point is that the European encouragement of an American presence in Europe served a variety of national needs. The room for maneuver within that hegemonic system ensured that those needs would at least in part be met. Moreover, to tie the United States to a formal security relationship with Europe would provide a much more effective basis for the Europeans to influence and shape the American exercise of hegemonic power than would be the case with a less encumbered America. Even as Britain and the continental governments invited America's political and military presence in Europe, it ensured that the international economic system that would attend that new relationship was sufficiently based on European terms.

From Liberal Multilateralism to "Embedded Liberalism"

The United States failed in its initial attempt to bring liberal multilateralism to Europe. The coercive use of American hegemonic power, most explicitly evident in the British loan, was largely self-defeating. The Marshall Plan represented a shift in policy toward regional reconstruction and a politically independent and integrated Europe. The Europeans took the aid but declined the invitation to move toward a third force in a multipolar world. At the same time, as we have seen, the Europeans (with leadership from British Foreign Minister Bevin) actively sought to extend the American security presence to Western Europe.

The United States was prevailed upon to defend a grouping of Western industrial democracies. But what kind of grouping? In late 1949 officials within the Truman administration were uncertain. "It is not yet clear," Acheson argued, "what is the most desirable ultimate pattern of deeper international association of the United States, British Commonwealth, and Europe, and I do not believe that anyone should blueprint a course far ahead with any great rigidity."[78] Nonetheless, even as American policy shifted, the Truman administration clung to a now more distant objective of liberal multilateralism. Liberal economic internationalism, although initially blocked by the imperatives of European reconstruction and the unfolding Cold War, was not abandoned, at least in rhetoric. William Clayton noted this in a broadcast on November 22, 1947: "The Marshall Plan, or the European Recovery Program, has to do with the short-term emergency needs of one part of the world. The International Trade Organization has to do with long-range trade policies and trade of all the world. They are highly complementary and interrelated."[79]

This observation was more a hope than anything else. The Marshall Plan was not simply an interim step to place the European economies in a position to participate in a system based on earlier elaborated American plans for liberal multilateralism. Rather, the working out of these policy shifts served to alter the substantive character of those liberal, multilateral designs. This policy retreat and what it reveals about American hegemonic power is noted by Fred Hirsch and Michael Doyle:

> The limited capacity of the United States to determine the international economic order actually in force, even at the peak of American military-economic predominance in the immediate aftermath of World War II, is a striking indication of the extent to which relationships between the United States and other major Western powers at this time fell short of unqualified American hegemony. For the striking fact is that the United States was not able to impose its preferred multilateral trading order on the major trading countries. It was able to set the frame for such an order, as embodied in the major provisions of the IMF [International Monetary Fund] and the proposed International Trade Organization (ITO). But these provisions themselves had to be considerably modified, as compared with the original United States proposals, to make them acceptable to other governments. The original United States conception was thus weakened substantially by the resulting allowance made for transitional provisions, for exceptions to nondiscrimination and absence of restrictions, and for the ultimate escape by countries from the discipline of the international system through exchange adjustment.[80]

Through out the period, these concessions and compromises were indirect and were manifest as the United States sought to promote political stability and non-communist regimes in Western Europe. The effort to encourage non-communist alternatives in continental Europe was pursued from many quarters of the American government. At the State Department Charles Bohlen argued in 1946 that the United States should direct the Left in democratic directions. "It is definitely in the interest of the United States to see that the present left movement throughout the world, which we should recognize and even support, develops in the direction of democratic as against totalitarian systems."[81] Later, George Kennan argued that the Marshall Plan itself was the key to building the strength of anti-communist forces.[82] Where serious communist parties contended for power, such as in Italy and France, the United States was willing to come to the aid of all parties to their right, including socialists.

United States involvement in support of non-communist forces in Italy during the crucial 1948 national elections reveals this strategy. An immediate aim during this period was the bolstering of the non-communist Italian Socialists. The American ambassador, James Dunn, searched for ways to channel funds to strengthen the fragile political base of the Socialists as well as those to the Right.[83] The attempt was made to prevent the Italian Socialist Party from joining the ranks of the communist-led electoral alliance. In the end, with massive American covert aid and threats of the cut-off of Marshall Plan assistance, the Christian Democrats won a commanding electoral victory and a majority in parliament.

The primacy of stability in Western Europe, built around non-communist political parties, had larger ramifications for American foreign economic policy. Indirectly at least, this commitment meant that the United States would need to accommodate social democratic goals in the construction of international economic order. The successful political reconstruction of Europe meant not just a delay in the realization of liberal, multilateral goals, but their permanent alteration.

Although not framed as an explicit shift in international economic objectives, the United States did gradually move to accept a modified liberal, multilateral order. For the most part this took the form of exemptions and abridgements in trade and financial arrangements. Together, these compromises allowed a larger measure of national economic autonomy and a stronger role of the state in pursuing full employment and social welfare. The discipline of the international market would be softened by the welfare state. The differences between Britain and the United States over postwar economic arrangements were representative of the larger American–European split. At each turn during negotiations over monetary and trade rules and institutions, Britain sought arrangements that would be congenial with an expanded domestic state role in employment and social welfare.

Compromises between multilateralism in international economic relations and state intervention in the domestic economy and society are what John Ruggie has termed "embedded liberalism."[84] "The task of postwar institutional reconstruction," Ruggie argues, was to "devise a framework which would safeguard and even aid the quest for domestic stability without, at the same time, triggering the mutually destructive external consequences that had plagued the interwar period."[85] In other words, rules would be devised to allow for nondiscrimination in commercial and monetary relations, but also to facilitate the welfare state.

Ruggie argues that a loose consensus existed among the industrial democracies, even during the war, on the need to make compromises between postwar liberal multilateralism and domestic interventionism. This was the case, however, only at the most general level. The types of compromises were achieved in piecemeal fashion over the course of the entire 1940s. European countries gave ground on the American insistence that multilateralism be at the core of international economic arrangements. The United States came to accept the need to protect newly emerging Keynesian economic policies and the provisions of the welfare state. But these compromises were less explicit and negotiated than a product of the failure of such instruments of liberal multilateralism as the Anglo-American Financial Agreement and the International Trade Organization.

At each stage of negotiation the British sought to make American monetary and commercial proposals contingent on expanded production and employment. Behind Britain's conditional response to American initiatives were various factions on the Left and Right that opposed liberal multilateralism.[86] Uniting these groups was a skepticism of economic liberalism at home or abroad. A British newspaper of the day noted: "We must . . . reconcile ourselves once and for all to the view that the days of *laissez-faire* and the unlimited division of labor are over; that every country – including Great Britain – plans and organizes its production in the light of social and military needs, and that the regulation of this production by such 'trade barriers' as tariffs, quotas, and subsidies is a necessary and integral part of this policy."[87]

In British debates on the various trade and financial agreements, as Gardner notes, officials "devoted considerable efforts to showing that full employment and domestic planning would not be impeded by the multilateral arrangements."[88] In negotiations over the ITO these concerns were manifest in safeguards and escape clauses, in the removal of agriculture from the framework, and in transition periods to multilateralism. As one British official noted in discussions over trade arrangements, "there must be in the international settlement which we are now devising sufficient escape clauses, let-outs, special arrangements, call them what you will, which will enable those countries which are adopting internal measures for full employment to protect themselves."[89]

These efforts to protect domestic economic and social obligations of the state came primarily from Britain and the other European countries. The Europeans themselves were crucial in recasting the terms of liberal multilateralism – if only in resisting, modifying, and circumventing American proposals. In insisting on the primacy of domestic stability in the development of international economic rules and institutions, the Europeans (and most importantly the British) successfully recast the character of postwar economic order. The story of postwar international political economy is as much that of the triumph of the welfare state as of the halting and partial emergence of liberal multilateralism.

Conclusion

The structure of the early postwar system bears the profound marks of American ideas and the projection of its power; about this there is no dispute. The task here has been to reconsider the conventional understanding of that power and the fate of those ideas. American power was unprecedented, but it was not unalloyed. The United States was not able to implement the full range of its proposals for postwar order; but it did get drawn into a larger hegemonic role in Europe than it anticipated or wanted. In understanding this duality of the American postwar experience, we are better able to appreciate the substance, scope, and limits of American hegemonic power.

The failure of the first efforts at multilateralism and the failure of policies to promote European unity say a great deal about the character of American hegemonic power after the war. The direct use of American power to coerce European acceptance of liberal, multilateral designs (seen most clearly in the British loan episode) were singularly unsuccessful. Less direct methods of pursuing even a revised plan for European regional cooperation also fell short. The purpose of the Marshall Plan was to restore the political confidence of the Europeans. Yet as Gaddis notes, once this was the objective, it was the Europeans who could dictate what it would take to produce confidence.[90] In the end, this required a direct American military commitment.

The Europeans wanted a stronger and more formal hegemonic system than the United States was initially willing to provide. The initial one world plans of collective security and economic universalism would have been a very cost-effective form of *Pax Americana*. The obligations to Europe would have been minimal and they would have accorded with prevailing US congressional and popular public opinion. The system, once constituted, was envisaged to be self-regulating. Given American economic size and competitiveness, this global open door would both serve its own interests and resonate with time-honored American liberal ideas of politics and economics. However, not only were the assumptions behind this vision of postwar order wrong, but the United States, despite its preponderance of economic and military resources, was unable to implement its essential parts.

The revised strategy of a European third force and the construction of a multipolar order was equally elusive. It again revealed the limits of American postwar power. These limits were recognized by many of the American officials themselves. In promoting the idea of a united Europe in the context of Marshall Plan aid, the Truman administration insisted that Europe itself take the initiative. More direct American pressure would have been self-defeating, but its absence also ensured that the Europeans could set the limits on cooperation and integration. It was the very weakness of the European economies and societies that prevented the United States from translating its array of power resources into bargaining assets. The United States could not push too hard. The Europeans, in turn, could set the terms upon which to pull the United States into economic and security relationships.

In the end the United States had to settle for a more traditional form of empire – a *Pax Americana* with formal commitments to Europe. The result was an institutional relationship that diverted American resources to Europe in the form of a security commitment, allowing the Europeans to employ their more scarce resources elsewhere and providing the ongoing institutional means for the Europeans to influence and render predictable American hegemonic power. In blunting and altering the substantive character of international economic relations to ensure the survival of budding welfare states, the Europeans succeeded in drawing the United States into protecting a system that they were able to effectively redefine. As students of empire have often noted, the flow of ideas and influence between empirical center and periphery works in both directions.[91] Unable to secure a less formal and more ambitious *Pax Americana*, the United States found itself experiencing the similar two-way flow of ideas and influence.

The sequence of shifts in American policy toward postwar order is often understood as a set of adjustments to the emergence of East–West hostilities. It was the rise of perceptions of threat from the Soviet Union that forced the compromises and that shifted the center of gravity from economic-centered postwar designs to security-centered designs. There are at least two problems with this understanding. First, this interpretation obscures the failures of American policy and the limited ability of the United States to exercise hegemonic power on its own terms. The focus on failure to implement policy in the first two phases of US policy reveals these limits and the striking ability with which the Europeans could resist American initiatives from a position of weakness.

Second, perhaps more fateful for the way in which American policy unfolded after World War II was the utter collapse of Great Britain, not the rise of the Soviet Union. In a meeting of American ambassadors in Paris in the autumn of 1949, John J. McCloy, the high commissioner for Germany, argued that perhaps too much emphasis had been given to "the increase of Russian power in the world and too little thought to the enormously important factor that is the collapse of the British Empire."[92] Scholars may have suffered a similar problem. This decline of British power, recognized for decades, accelerated by the destruction of the war, and taking a dramatic turn in 1947, was crucial in weakening the overall political and economic position of Europe in the late 1940s. If the argument made above has merit, it was precisely the weakness of Britain and continental Europe that undermined the ability of the United States to successfully employ its hegemonic position after the war. Ironically, it might well be the case that less disparity in the relationship between

Europe and the United States after the war could possibly have provided the basis for the realization of more of the American postwar agenda.

Notes

The author wishes to thank John Lewis Gaddis, Lloyd Gardner, and Klaus Knorr for helpful comments and suggestions. An earlier version of the paper was presented to a seminar on Postwar American Foreign Policy at Rutgers University. Research was supported by funds from the J. Howard Pew Freedom Trust and the Center of International Studies, Princeton University.

1 Recent discussions of the implications of American decline include Robert Gilpin, "American Policy in the Post-Reagan Era," *Daedalus* 116 (Summer 1987): 33–67; and Paul Kennedy, *The Rise and Fall of the Great Powers* (New York: Random House, 1988); David P. Calleo, *Beyond American Hegemony: The Future of the Western Alliance* (New York: Basic Books, 1987).

2 Robert O. Keohane, *After Hegemony: Cooperation and Discord in the World Political Economy* (Princeton, NJ: Princeton University Press, 1984), p. 37.

3 Robert Gilpin, *War and Change in World Politics* (New York: Cambridge University Press, 1981), p. 145.

4 Charles P. Kindleberger, *The World in Depression, 1929–39* (Berkeley: University of California Press, 1973).

5 Gilpin, *War and Change*. An earlier formulation of hegemonic power emphasizing similarities in the rise and decline of *Pax Britannica* and *Pax Americana* is in Gilpin, *US Power and the Multinational Corporation* (New York: Basic Books, 1975).

6 Gilpin, *War and Change*, p. 203.

7 Gilpin, *US Power and the Multinational Corporation*.

8 Gilpin notes: "Much as it happened in the latter part of the nineteenth century and the interwar period, the relative decline of the dominant economy and the emergence of new centers of economic power have led to increasing economic conflicts. During such periods of weak international leadership, international economic relations tend to be characterized by a reversion to mercantilism (economic nationalism), intense competition and bargaining among economic powers, and the fragmentation of the liberal interdependent world economy into exclusive blocs, rival nationalisms, and economic alliances." "Economic Interdependence and National Security in Historical Perspective," in Klaus Knorr and Frank N. Trager, eds., *Economic Issues and National Security* (Lawrence: Regents Press of Kansas, 1977), p. 61.

9 Keohane, *After Hegemony*, p. 32.

10 Ibid., p. 37.

11 Duncan Snidal makes a distinction between hegemony that is benign and exercised by persuasion, hegemony that is benign but exercised by coercion, and hegemony that is coercive and exploitive. Snidal, "Hegemonic Stability Theory Revisited," *International Organization* 39 (Autumn 1985). In another

effort to distinguish between types of hegemonic power, Hirsch and Doyle note those of cooperative leadership, hegemonic regime, and imperialism. See Fred Hirsch and Michael Doyle, *Alternatives to Monetary Disorder* (New York: McGraw Hill, 1977), p. 27.

12	Kindleberger, *World in Depression*; see also Kindleberger, "Dominance and Leadership in the International Economy," *International Studies Quarterly* 25 (June 1981): 242–54.

13	Gilpin, *War and Change*; Stephen Krasner, "State Power and the Structure of International Trade," *World Politics* 28 (April 1976): 317–43.

14	For an overview of this literature, see Stephan Haggard and Beth Simmons, "International Regimes," *International Organization* 41 (Summer 1987). Some scholars, employing a sociological perspective, focus on the role of regimes as institutions that inform the process by which nations define and pursue their interests. See Stephen Krasner, ed., *International Regimes* (Ithaca, NY: Cornell University Press, 1983). Others have developed micro-economic models that relate the maintenance of regimes to strategic interactions of states. See Keohane, *After Hegemony*.

15	Bruce Russett, "The Mysterious Case of Vanishing Hegemony; or Is Mark Twain Really Dead?" *International Organization* 39 (Spring 1985); Susan Strange, "The Persistent Myth of Lost Hegemony," *International Organization* 41 (Autumn 1987).

16	Strange, "The Persistent Myth of Lost Hegemony," p. 555.

17	US national output more than doubled in real terms during the war: American GNP rose from $91 billion in 1939 to $210 billion in 1945.

18	Krasner, "American Policy and Global Economic Stability," in William P. Avery and David P. Rapkin, eds., *America in a Changing World Political Economy* (New York: Longman, 1982), p. 32.

19	This does not in itself argue against the presence of hegemonic power, but it does suggest the importance of congenial domestic coalitions to support its exercise.

20	Strange, "The Persistent Myth of Lost Hegemony," pp. 560–1.

21	Michael Mastanduno, "Postwar East–West Trade Strategy," *International Organization* 42 (Winter 1987/8).

22	Franz Schurmann argues that the isolationist heritage made a postwar internationalist strategy difficult to sustain unless it was clothed in liberal ideals. The reluctance of portions of American public opinion to get involved in the atavistic power politics of Europe weighed heavily on foreign policy officials. Such involvement, it was argued, had a corrupting influence on the exceptionalism of American politics. Internationalism, consequently, would need to involve reforming and remaking European power politics in an American image – to export American exceptionalism. Schurmann, *The Logic of World Power* (New York: Pantheon, 1974).

23	American liberal multilateral ideas have long historical roots. They can be traced to John Hay's "Open Door" and to the third of Woodrow Wilson's Fourteen Points: "the removal, so far as possible, of all economic barriers."

Richard N. Gardner's study remains the most comprehensive account of these ideas and their fate in postwar economic diplomacy. Gardner, *Sterling-Dollar Diplomacy: The Origins and the Prospects of Our International Economic Order* (New York: McGraw Hill, 1969).

24 Ibid., p. 4.

25 Ibid., p. 12.

26 Ibid., pp. 31–5.

27 Article Seven to the Mutual Aid Agreement was the object of these negotiations.

28 Gardner, *Sterling-Dollar Diplomacy*, p. 68. On American wartime efforts to extract British concessions on the postwar trading system, see Lloyd C. Gardner, "Will Clayton, the British Loan, and the Political Economy of the Cold War," in Gardner, *Architects of Illusion: Men and Ideas in American Foreign Policy, 1941–1949* (Chicago: Quadrangle Books, 1970), pp. 113–38.

29 For systematic accounts of these monetary agreements, see Gardner, *Sterling-Dollar Diplomacy*; and Armand Van Dormael, *Bretton Woods: Birth of a Monetary System* (London: Macmillan, 1978).

30 For a summary of differences in American and British understandings of Bretton Woods, see Gardner, *Sterling-Dollar Diplomacy*, pp. 143–4. See also Alfred E. Eckes, Jr., *A Search for Solvency: Bretton Woods and the International Monetary System, 1941–1971* (Austin: University of Texas Press, 1975); and Van Dormael, *Bretton Woods*.

31 Gardner, *Sterling-Dollar Diplomacy*, p. 158.

32 Quoted in ibid., p. 198.

33 See Robin Edmonds, *Setting the Mould: The United States and Britain 1945–1950* (New York: Norton, 1986), ch. 8.

34 Gardner, *Sterling-Dollar Diplomacy*, p. 382.

35 Ernst H. Van Der Beugel, *From Marshall Aid to Atlantic Partnership: European Integration as a Concern of American Foreign Policy* (Amsterdam: Elsevier Publishing Co., 1966), p. 19.

36 Gardner, *Sterling-Dollar Diplomacy*, p. 294.

37 Quoted in John Gaddis, "Spheres of Influence: The United States and Europe, 1945–1949," in Gaddis, *The Long Peace* (New York: Oxford University Press, 1987), p. 57.

38 Bohlen memorandum, August 30, 1947, *Foreign Relations of the United States* [henceforth FRUS] *1947* (Washington, DC: US Government Printing Office, 1973), vol. I, pp. 763–4.

39 On the role of Europe in American wartime planning and the "relative indifference of the administration to regionalist ideas," see Max Beloff, *The United States and the Unity of Europe* (Washington, DC: Brookings Institution, 1963), ch. 1.

40 See Beugel, *From Marshall Aid to Atlantic Partnership*, pp. 41–5. For a fascinating account of the emerging policy views of State Department and other top government officials concerning the rebuilding of Europe, see Walter

Isaacson and Evan Thomas, *The Wise Men: Six Friends and the World They Made* (New York: Simon and Schuster, 1987), pp. 402–18.

41   Kennan to Cecil B. Lyon, October 13, 1947, Policy Planning Staff Records. Quoted in Gaddis, "Spheres of Influence," p. 58.

42   Kennan quotes the memorandum in his memoirs. George Kennan, *Memoirs: 1925–1950* (Boston: Little, Brown, 1967), p. 336.

43   Beugel, *From Marshall Aid to Atlantic Partnership*, p. 43.

44   Kennan, *Memoirs: 1925–1950*, pp. 325–53; *FRUS, 1947*, III, pp. 223–30.

45   Kennan, *Memoirs: 1925–1950*, p. 337.

46   The document was dated June 12, 1947, a week after Marshall's Harvard speech; but the main ideas were circulated earlier. This group, composed of H. van D. Cleveland, Ben T. Moore, and Charles Kindleberger, prepared the memorandum for a major State-War-Navy Coordinating Committee report. Parts of the document are reprinted in Charles P. Kindleberger, *Marshall Plan Days* (Boston: Allen & Unwin, 1987), pp. 4–24. See also Michael Hogan, "European Integration and the Marshall Plan," in Stanley Hoffman and Charles Maier, eds., *The Marshall Plan: A Retrospective* (Boulder, Colo.: Westview Press, 1984), pp. 4–5.

47   Beugel, *From Marshall Aid to Atlantic Partnership*, p. 45.

48   "The European Situation," Memorandum by the Under-Secretary of State of Economic Affairs, *FRUS, 1947*, III, pp. 230–2. Joseph Jones argues that this report had a decisive influence on Marshall's speech and may have prompted the speech itself: *The Fifteen Weeks* (New York: Viking Press, 1955), p. 203. Clayton's memo reportedly moved Marshall to confirm his tentatively scheduled appointment to speak at Harvard's commencement exercises. The next day Marshall gave a copy of Clayton's memorandum and Kennan's Policy Planning paper to Bohlen and instructed him to write a speech that would invite Europe to request American aid.

49   Summarized by Beugel, *From Marshall Aid to Atlantic Partnership*, pp. 47–9; also see Dean Acheson, *Present at the Creation* (New York: New American Library, 1966), pp. 277–30.

50   "Summary of Discussion on Problems of Relief, Rehabilitation and Reconstruction of Europe," May 29, 1947, *FRUS, 1947*, III, p. 235.

51   Section 102(a) of the Economic Cooperation Act of 1948, as amended, stated that: "It is further declared to be the policy of the people of the US to encourage the unification of Europe."

52   Gaddis, "Spheres of Influence," p. 59. See also Michael J. Hogan, *The Marshall Plan: America, Britain, and the Reconstruction of Western Europe, 1947–1952* (New York: Cambridge University Press, 1987).

53   Beugel, *From Marshall Aid to Atlantic Partnership*, p. 42.

54   Ibid., pp. 121–2.

55   W. W. Rostow, *The United States in the World Arena, an Essay in Recent History* (New York: Harper & Row, 1960), p. 216. See also Alan S. Milward, *The Reconstruction of Western Europe, 1945–51* (Berkeley: University of California Press, 1984).

56 "The Secretary of State to the Embassy in France," October 19, 1949, *FRUS, 1949*, IV, pp. 469–72. In the subsequent meeting of American ambassadors in Paris, agreement was reached among them that European integration could not proceed without British participation.

57 Beugel, *From Marshall Aid to Atlantic Partnership*, pp. 220–1.

58 *The Economist*, May 31, 1947.

59 Quoted in Gaddis, "Sphere of Influence," p. 66.

60 "Summary Record of a Meeting of United States Ambassadors at Paris," October 21–22, 1949, *FRUS, 1949*, IV, p. 492.

61 David P. Calleo, *Beyond American Hegemony: The Future of the Western Alliance* (New York: Basic Books, 1998), p. 35.

62 Beloff, *The United States and the Unity of Europe*, p. 69.

63 John Lewis Gaddis, "The Emerging Post-Revisionist Synthesis on the Origins of the Cold War," *Diplomatic History* 7 (Summer 1983). This statement is based, at least in part, on newly opened records of the British Foreign Office.

64 "Summary of a Memorandum Representing Mr. Bevin's Views on the Formation of a Western Union," enclosed in Inverchapel to Marshall, January 13, 1948, *FRUS, 1948*, III, pp. 4–6.

65 See Maier, "Supranational Concepts and National Continuity in the Framework of the Marshall Plan," in Stanley Hoffmann and Charles Maier, eds., *The Marshall Plan: A Retrospective* (Boulder, CO: Westview Press, 1984). p. 34.

66 Calleo, *Beyond American Hegemony*, p. 35. See also Michael M. Harrison, *The Reluctant Ally: France and Atlantic Security* (Baltimore: Johns Hopkins University Press, 1981).

67 Calleo, *Beyond American Hegemony*, p. 35.

68 Memorandum by the British Foreign Office, undated, *FRUS, 1947*, III, pp. 818–19. See also Geir Lundestad, *America, Scandinavia, and the Cold War, 1945–1949* (New York: Columbia University Press, 1980), pp. 171–2.

69 Lundestad, *America, Scandinavia, and the Cold War, 1945–1949*, p. 172.

70 *FRUS, 1948*, III, p. 14. In his memoirs, British Prime Minister C. R. Attlee referred to the "making of the Brussels treaty and the Atlantic Pact" as "the work of Bevin." Attlee, *As It Happened* (London: Heinemann, 1954), p. 171. See also Escott Reid, *Time of Fear and Hope: The Making of the North Atlantic Treaty, 1947–1949* (Toronto: McClelland and Stewart, 1977).

71 Quoted in Lundestad, "Empire by Invitation? The United States and Western Europe, 1945–1952," *Journal of Peace Research* 23 (1986): 270.

72 Hickerson memorandum, *FRUS, 1948*, III, pp. 6–7.

73 Kennan memorandum to Secretary of State, January 20, 1948, *FRUS, 1948*, III, pp. 7–8. See also Kennan, *Memoirs: 1925–1950*, pp. 397–406.

74 Lovett to Inverchapel, February 2, 1948, *FRUS, 1948*, III, pp. 17–18.

75 Ibid., p. 48.

76 Calleo, *Beyond American Hegemony*, p. 35.

77 Maier, "Supranational Concepts and National Continuity," p. 34.

78 "The Secretary of State to the Embassy in France," October 19, 1949, *FRUS, 1949*, IV, p. 469.
79 Quoted in Beloff, *The United States and the Unity of Europe*, p. 28.
80 Hirsch and Doyle, *Alternatives to Monetary Disorder*, p. 29.
81 Quoted in Gaddis, "Dividing Adversaries" in Gaddis, *The Long Peace*, p. 150.
82 Ibid., p. 154.
83 James Edward Miller, *The United States and Italy, 1940–1950: The Politics and Diplomacy of Stabilization* (Chapel Hill: University of North Carolina Press, 1986), pp. 243–9.
84 John Gerard Ruggie, "International Regimes, Transactions, and Change: Embedded Liberalism in the Postwar Economic Order," *International Organization* 36 (Spring 1982): 379–415. See also Robert Keohane, "The World Political Economy and the Crisis of Embedded Liberalism," in John H. Goldthorpe, ed., *Order and Conflict in Contemporary Capitalism: Studies in the Political Economy of Western European Nations* (Oxford: Clarendon Press, 1984), pp. 15–38.
85 Ruggie, "International Regimes, Transactions, and Change," p. 393.
86 See Gardner, *Sterling-Dollar Diplomacy*, pp. 30–5.
87 *The Times* (London), January 11, 1941. Quoted in Gardner, *Sterling-Dollar Diplomacy*, p. 31.
88 Gardner, *Sterling-Dollar Diplomacy*, p. 234.
89 Ibid., p. 277.
90 Gaddis, "Spheres of Influence," p. 62.
91 See Michael W. Doyle, *Empires* (Ithaca, NY: Cornell University Press, 1986).
92 "Summary Record of a Meeting of United States Ambassadors at Paris," October 21–22, 1949, *FRUS, 1949*, IV, p. 485.

2

Socialization and Hegemonic Power

Most historical ages are marked by the presence of great powers, nations capable of dominating the course of international politics. An ongoing task of scholarship is to explore the nature of the shadow that hegemonic nations cast. How do hegemons assert control over other nations within the international system? Through what mechanisms does control get established, and by what processes does it erode? How is compliance achieved, and how is it maintained?

Most observers would argue that the manipulation of *material incentives* – the use of threats and promises to alter the preferences of leaders in secondary nations – is the dominant form through which hegemonic power is exercised. Power is directly related to the command of material resources. Acquiescence is the result of coercion. Inducements and sanctions are used by the hegemon to ensure that secondary states prefer cooperation to non-cooperation.

But there is also a more subtle component of hegemonic power, one that works at the level of *substantive beliefs* rather than material payoffs. Acquiescence is the result of the socialization of leaders in secondary nations. Elites in secondary states buy into and internalize norms that are articulated by the hegemon and therefore pursue policies consistent with the hegemon's notion of international order. The exercise of power – and hence the mechanism through which compliance is achieved – involves the projection by the hegemon of a set of norms and their embrace by leaders in other nations.

The goal of this article is to develop an understanding of socialization in the international system and to define the conditions under which it comes about and can function effectively as a source of power. Socialization is an important element of power, but we have meager analytic tools with which to understand the mechanisms and conditions of its operation. Our purpose is not to diminish the importance of the manipulation of material incentives as a source of hegemonic power. Rather, it is to develop the means to identify and explain a different aspect of hegemonic power in which acquiescence emerges from the diffusion of a set of normative ideals.

We begin by developing the notion of socialization within an international context, drawing on the literature on socialization and learning at the domestic level. We then elaborate on the mechanisms through which norms and beliefs become embedded in the elite communities of secondary states. We next set forth and examine three hypotheses concerning the conditions under which socialization comes about. The first hypothesis is that socialization occurs primarily after wars and political crises, periods marked by international turmoil and restructuring as well as the fragmentation of ruling coalitions and legitimacy crises at the domestic level. The simultaneity of international and domestic instability creates the conditions conducive to socialization. At the international level, the emerging hegemon articulates a set of normative principles in order to facilitate the construction of an order conducive to its interests. At the domestic level, crisis creates an environment in which elites seek alternatives to existing norms that have been discredited by events and in which new norms offer opportunities for political gains and coalitional realignment. The second hypothesis is that elite (as opposed to mass) receptivity to the norms articulated by the hegemon is essential to the socialization process. Norms may first take root among the populace, but they must then spread to the elite level if they are to have important effects on state behavior. Coalitional realignment most often serves as the mechanism through which norms move from the public into the elite community. The third hypothesis is that when socialization does occur, it comes about primarily in the wake of the coercive exercise of power. That is, socialization is distinct from, but does not occur independently of, power manifest as the manipulation of material incentives. Material inducement triggers the socialization process, but socialization nevertheless leads to outcomes that are not explicable simply in terms of the exercise of coercive power. These hypotheses are explored in the historical case studies of US diplomacy after World Wars I and II and the British colonial experience in India and Egypt.[1]

Power as Coercion and Power as Socialization

There are two basic ways in which a hegemonic nation can exercise power and secure the acquiescence of other nations.[2] The first is by manipulating *material incentives.* Through threats of punishment or promises of reward, the hegemon alters the political or economic incentives facing other states. This manipulation of material incentives induces policy change that is congenial with hegemonic order. In effect, the hegemon exercises power by using sanctions and inducements to change the costs and benefits that other states face in pursuing particular policies. The second basic way in which a hegemonic nation can exercise power is by altering the *substantive beliefs* of leaders in other nations. Hegemonic control emerges when foreign elites buy into the hegemon's vision of international order and accept it as their own – that is, when they internalize the norms and value orientations espoused by the hegemon and accept its normative claims about the nature of the international system. These norms and value orientations occupy the analytic dimension that lies between deep philosophical beliefs about human nature and more narrow beliefs about what set of policies will maximize short-term interests,[3] and they therefore serve to guide state behavior and shape the agenda from which elites choose specific policies.[4] Power is thus exercised through a process of socialization in which the norms and value orientations of leaders in secondary states change and more closely reflect those of the dominant state. Under these circumstances, acquiescence is achieved by the transmission of norms and reshaping of value orientations and not simply by the manipulation of material incentives.[5]

These two ways of exercising hegemonic power are mutually reinforcing and frequently difficult to disentangle. Yet it is useful to distinguish between them analytically because they rely on quite different mechanisms and suggest quite different notions of the underlying fabric and durability of hegemonic power. In theoretical terms, broadening our understanding of hegemonic power to include socialization will lead to new insights into how order emerges and evolves in the international system. The socialization of elites into the hegemonic order leads to a consolidation of hegemonic power; rule based on might is enhanced by rule based on right. Furthermore, it is less costly: the hegemon can expend fewer economic and military resources to secure acquiescence because there is a more fundamental correspondence of values and interests. This added dimension of hegemonic power can also explain why the ordering principles and norms of a given system are not isomorphic with changes in the relative distribution of military and economic capability within that system. The norms and value orientations of secondary states may be altered before a substantial decline in the hegemon's wealth and military strength occurs, or they may outlast periods of hegemonic decline and thereby perpetuate the system "beyond its time." In short, socialization may be a key component in understanding the functioning of and change within hegemonic systems.

Demonstrating empirically the importance of socialization is more difficult. The core of the problem is that the outcomes we would expect to see if coercion were solely at work may not differ substantially from those associated with socialization. In inducing secondary states to adopt certain policies, the hegemon may in fact resort to both coercion and socialization to achieve the same end. It is therefore difficult to determine the extent to which a specific outcome follows from either the manipulation of material incentives or the alternation of substantive beliefs. Outcomes that can be explained solely in terms of material inducement do not undermine the case for socialization. On the contrary, it is only because concern about material forms of power has tended to dominate the study of hegemonic order that the burden of proof falls on those arguing that socialization has consequential effects on outcomes. We suggest that no single paradigm should be accorded this predominance if only because it impairs a more nuanced inquiry into the relative weights that should be assigned to socialization and material inducement in explaining outcomes.

Another problem in demonstrating empirically the implications of norm change is that, in methodological terms, the importance of socialization is easiest to observe when the hegemon's preponderance of material resources is declining. During periods in which the hegemon's coercive capacities are no longer sufficient to explain the perpetuation of hegemonic order, the importance of norms becomes most evident. Because the purpose of this essay is to understand when and how socialization works in the early stages of interaction between a hegemon and secondary states, probing more deeply into how socialization affects outcomes later in the trajectory of hegemonic systems goes beyond the scope of our inquiry.

Despite these methodological problems, our case studies do indicate that socialization has played an important role in shaping hegemonic orders. During the closing years of World War I, President Wilson's normative appeal to the European Left markedly influenced the terms of the Versailles Treaty. If Wilson had succeeded more fully in implanting among European elites the ideas embodied in the Fourteen Points, the postwar order would likely have looked dramatically different. After World War II, US officials were more successful in embedding a set of norms among European elites. By convincing the Europeans to depart from notions of colonialism and economic nationalism, the United States was able to forge a normative consensus around which the postwar order took shape. An examination of British rule in India and Egypt also reveals the importance of socialization. Britain's ability to penetrate and reshape Indian political culture facilitated British rule and meant that the period of British hegemony had a lasting effect on Indian politics. In Egypt, where Britain relied more heavily on coercive leadership, British hegemony was more fragile and had a less profound impact on Egyptian political culture.

Developing Theory of Socialization in International Relations

Hegemonic order built on inducements and threats depends exclusively on the hegemon's control of preponderant material resources. A variety of resources may be useful in altering the incentives of other nations. For example, economic sanctions can be imposed or lifted, foreign aid or military support can be offered or withheld, military intervention can be threatened or used, and international market power can be wielded by allowing or denying foreign access to the hegemon's own domestic economy.[6] Taken together, the constitutive elements of hegemonic power include military capabilities; control over raw materials, markets, and capital; and competitive advantages in highly valued goods.[7]

Few scholars, even those who stress the centrality of coercive forms of hegemony, are willing to leave it at this. Robert Keohane, for example, notes that "theories of hegemony should seek not only to analyze dominant powers' decisions to engage in rule-making and rule-enforcement, but also to explore why secondary states defer to the leadership of the hegemon," and stresses that these theories "need to account for the legitimacy of hegemonic regimes and for the coexistence of cooperation."[8] Likewise, Robert Gilpin argues that the "governance" of the international system is in part maintained by the prestige and moral leadership of the hegemonic power. While the authority of the hegemonic power is ultimately established by military and economic supremacy, "the position of the dominant power may be supported by ideological, religious, or other values common to a set of states."[9] Such arguments suggest the importance of non-material resources in the creation and maintenance of hegemonic order.[10]

Other scholars have noted that power can be exercised by shaping the norms and value orientations within which policy is conducted. Robert Cox, working within the Gramscian tradition, argues that hegemonic structures are sustained by "universal norms, institutions, and mechanisms which lay down general rules of behavior for states and for those forces of civil society that act across national boundaries."[11] Hegemony, according to this view, is the outgrowth of the intertwining of socioeconomic, political, and ideological structures, all of which are rooted in a particular mode of production. This complex set of structures limits the bounds of what is understood to be legitimate policy choice, thereby securing the continuing dominance of the hegemon.

These arguments, made by scholars working in otherwise very different theoretical traditions, acknowledge a component of power that is not reducible to the coercive capacities of the hegemonic nation. The ability to generate shared beliefs in the acceptability or legitimacy of a particular international order – that is, the ability to forge a consensus among national elites on the normative underpinnings of order – is an important if elusive dimension of hegemonic power.

Underlying this view is the notion of legitimate domination advanced by Max Weber. Although Weber is concerned with the exercise of power within the nation-state, his analysis is also relevant to the exercise of power between nation-states. Weber argues that there are systematic incentives for rulers to organize power in ways that establish or preserve the legitimacy of government institutions and decision-making. "Experience shows that in no instance does domination voluntarily limit itself to the appeal to material or affectual or ideal motives as a basis for its continuance. In addition every such system attempts to establish and to cultivate the belief in its legitimacy."[12] Weber notes a seemingly universal need for those who wield power to exercise that power as legitimate domination.

Weber and other scholars argue that the legitimacy of power has its foundation in a set of shared beliefs in a normative order. Rulers enjoy legitimacy when the values that they espouse correspond with the values of those they rule. "If binding decisions are legitimate," Jürgen Habermas argues, "that is, if they can be made independently of the concrete exercise of force and of the manifest threat of sanctions, and can be regularly implemented even against the interests of those affected, they must be considered as the fulfillment of recognized norms."[13] It is the common acceptance of a consensual normative order that binds ruler and ruled and legitimates power.

In general terms, we conceptualize socialization as a process of learning in which norms and ideals are transmitted from one party to another.[14] In specific terms related to hegemonic power, we conceptualize it as the process through which national leaders internalize the norms and value orientations espoused by the hegemon and, as a consequence, become socialized into the community formed by the hegemon and other nations accepting its leadership position.[15] The vision of international order articulated by the hegemon comes to possess a "quality of 'oughtness.' "[16] In this way, socialization can lead to the consolidation of the hegemon's position and to acquiescence among the states participating within the system.[17]

How socialization works

Socialization can occur through three mechanisms: normative persuasion, external inducement, and internal reconstruction.

When socialization occurs through *normative persuasion*, the hegemon is able to secure the compliance of secondary states without resorting to material sanctions and inducements. The hegemon relies instead on ideological persuasion and transnational learning through various forms of direct contact with elites in these states, including contact via diplomatic channels, cultural exchanges, and foreign study. The elites then internalize the hegemon's norms and move to adopt new state policies which are compatible with those of the hegemon and which produce cooperative outcomes. In this formulation, then, socialization occurs independently of and prior to changes in policy; this is a case of "beliefs before acts." Acquiescence follows from shifts in the values and norms held by elites in secondary states. The causal chain is as follows: normative persuasion → norm change → policy change (cooperation through legitimate domination).

When socialization occurs through *external inducement*, the hegemon initially uses economic and military incentives to induce smaller states to change their policies. This manipulation of the preferences of elites secures compliance through coercion. It is only after secondary states have adjusted their policies to accord with those of the hegemon that the normative principles underlying the hegemon's policies come to be embraced as rightful by the elites. Belief in the normative underpinnings of the system emerges gradually as elites seek to bring their policies and value orientations into line. This is a case of "acts before beliefs." The causal chain is as follows: external inducement → policy change (cooperation through coercion) → norm change (cooperation through legitimate domination).

Policy coercion can lead to socialization for three main reasons. First, entering into a subsidiary relationship with a hegemon could create domestic political problems for those in power and opportunities for those not in power. The public of the secondary state may associate compliant behavior with imperial manipulation and weakness on the part of its own leaders. Elites in power can circumvent this problem by basing their participation in the hegemonic system on normative claims. Alternatively, elites not in power, especially during the periods of political flux that surround major shifts in coalitional alignment or foreign policy, can espouse a new set of norms to challenge the authority of existing elites and take the opportunity to form new ruling coalitions. This becomes a particularly compelling political strategy if the elites in power continue to embrace traditional norms that are at odds with the new policies they have adopted. In other words, elites may embrace and espouse the norms articulated by the hegemon for instrumental reasons, either to minimize the potential domestic costs of compliant behavior or to take advantage of elite restructuring to build new coalitions.

Second, psychological pressures can induce a change in beliefs. Elites in secondary states may feel some degree of cognitive dissonance because the policies they implement do not correspond fully with their beliefs.[18] This dissonance can be reduced if the norms that guide the policies come to correspond more closely with those policies. Alternatively, as Daryl Bem's self-perception theory contends, individuals may feel a need to adopt beliefs that explain their actions, that give meaning and justification to their behavior.[19] This search for compatibility between policies and normative orientation drives forward the socialization process.

Third, the web of interactions created by participation in the hegemonic system can, through a gradual process of learning and adjustment, induce elites to buy into the normative underpinnings of that system.[20] Through frequent participation in the institutions erected by the hegemon, elites in secondary states are exposed to and may eventually embrace the norms and value orientations that those institutions embody. This form of social-ization has been particularly prevalent during the period of US hegemony because of the proliferation of formal international organizations erected to facilitate policy coordination.

Socialization can also occur through *internal reconstruction*. In this formulation, the hegemon directly intervenes in the secondary state and transforms its domestic political institutions. Such extensive intervention can occur only in the aftermath of war or as a result of "formal" empire – that is, it can only occur when the victorious hegemon occupies the defeated secondary state and assumes responsibility for its reconstruction or when an imperial power colonizes a peripheral state. In either case, the hegemon imports normative principles about domestic and international political order, often embodying these principles in institutional structures and in constitutions or other written proclamations. The process of social-ization takes place as elites in the secondary state become accustomed to these institutions and gradually come to accept them as their own. The causal chain is as follows: internal reconstruction → policy change (through imposition) → norm change (cooperation through legitimate domination).

When socialization works

Our first hypothesis is that socialization serves as an effective instrument of hegemonic power during critical historical periods in which interna-tional change coincides with domestic crisis in secondary states. As indicated above, socialization is most likely to occur shortly after war or imperial penetration. It is during these periods that the hegemon seeks to adjust to a new constellation of international power and to consolidate its dominant position. It is also during these periods that both defeated and victorious secondary states must cope with discredited elites, domestic fragmentation, and the task of political and economic reconstruction. Stated differently, there are two necessary conditions for socialization to occur. First, the hegemon must be seeking to recast the international order in a way that is more compatible with its interests. As part of its effort to shape the international system, the hegemon must actively attempt to alter the normative orientation of elites in secondary states and, in doing so, must articulate a clear set of normative claims about the international order. Second, domestic conditions in secondary states must make the elites receptive to the importation of new ideas and normative claims about state behavior. This receptivity is most pronounced during periods of domestic political turmoil in which the legitimacy of existing elites is threatened. Socialization and the emergence of legitimate domination at the international level are thus integrally linked to legitimacy at the domestic level.

Our second hypothesis is that socialization occurs only when normative change takes place within the elite community. Although normative claims articulated by the hegemon may take root in the public at large, it is ruling elites that must embrace these claims if they are to have a long-term and consequential impact on the behavior of secondary states. While public opinion can influence elite restructuring, it is through the dynamics of elite politics and coalition-building that socialization takes place.

Our third hypothesis is that even though socialization is a component of power that works at the level of beliefs, it is integrally related to material components of power inasmuch as it occurs primarily after war and the restructuring of material incentives and opportunities at the domestic level. This means that normative persuasion alone is insufficient to drive the socialization process. Rather, elites are driven to embrace the norms articulated by the hegemon for more instrumental reasons: to further coalitional realignment and restore domestic legitimacy and to bring beliefs into line with policies that have been adopted following hegemonic coercion or institutional reconstruction. Material incentives and opportunities for political advancement thus play a crucial role in making elites susceptible to the socializing efforts of the hegemon.

Three additional theoretical concerns, though not cast as testable propositions, also warrant mention. First, the degree to which socialization takes place depends, at least to some extent, on the intrinsic qualities of the norms and ideas being articulated by the hegemon. British liberalism, for example, is for ethical and moral reasons likely to take root more readily among elites in secondary states than, say, Naziism. Of relevance in this regard is not only the intrinsic appeal of a set of ideas but also the

conceptual distance or gap that separates proposed norms from those existing in the elite community. How far is the hegemon asking secondary elites
to move? Will the adoption of new norms put elites in a position to build
new coalitions, or will it push them to the fringe of the political community? Such considerations will color the appeal of a new set of norms
and will therefore affect the extent to which they take root in secondary states.

Second, it is important to recognize that socialization is a two-way
process. Interaction can affect not only the normative orientation of elites
in the secondary state but also that of elites in the hegemonic state. If
hegemonic elites find that their initial efforts at socialization are rebuffed,
they may rework the set of principles upon which they are attempting to
base a new international order. Alternatively, elites from both hegemonic
and secondary states may engage in a process of compromise and together
reshape the conceptions of a desirable normative order. The case studies
discussed below provide numerous instances in which the hegemon's initial
formulation of order was modified through interaction with elites in secondary states.

Third, although socialization usually facilitates cooperation, it can also
lead to discord between the hegemon and the socialized secondary states.
Ideas are by no means static in nature: once implanted among elites in
secondary states, they may follow a trajectory of their own and combine
with pre-existing norms to produce orientations and policies that are at
odds with the hegemon's aspirations. The surge of anti-imperialism that
eventually led to the demise of the British empire, for example, was rooted
in the same liberal notions of justice and representative government that
initially served to facilitate British rule. Socialization can also lead to
discord when the hegemon finds it necessary to pursue policies that are at
odds with the norms it initially articulated. Under these circumstances,
elites in secondary states may question the sincerity and credibility of the
hegemon's normative program. The United States faced this predicament
during the 1960s and 1970s: after decades of persuading the Europeans to
abandon empire and uphold the right of all nations to self-determination,
the United States began to pursue a more interventionist policy toward the
Third World.

Examining the earlier-mentioned hypotheses through historical case
studies and assessing the role of socialization in the exercise of hegemonic
power entail thorny methodological problems. Providing evidence that the
elites of hegemonic nations are concerned with legitimating their position
presents few difficulties. The papers, memoirs, and policy memoranda of
British officials in the nineteenth century and US officials in the twentieth
century contain frequent allusions to both the need to articulate a set of

norms that legitimate their designs for international order and the need to socialize other states into a community bound by shared norms and values. Identifying the process of socialization within secondary nations is a far more difficult task. The process of discerning and measuring shifts in substantive beliefs is difficult when dealing with isolated individuals and is even more problematic when dealing with diffuse elite communities. The normative orientation of a ruling elite is not often clearly articulated, and even if it is possible to show that norms change over time, it is difficult to determine which mechanisms are at work. To do so requires a nuanced reading of history and efforts to infer beliefs from statements and behavior. These obstacles should be kept in mind as we examine the historical materials.

Historical Case Studies

We now turn to several empirical case studies to examine our notion of socialization in more depth and to test our initial propositions about the mechanisms through which and the conditions under which socialization functions effectively as a source of power in international relations.[21]

US diplomacy and the end of World War I: Woodrow Wilson and collective security

The negotiations leading to the end of World War I and the drafting of the Versailles Treaty provide a unique opportunity to study the problem of international socialization. Few, if any, instances of international diplomacy were as steeped in argument about ideals and a normative world order as President Wilson's peacemaking efforts between 1917 and 1919. Wilson's peace program was motivated by a desire to discredit and discard the old diplomacy that he believed led to the outbreak of the war. He proposed that secret diplomacy, balances of power, and trade barriers be replaced by a system of collective security based on popular control of foreign policy, disarmament, free trade, and a community of nations united by the moral and ideological principles of progressive democracy. In this case, the spread of Wilsonian norms was not preceded by the extension into Europe of US military and economic power. This affords us the opportunity to examine the spread of norms in an international community in which no single nation claimed to be in a position of clear economic, military, or ideological dominance.

The terms of the Versailles Treaty and the establishment of the League of Nations indicate that Wilsonian norms, at least to some extent, did shape

Allied conceptions of the postwar order. Nevertheless, the unwillingness of British and French governments to acquiesce to a number of Wilson's requests – that war reparations be kept to a minimum, that Germany not be occupied, that general disarmament be pursued, and that minorities be granted self-determination – is indicative of European resistance to principles central to Wilson's notion of liberal peace and collective security. In this case, we argue that there were two main reasons why socialization did not take place on a more thorough basis. First, while the public, particularly in Britain, did show considerable enthusiasm for Wilson's program, elites were far less receptive. This was largely because military success in 1918 confirmed the stability of incumbent conservative coalitions in both Britain and France, thereby preventing a domestic political crisis that would have led to the fragmentation and realignment of coalitions. Second, because of continuing US isolationism, Wilson's program was not backed up by offers of economic or military assistance. However appealing the program may have been in normative terms, the absence of both political and material incentives dampened its appeal to elites.

Even a cursory glance at the context and tone of Wilson's peacemaking program reveals the extent to which the President was committed not only to ending the war but also to creating a postwar order based on a new conception of international relations. In January 1917, Wilson told the Senate that "there must be, not a balance of power, but a community of power; not organized rivalries, but an organized common peace."[22] The cessation of fighting was not sufficient for Wilson. Unless peace were based "on the highest principles of justice, it would be swept away by the peoples of the world in less than a generation."[23] These principles of justice included notions of democracy, self-determination, and the conviction that territorial settlements and the balance of power should not be allowed to tread on the rights and welfare of peoples, regardless of whether they were members of victorious or defeated states.[24]

These principles were embodied in Wilson's proposals for the terms of peace: open diplomacy, disarmament by all powers, freedom of the seas, removal of trade barriers, self-determination for minorities, restraint in reparations imposed on Germany, and the formation of a league of nations to enforce the peace. The President attempted to win European acceptance of these terms more through mass ideological persuasion than through diplomatic tact. He used the media as well as personal tours of Europe to launch an "ideological crusade" that would appeal to the moral instincts of Europe's masses and induce them to reject the injustices of the old diplomacy.[25] Wilson was attempting to speak directly to Europe's conscience and to instill a new conception of world order through moral persuasion. As one historian stated, "President Wilson applied the idea of

international social control to American foreign relations, promoting collective security to restrain national egoism."[26]

The terms of the Versailles Treaty indeed reflected incorporation of
significant elements of the Wilsonian program. The British and French
agreed to provisions that ensured open diplomacy, a reduction of trade
barriers and armaments, and the establishment of the League of Nations.
In return, Wilson acquiesced to the French demand for occupation of the
Rhineland and the imposition of relatively harsh reparation terms, concessions that indicated European rejection of central elements of the Fourteen
Points.

The incorporation of these important elements of the Wilsonian program
in the treaty was not simply the result of Wilson's bargaining influence at
Versailles. Liberal principles were gaining support in Europe throughout
1917 and 1918, partly as a result of events in Russia. The Russian Revolution gave momentum to leftist parties in Europe and caused intellectual
ferment across the political spectrum. The Bolshevik peace plan, issued
soon after the provisional government was formed in Petrograd, was boldly
progressive and placed pressure on the Allies for a substantive response.[27]
Radicals in Britain were also clamoring for a moderation of war aims and
a more liberal international order.[28]

The extent to which Wilson had established himself as the champion of
liberal peace and democracy among the French and British public became
evident during the President's trip to Europe in December 1918. In France,
Wilson was greeted by throngs of supporters and given a hero's welcome
by trade unions and parties on the Left. His reception in Britain was
similar. Even the conservative *Times* of London commented that "we are
all idealists now in international affairs, and we look to Wilson to help us
realize these ideals and to reconstruct out of the welter a better and fairer
world."[29]

The historical record also suggests that the French and British public
embraced Wilsonian liberalism for ideological and normative reasons and
not simply because the United States entered into the war and was willing
to devote material resources to defeat Germany. The prosecution of the
war clearly had a profound impact on the political and intellectual climate
in Britain and France. The resurgence of the Left and the rising popularity
of Wilsonian war aims early in 1918 were associated not only with growing
disaffection with the war effort but also with fear that the dissolution of
the eastern front which followed the Brest-Litovsk Treaty would give
Germany overwhelming numerical superiority in the West.[30] US assistance
was becoming increasingly important.

Yet to claim that the Europeans were simply mouthing Wilsonian
platitudes to secure US involvement in the war effort does not withstand

scrutiny. As Laurence Martin points out, Wilson was garnering support for a peace program "the principles of which bore a marked resemblance to those long professed by the British Liberal party."[31] The wave of popular support for Wilson emerged in 1918, well after the United States had entered the war. Furthermore, neither the British nor the French government behaved in a way suggestive of disingenuous posturing. As discussed below, Lloyd George offered only reluctant support for Wilsonian diplomacy, while Clemenceau remained one of Wilson's most formidable foes throughout 1918 and 1919. Wilson succeeded in appealing to the people of Europe on moral and ideological, rather than material, grounds. To the extent to which Wilsonian ideals took root, they represented the transmission of normative claims about world order, not the opportunistic acquiescence to US military or economic power.

Although Wilsonian liberalism appealed to the British and French public, it gained little support from European elites. That socialization occurred among the masses but not among decision-makers was largely attributable to coalitional dynamics. At the end of 1917, the conservative forces initially strengthened by the outbreak of war still maintained firm control of the war cabinets of Britain and France. In fact, according to Arno Mayer, between 1914 and 1917 "the forces of order achieved a position of power to which they had aspired only in their most daring dreams before the war."[32] Steeped in the practices and assumptions of the old diplomacy, war policy was characterized by secret negotiations, plans for territorial annexation, and hopes of total defeat of Germany.

During 1918, however, conservative control of the war cabinets, particularly in Britain, eroded considerably. The Russian Revolution and the political crisis of 1917–18 led to the formation of a strong Center/Left coalition in both countries. In Britain, growing popular support for the radical cause forced Labourites to move to the Left. To maintain control of the government, Lloyd George had to incorporate liberal war aims into official policy.[33] In other words, the legitimation of Wilsonian diplomacy among the British public led to the delegitimation of the Conservative government, which in turn brought about a moderation of war aims. A similar policy shift did not occur in France precisely because the Center/Left coalition was not strong enough to undermine Clemenceau's position.

After the defeat of Germany, the political pendulum in Britain again swung to the Right, given a strong push by the nationalistic and patriotic sentiment stimulated by victory. The waning of support for the liberal peace program corresponded with the relegitimation of the Right in the wake of military victory. Lloyd George accordingly paid increasing attention to the Conservatives and their preferences for the shape of a negotiated peace.[34] The Center/Left coalition eroded and the Left grew fragmented, leading to the dissolution of the locus of political activism and idealism that Wilson had tapped to win support for the Fourteen Points. Wilsonian ideals had by no means been rejected, but those still committed to his peace plan were unable to wield effective political power. Thus, socialization of the elite did not occur, since the domestic political context was not conducive to coalitional realignment and hence to elite internalization of a new set of international norms. The relegitimation of the Right prevented a domestic political crisis from emerging in Britain and France, a crisis that could well have produced a vastly different postwar order.

With opportunities for political advancement closed off by the resurgence of the Right, Wilson's peace program had little to offer European decision-makers; material incentives were essentially nonexistent. The norms espoused by Wilson challenged the traditional notion of power-as-resource and worked against British and French interests defined in such traditional terms. Wilson called for the reduction of war reparations, the disarmament of the victors as well as the vanquished, and the adoption of liberal trade ideas that contradicted current British and French practices. Without political, economic, or military incentives, there was little to induce elites to undertake what would have constituted a revolutionary change in their conception of international order. Nevertheless, through normative persuasion, Wilson had left an indelible mark on the European Left. Especially in Britain during the 1930s, notions of collective security and disarmament had a profound effect on the pace of rearmament.[35] Yet in the absence of coalitional realignment and material incentives, intellectual ferment among the Left was insufficient to alter the normative orientation of ruling elites.

US diplomacy and the end of World War II:
liberal multilateralism in Europe and Japan

During World War II and in its immediate aftermath, the United States articulated a remarkably elaborate set of norms and principles to guide the construction of a postwar international order. In the initial formulation, as articulated by the Roosevelt administration, these norms represented a vision of political and economic order organized around the ideas of liberal multilateralism. In the political realm, great power cooperation, embodied in the United Nations Charter, would replace balance-of-power politics. In the economic realm, a system of liberal, nondiscriminatory trade and finance, embodied in the Bretton Woods agreement and the proposals for an international trade organization, would be established.[36]

In the years following World War II, as described in further detail below, the exercise of US hegemonic power involved the projection of a set of norms and their embrace by elites in other nations. Socialization did occur, since US leaders were largely successful in inducing other nations to buy into this normative order. But the processes through which socialization occurred varied from nation to nation. In Britain and France, shifts in norms were accomplished primarily by external inducement; in Germany and Japan, they resulted from direct intervention and internal reconstruction. In all cases, the spread of norms of liberal multilateralism was heavily tied to US military and economic dominance. Just as important was the fact that socialization was a two-way process: the Europeans themselves found opportunities to shape the substantive content of the newly emerging Atlantic order.

The normative order that the United States began to articulate during the war drew on the ideals of liberal multilateralism. These ideals had long historical roots that could be traced to John Hay's "Open Door" and to the third of Woodrow Wilson's Fourteen Points: "the removal, so far as possible, of all economic barriers." The Atlantic Charter, signed by Roosevelt and Churchill during the war, also represented US efforts to elaborate a set of ideals around which a postwar order could be constructed.[37]

Britain and France   Among the democratic nations, the search for agreement on norms and principles was facilitated by shared Western economic and social values. Yet in 1945, as David Watt has pointed out, US ideas for a liberal multilateral order faced several obstacles and had few enthusiastic proponents in Europe:

> Whatever the underlying realities of power, Britain and France started from the assumption that their own pre-war spheres of influence would be maintained or restored to them. Britain still believed in its destiny in the Empire, in the Middle East, in the Eastern Mediterranean and initially in Germany itself. France, in the person of De Gaulle, had spent most of the war years attempting to demonstrate total independence, and had every intention of asserting an equal right to impose a repressive settlement on Germany as well as to repossess its patrimony in Africa, Indo-China and the Middle East. These ambitions did not fit in very easily to a framework of American tutelage or dominance.[38]

US efforts to overcome these obstacles and to induce European acceptance of a more liberal order began with the use of coercive power. This was reflected most strikingly in 1945–6, when US officials attempted to use financial assistance to Britain as a means of forcing a British pledge to lift discriminatory controls and dismantle the imperial preference system.

Reflecting the attitude of Congress at the time, a congressional report stated that "the advantages afforded by the United States loans and other settlements are our best bargaining asset in securing political and economic concessions in the interest of world stability."[39] The British needed financial assistance and were forced to accept the unfavorable terms of the loan, which led in only a matter of weeks to a massive drain on British reserves and forced suspension of convertibility.[40]

The utter devastation of Britain and continental Europe, underestimated at the time by US officials, limited the effectiveness of economic coercion aimed at immediate policy change. In the wake of the failure of the British loan to encourage reform, the Truman administration policy shifted toward less severe sanctions and inducements. Beginning in 1947, the Marshall Plan became the central vehicle for Europe's economic renewal and also for its political reconstruction along lines congenial with US normative designs. "No matter how nebulous the ideas when Marshall spoke," Alan Milward argues, "the political and economic intentions behind the decision to announce the provision of aid were extraordinarily far-reaching and ambitious. The United States did not only intend to reconstruct western Europe economically, but also politically."[41] Beginning with financial assistance, US officials promoted alternatives to economic nationalism and empire. Their immediate political objective was to use Marshall Plan assistance in a way that would promote European integration. A more united Europe built on a common social and economic foundation would help prevent the re-emergence of political antagonisms and economic failure that doomed the settlement of Versailles. But US officials were also convinced that European unity would facilitate the construction of a larger system of liberal multilateral order.[42] Through the Marshall Plan, the United States became directly engaged in the political reconstruction of Europe.

The process by which European elites came to embrace liberal multilateral norms (and disengage from national and imperial alternatives) was gradual and was sustained by the massive flow of money and resources to Europe. Because the European economies grew rapidly during the Marshall Plan years, the norms underlying the plan became associated with economic success and were therefore more appealing to the elites.[43] Efforts other than economic inducements, such as Roosevelt's earlier push for an Atlantic charter, were also designed to convince Churchill and other European leaders of the normative virtues of liberal multilateralism.[44] Before the leaders could be convinced, however, a variety of compromises had to be made along the way.

Agreement emerged over the desirability of a loose system of liberal multilateralism. Two specific processes facilitated the emergence of a new normative order. One involved the reworking of the normative ideas themselves; a two-way process was clearly at work. Although the modified set of liberal designs was not framed as an explicit shift in international economic objectives, the United States gradually accepted exemptions and abridgments in trade and financial arrangements, which together allowed a larger measure of national economic autonomy and a stronger role for the state in pursuing full employment and social welfare. These compromises between multilateralism in international economic relations on the one hand and state intervention in the domestic economy and society on the other constituted what John Ruggie has termed "embedded liberalism."[45] A loose consensus on the norms of international economic order emerged. The British and French moved slowly to multilateralism, and the United States came to accept the primacy of the welfare state in the organization of the international political economy.

The other process that served to yield a consensus on modified liberal multilateralism was more directly associated with domestic politics in Britain and France as well as in Italy. The resistance to US ideas after World War II came from both the Left and Right within Western Europe. Right-wing parties sought to protect the fragments of empire and preserve their status as great powers, a status that liberal multilateralism would necessarily undermine. Left-wing parties feared the erosion of national autonomy and the effects of multilateralism on independent economic planning. Both groups were vocal in seeking to protect and extend programs of full employment and social welfare.[46] European movement toward a loose liberal multilateral system involved the gradual decline of these positions. On the Right, the ravages of war utterly weakened the capacity of Britain and France to maintain the cloakings of colonial empire. Indeed, this weakness was in part responsible for their willingness to invite the United States into a security relationship with Western Europe. Likewise, the watering down of the liberal multilateral agreements – modifications that served to protect the obligations of the welfare state – served to undercut the impact of the Left.

In summary, the norms of liberal multilateralism, backed by the massive flow of Marshall Plan aid, provided a basis for the building of centrist coalitions in postwar Britain, France, and Italy. The gradual economic recovery of Europe also served to weaken the positions of left- and right-wing elites who argued for national socialist or imperial alternatives to liberal multilateral policies. Moreover, the compromises reached between US and European officials over the terms of an embedded liberal system are indicative of the importance that both groups of elites attached to the development of a normative consensus about the terms of postwar order.

Germany and Japan   The conviction of US leaders that postwar order had to be based on normative principles is also revealed in the government's deliberations over the postwar fate of Germany and Japan. In early 1945, President Roosevelt agreed to the State Department's recommendation for "assimilation – on a basis of equality – of a reformed, peaceful and economically nonaggressive Germany into a liberal system of world trade."[47] The emphasis was on "normative" rehabilitation and not punishment. Several years later, with the rise of Cold War tensions, the plan for a reconstructed and "assimilated" Germany also made good geopolitical sense. But the fact that US officials were planning to promote liberal political and economic institutions in Germany well before US–Soviet hostilities emerged is an indication of the importance they attached to the spread of liberal norms.

The US occupation of Germany had a profound impact on the character of German postwar institutions and the political values that guided German behavior at home and abroad. The occupation policy (in both Germany and Japan), as John Montgomery notes, "aimed at a programmed installation of democracy, first, through the elimination of despotic elites, second, through the encouragement and support of a new leadership, and, finally, through constitutional, legal, and institutional assurances of a new order."[48] These efforts to purge the old elite and build new democratic institutions had uneven success. The occupation forces found it easier to promote the demilitarization and democratization of Germany than to promote the restructuring and decartelization of the German economy. Moreover, it is quite likely that postwar Germany would have moved in the direction of political reform and economic liberalization even in the absence of the Allied occupation. Nonetheless, the process of internal reconstruction during the occupation left a lasting impact on the institutions and values that have shaped postwar German politics.

A central legacy of the Allied occupation was the decentralization of the German political system. As Peter Katzenstein argues, "Although American, British, and French authorities disagreed on the degree and type of political decentralization that they preferred, they strongly agreed that a territorial decentralization of the Federal Republic would shield democratic institutions from the possible reemergence of centralizing, totalitarian political movements."[49] This federal system restricted the power of the national government by assigning major responsibilities (such as education, law enforcement, and administration) to the states. The result was a system of dispersed political power in which federal officials had to negotiate and share power with regional elites.

The most enduring economic reforms carried out during the Allied occupation were those of currency reform and trade liberalization. The impulse for reform came at the behest of the Allied occupation, but it was also championed by a few leading German officials. Currency reform, a vital factor in German economic recovery, was initiated by Economics Minister Ludwig Erhard, who used the occupation period to articulate a distinctively German vision of market economy.[50] Other reforms, such as trade liberalization, were carried out at the insistence of Allied officials. As Henry Wallich argues, "American authorities in Washington and Paris had decided to make Germany into a test or showcase of liberalization."[51] Through these efforts (as well as through less direct programs of political re-education and cultural exchange), the United States encouraged the growth of a set of political and economic norms that were soon embraced widely by German elites.

There were limits on the ability of US officials to give shape to German political and economic institutions. "It is doubtful that new ideas and new leaders, however worthy, can survive alone," Montgomery argues. "Both require a degree of support that cannot be achieved by promises, propaganda, or external pressure."[52] But Allied forces did give shape to institutions that reinforced political values congenial with the US policy of liberal multilateralism.

Similar postwar policies emerged in regard to Japan.[53] Through its role as an occupying power, the United States in the early postwar years reshaped the norms that guided Japanese behavior in the domestic and international arenas. The US decision to intervene directly in the reconstruction of Japan's domestic political institutions set the stage for a striking episode of socialization through internal reconstruction. The occupation reforms were based on norms of democratization and liberalization, norms that were embraced by elites and masses alike. Although historians continue to dispute whether the Japanese would have chosen a similar path of democracy and political reform in the absence of the US occupation,[54] there is widespread acknowledgment that the United States played a central role in the proliferation of the norms and political institutions that eased Japan's reintegration into the postwar order.

Despite the existence of the Allied Council for Japan, responsibility for Japan's postwar reconstruction fell almost exclusively into American hands under the guidance of the Supreme Commander for the Allied Powers (SCAP). In the short term, SCAP was to restore order to Japanese society and to destroy the country's military capability. In the long term, however, US officials believed that democratization and political reform were needed to ensure the eradication of militaristic tendencies from Japanese society.[55]

The goal was not only to graft democratic institutions onto the Japanese polity but also to inculcate among the Japanese people values that would allow political reforms to plant deep roots. As Edwin Reischauer stated, "The occupation did not stop at political reform but went on to a bold attempt to reform Japanese society and the economy in order to create conditions which were thought to be more conducive to the successful functioning of democratic institutions than the old social and economic order had been."[56]

Reforms that were introduced by SCAP and accepted by the Japanese government penetrated the political, economic, and social realms. A new constitution, drafted by SCAP and put into effect on May 3, 1947, served as the foundation for Japan's postwar political structure. The constitution contained several key features. First, it established a parliamentary system based on the British model.[57] Provisions were included to ensure that the Diet would not again be subordinate to the executive, as it was during the interwar period. To protect further the parliamentary system, the emperor was relegated to a position of largely symbolic importance, and the judiciary was revamped so as to minimize executive interference.[58] Second, the constitution stipulated that the state grant and protect specified civil rights, including the right of workers to bargain collectively, the right of women to vote, and the right of all citizens to equal education. In addition, local governments were granted increased autonomy. Third, the constitution prohibited the maintenance of armed forces and explicitly expressed the will of the Japanese people to renounce war forever. Most of these constitutional provisions were implemented without delay, although the prohibition on armed forces fell by the wayside during the 1950s.

In the economic realm, SCAP pushed forward two major reforms. Prior to the war, close to 50 percent of agricultural land was owned by traditional elites and worked by tenants. Radical land reform reduced this figure to 10 percent.[59] SCAP also tried to dissolve the *zaibatsu*, the powerful conglomerates that dominated Japanese industry. The attempt was partially abandoned, however, in order to further the country's economic recovery. The *zaibatsu* were able to maintain their control over industry, though they were effectively stripped of the large holding companies that they had constructed prior to the war.[60]

In the social realm, SCAP focused on cultivating communal norms of equality and on educational reform. Reform was successful in enfranchising women but was only partially successful in breaking down the traditional authority of main families over branch families. Educational reform was widespread. The United States completely revamped the primary and secondary education system. The curriculum was based on the US model, and education through the high school level became compulsory. A new educational philosophy focused attention on the development of analytic skills rather than on memorization. These changes so challenged traditional patterns that they were implemented only gradually and with varying degrees of success.[61]

Through this broad package of reforms, the United States helped implant among Japanese elites and masses the norms of parliamentary government and anti-militarism that have guided Japan's domestic and foreign policy during the postwar era. Clearly, the pre-war system had been discredited by the disastrous consequences of Japanese expansion and aggression, and the Japanese people felt betrayed by the pre-war government and military elites. War had indeed made the polity ripe for change, and new political values and norms may even have emerged in the absence of the US occupation. Nevertheless, the US occupation deeply influenced the direction and content of the changes, and the extent to which they were compatible with the US vision of postwar order was by no means a coincidence.

That a process of socialization was at work during this period is confirmed by the extent to which elite personnel and structures remained unchanged by the occupation. As mentioned above, the *zaibatsu* continued to dominate industrial circles. Furthermore, many pre-war administrative and bureaucratic organs continued to function during and after the occupation period. This institutional continuity hampered the implementation of certain reforms and perpetuated traditional elite prerogatives and patterns of authority. But because of shifts taking place at the level of substantive beliefs and normative orientations, this continuity did not prevent the Japanese from embracing principles of liberal equality and democracy embodied in the new constitution. As one Japanese scholar notes, "As the years have passed, the influence of occupation reforms has penetrated into the very core of Japanese society."[62] And as another Japanese observer confirms, "The reforms themselves exercised a powerful influence on the character of Japanese postwar politics and in fact upon all of Japan's postwar history."[63]

In summary, socialization played an important role in the construction of a postwar order. The proliferation of liberal multilateral norms, both through external inducement and internal reconstruction, infused the system with a set of values that would eventually allow the system to function smoothly and in a manner consistent with US interests.[64] By the mid- to late 1950s, US efforts at international socialization proved successful. A set of liberal multilateral norms had, to varying degrees, taken root in Western Europe and Japan.

British experience in India and Egypt:
socialization through colonization

A necessary condition for the emergence of both informal and formal empire is the explicit, physical penetration of peripheral society by metropolitan agents. Whether officials, soldiers, traders, financiers, or missionaries, these agents serve as the medium through which socialization occurs.[65] During the middle decades of the nineteenth century, Britain was relatively successful in altering the normative orientation of Indian elites and thereby furthering the secularization and liberalization of political life. Socialization contributed significantly to the longevity of British rule in India, to the relatively low costs of maintaining the empire in South Asia, and to the lasting effect of the British presence on Indian political culture. The situation in Egypt was quite different; Britain did not penetrate Egyptian society or socialize Egyptian elites as it did in India. This more shallow form of colonial penetration increased British reliance on the use of force, meant that the period of colonial rule was relatively short, and tempered the long-term impact of Britain's presence on Egyptian society. To explain these differences between Britain's experience in India and Egypt, we examine both British policy and the effect of indigenous social and political structures on the interaction between metropole and periphery.

India Beginning in the seventeenth century, the East Indian Tea Company gradually established control over significant areas of the subcontinent. It was not until 1813, however, that the British Crown extended formal sovereignty to these areas. While the principal goal of the British was to govern India effectively and allow for lucrative trade with the metropole, it was clear that British intentions went far beyond efficient administration.

As one observer of the period stated, the British empire "has for its end the larger freedom, the higher justice whose root is in the soul not of the ruler but of the race."[66] This commitment to effect a deeper change in Indian society was driven not only by a desire to consolidate British power but also by the increasing strength of utilitarianism and evangelism within Britain itself. The former provided impetus for the improvement of living conditions and education in India. The latter brought missionaries seeking to propagate Christian morality in India. As Charles Grant expressed in an article contained in an 1832 parliamentary report on India, British rule is a question "not merely of increasing the security of the subjects and prosperity of the country, but of advancing social happiness, of meliorating the moral state of men, and of extending a superior light."[67]

Through what specific mechanisms did socialization take place? British efforts to effect change in Indian political culture were embodied or manifest in a wide range of policy tools. First, the Charter Act of 1813 was the first of several enactments that firmly established English as the primary language for the school system and government business. The spread of English made Western books and ideas accessible to educated Indians and made possible more extensive and meaningful contact between Indians and Englishmen. As Percival Spear noted, "The widespread knowledge of English provided an ideological bridge; ideas flowed over in the persons of British lawyers and officials, missionaries, and disinterested men of learning. . . . The essential fact is that these ideas did begin to take root."[68]

Second, the Indian judicial system was reformed along the British model. Beginning in 1835, English replaced Persian as the language of record. The principles and procedures of British law were also imported into India.[69] James Fitzjames Stephen held out high hopes for the effect of British law on Indian society:

> The establishment of a system of law which regulates the most important part of the daily life of a people constitutes in itself a moral conquest, more striking, more durable, and far more solid than the physical conquest which renders it possible. It exercises an influence over the minds of the people in many ways comparable to that of a religion. . . . Our law is, in fact, the sum and substance of what we have to teach them.[70]

The British also restructured the Indian education system, again relying on their own model. Sir Charles Wood's education dispatch of 1854 established universities in Calcutta, Bombay, and Madras, all of which adopted London's examination procedures.

These reforms and institutional changes led to the emergence of a new Indian middle class whose prosperity and professional success depended on its learning of English and adoption of British legal and business procedures.[71] The growth and rising stature of this class of collaborators in turn played a central role in allowing British ideas and practices to take root in India. According to Spear:

> Britain's supreme function has been that of a cultural germ carrier. . . . The introduction of the English language provided a vehicle for Western ideas, and English law a standard practice. Along with English literature came Western moral and religious ideas, and the admission of missionaries provided, as it were, a working model of Western moral precepts.[72]

To what extent did the British succeed in changing the norms and values shaping Indian political culture? During the nineteenth century, British rule deeply influenced the structure and normative orientation of Indian political life. Before the British presence, Indian politics was dominated by religious affiliation and practice, the caste system, and strong local and regional allegiances. By the end of the 1800s, Western notions of administrative efficiency and justice had led to the gradual secularization of politics; the importance of the caste system had declined somewhat; and the spread of English had helped overcome the political regionalism that had been perpetuated by linguistic diversity (some 179 distinct languages and 544 dialects had hampered communication). In short, British political values and practices had intermingled with and, in some instances, replaced the traditional norms eroding under the pressure of colonialism.

As mentioned above, these changes were possible largely because of the emergence of a new political elite within India. British administration of India took place through a new class of collaborators consisting of English-speaking and Western-educated professionals. Trained within an education system introduced by the British, these individuals – bureaucrats, lawyers, doctors, and teachers – quickly rose to prominent positions within Indian society. Induced by the opportunities for advancement and indoctrinated by Western education, this new political elite came to believe in and espouse the values and norms articulated by the Raj. They thus provided a mechanism for socialization, a medium through which British values seeped into Indian political culture.

By the late 1800s, the osmosis and spread of Western political values and teachings had stimulated an increasingly strong movement for democracy and Indian independence.[73] Given the principles embodied in the liberal notions imported to India, it is not surprising that the same educated elite co-opted by the British to facilitate their rule later became a key force behind the delegitimation of imperial domination.[74] Yet even after the opposition movement grew strong, the depth of British penetration of Indian political culture was evident. As Anil Seal points out, "The new politicians were impeccably constitutional. [They] spoke highly of British justice. They asked God to bless the British Queen. They had friends inside the British parliament."[75] This behavior suggests that the trajectory of British rule in India was shaped by the power of ideas as much as by military and economic might. The consolidation of British rule during the 1800s was due, at least in part, to a process of socialization. The observed changes in political values came about through policy coercion; that is, the transmission of ideas followed the forcible importation of Western political institutions and practices. Moreover, the collaborative elite was enticed by promises of financial or political gain. Nevertheless, India's political elite actually came to believe in Western values rather than simply mouthing acquiescence because of British coercion. And the subsequent rise of Indian nationalism and delegitimation of the British presence were also associated with changing beliefs, rather than with a changing constellation of military and economic power.

Egypt   British rule in Egypt after the occupation in 1882 stands in stark contrast to the British experience in India. Neither in intent nor in deed did the British penetrate and restructure Egyptian political culture as they did in India. British elites, from the outset of the occupation, never intended to incorporate Egypt into the formal empire as a lucrative and permanent outpost. On the contrary, they viewed Egypt primarily as a strategic asset needed to guard the Suez Canal and the route to India. They assumed that after restoring stability to Egypt following the revolt of Colonel Arabi, they could withdraw without jeopardizing Britain's strategic or economic interests.[76] The evangelical, moralistic, and normative orientation of British rule in India was strikingly absent from British policy in Egypt.

The British did not attempt to restructure the indigenous political, legal, and administrative apparatus through which Egypt was governed. They sought only to fine-tune and make more efficient the existing administrative apparatus. In Viscount Milner's words, "The object of the British officials has been, not to Anglicize the Egyptian bureaucracy in political opinion, but only to Anglicize it in spirit, to infuse into its ranks that uprightness and the devotion to duty which is the legitimate boast of the Civil Service of Great Britain."[77] John Marlowe agreed that "British administration was merely added as a superstructure to the existing fabric of government."[78]

As a result, no new political elite emerged in Egypt. On the contrary, both before and during the occupation, the British relied on well-established landlords and merchants as their collaborators. "They adopted the expedient of attempting to raise standards of living without changing class structures," as Robert Tignor points out, and "they attempted to make authority felt without undermining the position of the traditional ruling classes." In short, "they governed behind these ruling classes."[79] The ruling classes cooperated with the British not because they believed in Western values or justice but, rather, because they benefited from their role as collaborators and from the loans and improvements in irrigation that came with the British presence. They were not drawn into or psychologically co-opted by British rule. The very mechanism through which socialization occurred in India – the creation of a new political elite – was never set in motion in Egypt.

The absence of significant reform in the Egyptian education and legal systems was indicative of the superficial nature of British rule. The British had only partial success in spreading the use of English throughout the country.[80] English-language newspapers did not proliferate in Egypt as they did in India. This limited the extent to which Western ideas and values were absorbed even by the educated elite. Furthermore, the education system changed little under British rule and was given a low priority in terms of government expenditure.[81] Viscount Milner admitted that Britain did "very little for Egypt in the way of voluntary schools."[82] The lack of universities was also a significant problem. The British, in order to restrict the spread of nationalism, actually opposed the expansion of the university system.[83] Many Egyptians completed their secondary education but did not have the opportunity to attend university. They were therefore too well qualified for manual work but lacked the credentials for government or administrative work. This created a large body of disaffected youth easily swayed by nationalist sentiment.[84] The effect of British rule on the court system was similarly insignificant. Despite the importation of some Anglo-Indian legal procedures, the Egyptian judicial system continued to be modeled on that of the French.[85]

The superficial nature of British rule was also reflected in Britain's dependence on the cooperation of specific collaborators. During the early years of colonial rule, Khedive Tewfik played a key role in facilitating British administration. When Tewfik died in 1892, he was replaced by Abbas II, who was far less willing to cooperate with the British. Richard Cottam describes the result: "With the realization that Abbas II would not serve as the legitimating agent for the British presence . . . the British established a different type of control system – one which relied far more on direct coercive instruments."[86] In 1893, Lord Cromer requested and was granted the first of several increases in the size of the British garrison. Moreover, traditional elites, who were no longer willing to cooperate with the British, were replaced by British personnel. The collaborative network was breaking down. Between 1896 and 1906, the number of British officials serving in Egypt rose from 286 to 662.[87] To cope with resistance movements, the British were forced to implement a rigorous security system in the countryside and hire some fifty thousand informants to report on developments in local villages. As Timothy Mitchell describes this system, the British "transformed modern military methods of inspection, communication and discipline into an uninterrupted process of political power."[88] Only ten years after the initial occupation, the British found themselves scrambling to keep pace with a nationalist movement that made colonial rule increasingly difficult and costly.

The British thus attempted to rule Egypt through unadorned coercion and inducement. They sought to co-opt the traditional ruling elite by either forcing or inducing them to serve as peripheral collaborators. Yet once the benefits of cooperation with the British began to decrease, there was no corpus of beliefs or norms that had taken root in Egyptian society to justify or legitimate British rule and to counter the rise of nationalist and anti-British sentiment. As John Marlowe described this phenomenon, "The only moral justification for imperialism is the *pax* which accompanies the legions. Great Britain in Egypt tried to secure the presence of the legions without being prepared to enforce the *pax*." Britain initially enjoyed the privileges of occupation without paying the price but soon "destroyed the moral basis on which her position in Egypt rested."[89] In 1914, when the use of coercion in the absence of efforts to socialize Egyptian elites proved insufficient to subdue the swelling tide of nationalism, Britain unilaterally declared Egypt a protectorate and imposed martial law. By 1922, however, the British cabinet realized that the situation was untenable and granted Egypt formal independence.

The imposition of foreign rule unadorned by a corpus of beliefs and norms led to a period of occupation that was both difficult and relatively short-lived. Britain's experience of formal empire in India, though it also ended in acquiescence to nationalism, was far more durable and left a deeper impression on Indian society. The distinguishing feature of British hegemony in India was that Britain succeeded in building and socializing a new political elite, allowing it to penetrate and reshape Indian political culture.

Conclusion

In this essay, we have attempted to characterize and shed light on a neglected component of hegemonic order – power as socialization – and have articulated a theoretical framework for thinking about when and how socialization functions effectively as a source of power in the international system. The intersection between theory and historical cases corroborates our three main hypotheses.

First, the case studies suggest that the timing of socialization and the extent to which it occurs are highly dependent on the efforts of the hegemon to propagate its conception of international order and also on the susceptibility of secondary states to a restructuring and redefining of the terms of domestic political legitimacy. It is principally in the aftermath of war or colonial penetration that the hegemon articulates a new set of norms and that domestic political conditions make elites most susceptible to socialization. In the post-World War II case, the spread of US norms was intimately tied to the tasks of reconstruction and coalition-building. The reconstruction aid of the Marshall Plan and its ideological gift-wrapping strengthened the hands of government elites standing against both left-wing and right-wing opposition to liberal multilateralism. Moreover, after the initial failure of coercive efforts to promote liberal multilateralism, US officials grew more sensitive to European sovereignty and the need for European leaders to take the initiative in constructing a postwar order. It was only through struggle and compromise that the Europeans and Americans arrived at a consensus on the norms of the postwar order. A process of "thought reform," as Andrew Shonfield puts it, did take place, with the Europeans gradually shedding the norms of colonization and imperial preference.[90] In the case of India, the British were able to legitimate their rule because the colonial presence led to the emergence and co-optation of a new professional class that quickly established its stature and political power within Indian society. The British manipulated the standards of domestic political legitimacy, replacing traditional standards with their own. In doing so, they were able to consolidate and legitimate their rule. In the case of Egypt, precisely because the British administration depended on traditional elites, there was little change in the standards of domestic legitimacy. There was no opportunity for the transmission of norms; the consequent absence of interaction between British rule and domestic politics hindered the emergence of legitimate domination.

Second, the case studies confirm that socialization is principally an elite and not a mass phenomenon. For norms to have a consequential effect on state behavior, they must take root within the elite community. Wilson did not succeed fully in shaping the peace process, since his package of liberal norms found substantial support in Britain and France only among the public and was not greeted with enthusiasm in elite circles. The successful spread of British norms in India resulted from the creation and co-optation of a new political elite. In contrast, the shallow and fragile nature of British rule in Egypt was a function of the British decision to govern through traditional elite channels.

Third, the case studies suggest that socialization comes about principally through external inducement or internal reconstruction and that normative persuasion is insufficient to drive the socialization process. Elites in secondary states come to believe in the norms and ideals articulated by the hegemon only in conjunction with the provision of material incentives or through the imposition of those norms via direct intervention. Although Wilson's program found some followers in post-1918 Europe, its ultimate failure was at least partially due to the fact that it was not backed up with economic or military assistance. In Europe after World War II, US offers of material aid and opportunities for coalitional realignment drove forward the establishment of a normative consensus. In India, a new political elite emerged at least in part because of the opportunities for political advancement and material gain that accompanied collaboration with the British.

Although socialization is triggered by coercion and material inducements, the process of socialization can lead to outcomes that are not explicable simply in terms of the exercise of coercive power. Socialization affects the nature, the costs, and the longevity of the interactions that shape hegemonic systems. In particular, socialization leads to the legitimation of hegemonic power in a way that allows international order to be maintained without the constant threat of coercion. In this regard, it may be instructive to study the waning of hegemony – and especially that of *Pax Americana* – in terms of the legacies of socialization as well as in terms of the decline of the hegemon's military and economic dominance. As we have noted, the importance of socialization is most likely to be observed during periods when the hegemon's coercive capacities are in decline. According to our argument, the spread of liberal multilateral norms among elites in the late 1940s has given the contemporary hegemonic order more durability than would be expected by those who focus exclusively on the distribution of material resources. The socialization of hegemonic power has left a loose normative consensus embedded in the rules and institutions of the postwar system. These rules and institutions should persist well beyond the inflection point of hegemonic decline. *Pax Americana*, nonetheless, is in decline, and we are left to reflect on the nature of the normative principles that might be used by a future hegemon to legitimate a new order.

Notes

We gratefully acknowledge valuable comments and suggestions from Hayward Alker, Henry Bienen, George Downs, Michael Doyle, John Lewis Gaddis, Fred Greenstein, Steph Haggard, John Hall, Robert Jervis, Peter Katzenstein, Robert Keohane, Stephen Krasner, M. J. Peterson, David Rapkin, John Ruggie, Jack Snyder, and Steve Walt. Research for this article was supported by the Pew Charitable Trusts Program on Integrating Economics and National Security and by the Center of International Studies, Princeton University.

1   The groundwork for this essay was laid out in an earlier essay that sought to deepen our understanding of the nature of legitimacy in the international system. See G. John Ikenberry and Charles A. Kupchan, "The Legitimation of Hegemonic Power," in David Rapkin, ed., *World Leadership and Hegemony*, vol. 5 of *International Political Economy Yearbook* (Boulder, Colo.:

Lynne Rienner, 1990). Some of the historical material contained in the present essay draws on our earlier essay.

2   Some scholars have made general distinctions among political, economic, and ideological aspects of power. See Michael Mann, *The Sources of Social Power*, vol. 1, *A History of Power from the Beginning to AD 1760* (Cambridge: Cambridge University Press, 1986), especially pp. 22–8; and Kenneth Boulding, *The Three Faces of Power* (Newbury Park, Calif.: Sage, 1989).

3   See Alexander George, "The 'Operational Code': A Neglected Approach to the Study of Political Leaders and Decision Making," *International Studies Quarterly* 13 (June 1969): 190–222. George argues that the operational code consists of two levels of beliefs: deep philosophical beliefs and instrumental beliefs. Our notion of norms is similar to George's category of instrumental beliefs. For further discussion of this level of beliefs and how to measure them, see Charles A. Kupchan, "France and the Quandary of Empire, 1870–1939," paper presented at the annual meeting of the American Political Science Association, Atlanta, 1989. To clarify the presentation, we distinguish among norms, value orientations, interests, and preferences in the following way. Norms are general principles upon which a certain vision of international order is based. Value orientations are norm-based attitudes toward specific policy issues and types of behavior. Interests are the broad objectives of policy, such as prosperity, political stability, and security. Preferences are the ordering of alternative courses of action or policy choices.

4   As discussed below in the case studies, the content of norms changes over time. During the nineteenth century, for example, British hegemony in the European system was facilitated by principles of free trade. British domination in certain colonial areas, most notably India, was similarly facilitated by the importation and spread of liberalism. During the post-World War II era, the US hegemonic system has been infused with norms of liberal multilateralism and democratic government.

5   A similar distinction between types of acquiescence (or "acceptance") is made by Mann: "*pragmatic* acceptance, where the individual complies because he perceives no realistic alternative, and *normative* acceptance, where the individual internalizes the moral expectations of the ruling class and views his own inferior position as legitimate." See Michael Mann, "The Social Cohesion of Liberal Democracy," *American Sociological Review* 35 (June 1970): 423–39.

6   For a discussion of the use of international market power, see Scott C. James and David A. Lake, "The Second Face of Hegemony: Britain's Repeal of the Corn Laws and the American Walker Tariff of 1846," *International Organization* 43 (Winter 1989): 1–29.

7   See Robert O. Keohane, *After Hegemony: Cooperation and Discord in the World Political Economy* (Princeton, NJ: Princeton University Press, 1984), p. 32; and Stephen D. Krasner, "American Policy and Global Economic Stability," in William P. Avery and David P. Rapkin, eds., *America in a Chang-*

ing World Political Economy (New York: Longman, 1982), p. 32. The United States after World War II provides the premier case of the coercive potential of a remarkably diversified resource portfolio. "American leaders were able to bring into play a very wide range of resources with few opportunity costs for the United States," argues Krasner. "American threats were credible because the United States would not lose much if they were carried out. American leaders could usually construct a link that would enable them to compel other actors to alter their policy. Inducements could be offered because the United States had resources that others needed much more than they were needed by the United States."

8   Keohane, *After Hegemony*, p. 39.

9   Robert Gilpin, *War and Change in World Politics* (New York: Cambridge University Press, 1981), p. 34.

10 A variety of efforts have been made to develop more sophisticated models of hegemonic power, giving precision to its mechanisms and dynamics. Snidal outlines three forms of hegemony: that which is benign and exercised by persuasion; that which is benign but exercised by coercion; and that which is coercive and exploitative. See Duncan Snidal, "Hegemonic Stability Theory Revisited," *International Organization* 39 (Autumn 1985): 579–614. Hirsch and Doyle note three types of hegemonic power: cooperative leadership, hegemonic regime, and imperialism. See Fred Hirsch and Michael Doyle, *Alternatives to Monetary Disorder* (New York: McGraw Hill, 1977), p. 27.

11 Robert W. Cox, *Production, Power and World Order* (New York: Columbia University Press, 1987), p. 172. See also two works by Stephen Gill: "Hegemony, Consensus, and Trilateralism," *Review of International Studies* 12 (July 1986): 205–21; and "American Hegemony: Its Limits and Prospects in the Reagan Era," *Millennium: Journal of International Studies* 15 (Winter 1986): 311–36.

12 Max Weber, *Economy and Society*, vol. 1, edited by Guenther Roth and Claus Wittich (Berkeley: University of California Press, 1978), p. 213.

13 Jürgen Habermas, *Legitimation Crisis* (Boston: Beacon Press, 1975), p. 101.

14 Our notion of socialization corresponds closely with that in the literature on political socialization. As Sigel states, "Political socialization refers to the learning process by which political norms and behaviors acceptable to an ongoing political system are transmitted from generation to generation." See R. Sigel, "Assumptions About the Learning of Political Values," *Annals of the American Academy of Political and Social Sciences*, vol. 361 (1965): 1.

15 Our notion of socialization differs from that of Waltz. In Waltz's theory, socialization refers to a process through which actors come to conform to the structural norms of the international system. It is a process that "limits and molds" the behavior of states in ways that accord with the imperatives and constraints of international structures. See Kenneth Waltz, *Theory of International Politics* (New York: Wiley, 1979), pp. 74–6. We refer to social-

ization as a process through which the value orientations of a leading state are transmitted to elites in other nations, regardless of the structural setting.

16 Richard Merelman, "Learning and Legitimacy," *American Political Science Review* 60 (September 1966): 548. See also Alexander L. George, "Domestic Constraints on Regime Change in US Foreign Policy: The Need for Policy Legitimacy," in Ole Holst et al., eds., *Change in the International System* (Boulder, Colo.: Westview Press, 1980), pp. 233–62; and Thomas Trout, "Rhetoric Revisited: Political Legitimacy and the Cold War," *International Studies Quarterly* 19 (September 1975): 251–84.

17 Our notion of socialization in the international system has a clear parallel to Durkheim's "conscience collective" – a body of beliefs and values upon which moral consensus in domestic societies is based. The conscience collective, as Giddens suggests, provides domestic cohesion and conformity through "the emotional and intellectual hold which these beliefs and values exert over the perspectives of the individual." See Anthony Giddens, ed., *Emile Durkheim: Selected Writings* (Cambridge: Cambridge University Press, 1972), p. 5. We maintain that the emergence of shared norms and beliefs performs a similar role in the international context, facilitating cooperation and cohesion among sovereign states.

18 Merelman, "Learning and Legitimacy."

19 For an application of this theory to international relations, see Deborah Larson, *The Origins of Containment: A Psychological Explanation* (Princeton, NJ: Princeton University Press, 1985), pp. 42–50.

20 A related process, involving the spread of policy-relevant knowledge, is described by Hass as "consensual knowledge." See Ernst Hass, "Why Collaborate? Issue-Linkage and International Regimes," *World Politics* 32 (April 1980): 357–405. More generally, the literature on regimes addresses how norms and procedures guide state behavior. This literature, however, focuses more on how norms facilitate cooperation than on how norms emerge and take root among relevant states. Our notion of socialization may shed light on the processes through which regimes emerge. For a general review of the literature, see Stephan Haggard and Beth A. Simmons, "Theories of International Regimes," *International Organization* 41 (Summer 1987): 491–517.

21 Several considerations informed our selection of case studies. We were concerned primarily with understanding how and when socialization takes place, rather than with assessing the extent to which socialization affects outcomes. Accordingly, we focused on the early stages of interaction between a hegemon and secondary states. We also attempted to select a range of historical cases that would allow us to probe the different mechanisms through which socialization takes place. In Britain and France after World War II, socialization occurred through the thick network of political, economic, and military ties that emerged between Western Europe and the United States. In Germany and Japan, the United States resorted to military occupation and explicit

reconstruction of domestic institutions. The cases of India and Egypt allowed us to examine examples of colonial penetration. We were also careful to pick instances of both successful and unsuccessful efforts at socialization in order to enhance the analytic value of comparative analysis. Inasmuch as work in this area is relatively underdeveloped, we consider these cases to serve as "plausibility probes" in an effort to formulate and test initial hypotheses about the process of socialization in international relations.

22 Wilson, quoted in Arthur Link, *Wilson the Diplomatist: A Look at His Major Foreign Policies* (New York: New Viewpoints, 1974), pp. 96–7.

23 Wilson, quoted in Arno Mayer, *Politics and Diplomacy of Peacemaking: Containment and Counterrevolution at Versailles, 1918–1919* (New York: Knopf, 1967), p. 21.

24 Link, *Wilson the Diplomatist*, p. 105.

25 Mayer, *Politics and Diplomacy of Peacemaking*, p. 368.

26 Lloyd Ambrosius, *Woodrow Wilson and the American Diplomatic Tradition: The Treaty Fight in Perspective* (Cambridge: Cambridge University Press, 1987), p. 2.

27 The April 1917 statement included the following passage: "The purpose of free Russia [was] not domination over other peoples, nor spoilation of their national possessions, nor the violent occupation of foreign territories, but the establishment of a permanent peace on the basis of self-determination of peoples. The Russian people [were] not aiming to increase their power abroad at the expense of other people; they [had] no aim to enslave or oppress anybody." Quoted in Arno Mayer, *Political Origins of the New Diplomacy, 1917–1918* (New Haven, Conn.: Yale University Press, 1959), p. 75.

28 Laurence Martin, *Peace Without Victory: Woodrow Wilson and the British Liberals* (New Haven, Conn.: Yale University Press, 1958), ch. 3.

29 London *Times*, quoted in Mayer, *Politics and Diplomacy of Peacemaking*, p. 188.

30 Mayer, *Political Origins of the New Diplomacy*, p. 311.

31 Martin, *Peace Without Victory*, p. 21.

32 Mayer, *Political Origins of the New Diplomacy*, p. 14.

33 Martin, *Peace Without Victory*, pp. 132–4 and 148–54.

34 Ibid., p. 192.

35 Michael Howard, *The Continental Commitment* (London: Temple Smith, 1972), pp. 110 ff.

36 These ideas are summarized by Richard Gardner in *Sterling-Dollar Diplomacy: The Origins and the Prospects of Our International Economic Order*, expanded edition (New York: McGraw Hill, 1969). See also David P. Calleo and Benjamin M. Rowland, *America and the World Political Economy: Atlantic Dreams and National Realities* (Bloomington: Indiana University Press, 1973).

37 See Robert A. Pollard, *Economic Security and the Origins of the Cold War, 1945–1950* (New York: Columbia University Press, 1985), ch. 1.

38 David Watt, "Perceptions of the United States in Europe, 1945–83,"

in Lawrence Freedman, ed., *The Troubled Alliance: Atlantic Relations in the 1980s* (New York: St Martin's Press, 1983), pp. 29–30.

39 Congressional report, quoted in Gardner, *Sterling-Dollar Diplomacy*, p. 198.

40 See Robin Edmonds, *Setting the Mould: The United States and Britain, 1945–1950* (New York: Norton, 1986), ch. 8.

41 Alan S. Milward, *The Reconstruction of Western Europe, 1945–51* (Berkeley: University of California Press, 1984), p. 56.

42 See Michael J. Hogan, *The Marshall Plan: America, Britain, and the Reconstruction of Europe, 1947–1952* (New York: Cambridge University Press, 1987).

43 See Charles Maier, "The Politics of Productivity: Foundations of American International Economic Policy After World War II," in Peter Katzenstein, ed., *Between Power and Plenty: Foreign Economic Policies of Advanced Industrial States* (Madison: University of Wisconsin Press, 1978), pp. 23–49.

44 G. John Ikenberry, "Rethinking the Origins of American Hegemony," *Political Science Quarterly* 104 (Fall 1989): 375–400.

45 John Gerard Ruggie, "International Regimes, Transactions, and Change: Embedded Liberalism in the Postwar Economic Order," *International Organization* 36 (Spring 1982): 379–415.

46 For a discussion of these groups in Britain, see Gardner, *Sterling-Dollar Diplomacy*, pp. 31–5.

47 Roosevelt, quoted in Robert Dallek, *The American Style of Foreign Policy: Cultural Politics and Foreign Affairs* (New York: Knopf, 1983), p. 147.

48 John D. Montgomery, *Forced to Be Free: The Artificial Revolution in Germany and Japan* (Chicago: University of Chicago Press, 1957), pp. 4–5.

49 Peter J. Katzenstein, *Policy and Politics in West Germany: The Growth of a Semisovereign State* (Philadelphia: Temple University Press, 1987), p. 16.

50 Ibid., p. 87.

51 Henry C. Wallich, *Mainsprings of the German Revival* (New Haven, Conn.: Yale University Press, 1955), p. 372.

52 Montgomery, *Forced to Be Free*, p. 194.

53 The Truman administration, in a major statement of post-surrender policy on September 6, 1945, argued that the Japanese people were to "be encouraged to develop a desire for individual liberties and respect for fundamental human rights, particularly freedom of religion, assembly, speech, and the press." Most important, the Japanese were "to become familiar with the history, institutions, culture, and the accomplishments of the United States" and, by so doing, turn themselves into a "New Deal-style Democracy." Quoted in Dallek, *The American Style of Foreign Policy*, p. 149. Compliance with the precepts of a liberal multilateral order, in the view of US officials, must begin with liberal reforms at home. Only with these economic and political reforms could the nations of the industrial world, victors and vanquished alike, abide by American-inspired norms.

54 For contrasting views on this issue, see the contributions of Edwin Reischauer, J. W. Dower, Sodei Rinjiro, and Takemai Eiji in the following book: Harry Wray and Hilary Conroy, eds., *Japan Examined: Perspectives on Modern Japanese History* (Honolulu: University of Hawaii Press, 1983), pp. 331–63.

55 Edwin Reischauer, *The Japanese* (Cambridge, Mass.: Harvard University Press, 1977), p. 106.

56 Ibid., p. 107.

57 SCAP reasoned that Japan's experience with republican government during the 1920s made the British model more appropriate than the American model. See Reischauer, *The Japanese*, p. 106.

58 See Theodore H. McNelly, "'Induced Revolution': The Policy and Process of Constitutional Reform in Occupied Japan," in Robert E. Ward and Sakamoto Yoshikazu, eds., *Democratizing Japan: The Allied Occupation* (Honolulu: University of Hawaii Press, 1987).

59 Ibid., p. 108.

60 J. W. Dower, "Reform and Consolidation," in Wray and Conroy, *Japan Examined*, p. 348.

61 Reischauer, *The Japanese*, pp. 108–9.

62 Takemai Eiji, "Some Questions and Answers," in Wray and Conroy, *Japan Examined*, pp. 359–60.

63 Masataka Kosaka, *A History of Postwar Japan* (Tokyo: Kodansha International, 1972), p. 65.

64 Note that US policy in both Germany and Japan was predicated on the assumption that changes in domestic institutions and structures would lead to desired changes in foreign policy. In Britain and France, it was focused more narrowly on altering elite norms about international behavior. The more ambitious approach in Germany and Japan was at least in part due to the wide variance between the ideas being propagated and the norms existing in the target country.

65 For an insightful study of the dynamics of metropolitan penetration, see Michael Doyle, *Empires* (Ithaca, NY: Cornell University Press, 1986), pp. 141–231.

66 J. A. Cramb, cited in Francis Hutchins, *The Illusion of Permanence: British Imperialism in India* (Princeton, NJ: Princeton University Press, 1967), p. 149.

67 Grant, cited in ibid., p. 5.

68 Percival Spear, *The Oxford History of Modern India, 1740–1975*, 2nd edn. (Delhi: Oxford University Press, 1978), p. 137.

69 Ibid., p. 205.

70 Stephen, cited in Hutchins, *The Illusion of Permanence*, p. 126.

71 Spear, *The Oxford History of Modern India*, pp. 206–8.

72 Ibid., p. 7.

73 The gradual consolidation of British rule in the mid-1800s by no means removed all resistance to the colonial presence. The mutiny of 1857, which

came as a great surprise to the British, demonstrated the potential for latent resentment to be mobilized. It was not until the last two decades of the century, however, that an organized nationalist movement began to systematically undermine British rule.

74 See Hutchins, *The Illusion of Permanence*, pp. 190–1.

75 Anil Seal, *The Emergence of Indian Nationalism: Competition and Collaboration in the Later Nineteenth Century* (Cambridge: Cambridge University Press, 1968), pp. 14–15.

76 Robert Tignor, *Modernization and British Colonial Rule in Egypt, 1882–1914* (Princeton, NJ: Princeton University Press, 1966), pp. 24 and 48–9. See also Nadav Safran, *Egypt in Search of Political Community* (Cambridge Mass.: Harvard University Press, 1961), p. 54.

77 Viscount Milner, *England in Egypt* (London: Edward Arnold, 1920), p. 290.

78 John Marlowe, *Anglo–Egyptian Relations, 1800–1953* (London: Cresset Press, 1954), p. 251.

79 Tignor, *Modernization and British Colonial Rule in Egypt*, p. 105.

80 Milner, *England in Egypt*, p. 301.

81 Tignor, *Modernization and British Colonial Rule in Egypt*, p. 319.

82 Milner, *England in Egypt*, p. 299. See also Safran, *Egypt in Search of Political Community*, p. 55.

83 Tignor, *Modernization and British Colonial Rule in Egypt*, p. 338.

84 Marlowe, *Anglo–Egyptian Relations*, p. 189.

85 Tignor, *Modernization and British Colonial Rule in Egypt*, pp. 123–37.

86 Richard Cottam, *Foreign Policy Motivation: A General Theory and a Case Study* (Pittsburgh: University of Pittsburgh Press, 1977), p. 239.

87 Ibid., p. 236.

88 Timothy Mitchell, *Colonising Egypt* (Cambridge: Cambridge University Press, 1988), pp. 97–8.

89 Marlowe, *Anglo–Egyptian Relations*, p. 254.

90 Andrew Shonfield, "International Economic Relations of the Western World: An Overview," in Andrew Shonfield, ed., *International Economic Relations of the Western World, 1959–1971*, vol. 1 (London: Oxford University Press, 1976), p. 98.

3

The Nature and Sources of Liberal International Order

Introduction

The end of the Cold War has triggered new debates about international relations theory. Most of the attention has been focused on explaining the end of the Cold War. Equally important, however, this epochal development raises new questions about the impact of 40 years of East–West rivalry on the relations among the Western liberal democracies. This issue is not simply of passing historical interest, because it bears on our expectations about the future trajectory of relations among the great powers in the West. Will the end of the Cold War lead to the decline of cohesive and cooperative relations among the Western liberal democracies? Will major Western political institutions, such as NATO and the US–Japanese alliance, decay and fragment? Will "semi-sovereign" Germany and Japan revert to traditional great power status? Will the United States revert to its traditional less engaged and isolationist posture? Our answers to these questions depend upon the source of Western order: was the Cold War the primary source of Western solidarity or does the West have a distinctive and robust political order that predated and paralleled the Cold War?

Realism advances the most clearly defined – but pessimistic – answers to these questions. Neorealist theory provides two powerful explanations for cooperation within the West: balance of power and hegemony. Realist balance of power theory holds that Western institutions are the result of balancing to counter the Soviet threat, which provided the incentive for Western countries to cooperate.[1] With the end of the Cold War, balance of power theory expects Western security organizations, such as NATO, to weaken and eventually return to a pattern of strategic rivalry.[2] Realist hegemony theory holds that American power created and maintained the order in the West by offering incentives to the other Western democracies to participate, and that Western conflict will rise as American power declines.[3] The basic thrust of these realist theories is that the relations among the Western states will return to the patterns of the 1930s and early '40s, in which the problems of anarchy dominated: economic rivalry, security dilemmas, arms races, hypernationalism, balancing alliances, and ultimately the threat of war.

But realists overlook important facts. In the wake of World War II, the United States and its allies created a political, economic, and strategic order that was explicitly conceived as a solution to the problems that led to the depression and world war.[4] The origins of this order predated the full onset of the Cold War and it was institutionalized at least semi-independently of it. Major features of this order cannot be explained by realist theories. The Western order contains too many consensual and reciprocal relations to be explained as the product of balancing and hegemony. Nor can the degree of Western institutionalization, its multilateral pattern, and the stable "semi-sovereignty" of Germany and Japan be explained by balancing and American hegemony. The timing of its origins and many of its salient features provide a puzzle that can only be solved by looking beyond realist theories.

Of course, many liberal theories have attempted to understand and explain the distinctive features of the Western political order, and their overall picture of the West's future is much more optimistic than that of realism. Theories of the democratic peace, pluralistic security communities, complex interdependence, and the trading state attempt to capture distinctive features of liberal, capitalist, and democratic modern societies and their relations.[5] While offering important insights into the Western order, these liberal theories are incomplete and miss several of its most important aspects.

The aim of this essay is to develop a theory of "structural liberalism" that more adequately captures the unique features of this Western order in a way that builds on the strengths but goes beyond the weaknesses of current realist and liberal theories. Existing liberal theories do not give sufficient prominence to nor attempt to explain the prevalence of co-binding security practices over traditional balancing, the distinctive system-structural features of the West, the peculiarly penetrated and reciprocal nature of American hegemony, the role of capitalism in overcoming the problem of relative gains, and the distinctive civic political identity that pervades these societies. In contrast, structural liberalism seeks to capture the major components of the Western political order and their interrelationships. These core dimensions of Western political order

Structural liberalism		Neorealism	
Characteristic	Role	Characteristic	Role
security co-binding	mitigates dynamics of anarchy	balancing	maintains autonomy of units
penetrates reciprocal hegemony	enhances legitimacy through access and shared decision-making	coercive hegemony	provides public goods and maintain order
semi-sovereign and partial great powers	mechanism to incorporate problem states	full sovereignty and great powers	management of system by leading states
economic openness	exploit comparative advantage and create interdependence	self-reliance	avoids dependence and maintain military mobilization capacity
civic identity	moderates conflict and facilitates integration	national identity	reinforces state coherence, legitimacy and interdependence

Figure 3.1   Structural liberal vs neorealist order

and contrasting realist descriptions and theories of order are summarized in figure 3.1.

The argument unfolds in five sections, each focused on a component of the Western order. The first section examines the security practice of co-binding as a liberal solution to the problem of anarchy. The second section explores the penetrated character of American hegemony, the role of transnational relations in American hegemony, and its reciprocal rather than coercive character. The third section analyzes the role of the semi-sovereign and partial great powers of Japan and Germany as structural features of the Western political order. The fourth section examines structural openness, the political foundations of economic openness and its solutions to relative gains problems. The final section focuses on the distinctive Western civic identity and community and its role in underpinning the liberal institutions in the West. In the conclusion, the significance of this alternative conception of liberal political order is discussed.

Security Co-Binding

Neorealism provides a very strong argument relating system structure to unit-level practices. The core of neorealist theory is that states in an anarchical system will pursue a strategy of balancing. Anarchy means that there is no central government that the units can rely upon for security; and in such a situation, states seeking security will balance against other states that they perceive to be threats to their security. Balancing has both an internal and external dimension. Internally, it takes the form of the domestic mobilization of power resources (via armament and the generation of state capacity). Externally, balancing typically takes the form of *ad hoc*, counter-hegemonic alliances in which states join together with other states that fear for their security from threatening or powerful states.[6] Moreover, successful balancing, by undercutting the concentration of power at the system level, tends to reinforce and reproduce anarchy; in effect, balancing and anarchy are co-generative. Likewise, balancing in anarchy tends to strengthen the capacity of the state in its relation with society, which in turn makes the creation of system-wide governance more difficult. This pattern of balancing in anarchy has characterized the Western state system both in its early modern, Europe-centered phase as well as in the global system that has emerged in late-modern times. Because of this long pattern and deep logic, realists expect balancing to be pervasive in international politics wherever there is anarchy.

This realist view neglects a distinctive practice that liberal states have pioneered and which has given the West a distinctive structure unlike anarchy. Unrecognized by neorealists, liberal states practice co-binding – that is, they attempt to tie one another down by locking each other into institutions that mutually constrain one another.[7] This practice of co-binding constraint can be either asymmetrical or symmetrical. Asymmetrical binding is characteristic of hegemony or empire, but liberal states practice a more mutual and reciprocal co-binding that overcomes the effects of anarchy without producing hierarchy. This practice of co-binding does not ignore the problems and dynamics of anarchy, but rather aims to overcome them. By establishing institutions of mutual constraint, co-binding reduces the risks and uncertainties associated with anarchy. It is a practice that aims to tie potential threatening states down into predictable and restrained patterns of behavior, and it makes unnecessary balancing against such potential threats.

Co-binding practices are particularly suited to liberal states. When co-binding is successful, it reduces the necessity for units to have strong and autonomous state apparatuses. Moreover, democratic and liberal states are particularly well suited to engage in co-binding, because their internal structures more readily lend themselves to the establishment of institutions that constrain state autonomy. As with anarchy and balancing, co-binding creates an international situation that is congenial to the liberal states that are particularly suited to co-binding. This co-binding practice has been neglected by neorealist theory, but it has a robust logic that liberal states in the West have exhibited.

Co-binding is an important feature of the Western liberal order. While balancing and hegemony played a role in the formation of these Western institutions, this binding practice was significantly and independently motivated by an attempt to overcome anarchy and its consequences among the Western states. After World War I, the United States sought through the League of Nations to establish a system of binding restraints among the Western states, but this was not fully attempted in practice and, to the extent it was, it failed for a variety of reasons.[8] After World War II, the United States and liberal states in Europe sought again to bind themselves through NATO. Although realists dismiss failed efforts at binding as idealistic, and successful post-World War II institutions as purely the result of balancing, these institutions were created in significant part by Europeans and Americans who were eager to avoid the patterns that led to the two world wars.

The most important co-binding institution in the West, of course, is NATO. Although the Soviet threat provided much of the political impetus to form NATO, the alliance always had in the minds of its most active advocates the additional purpose of constraining the Western European states vis-à-vis each other and tying the United States into Europe.[9] Indeed, NATO was as much a solution for the "German problem" as it was a counter to the Soviet Union. As the first NATO Secretary-General, Lord Ismay, famously put it, the purpose of NATO was to keep the "Russians out, the Germans down, and the Americans in." These aims were all inter-related: in order to counter-balance the Soviet Union it was necessary to mobilize German power in a way that the other European states did not find threatening and to tie the United States into a firm commitment on the continent.

The NATO alliance went beyond the traditional realist conception of an *ad hoc* defense alliance, because it created an elaborate organization and drew states into joint force planning, international military command structures, and established a complex transgovernmental political process for making political and military decisions.[10] The co-binding character of this alliance is manifested in the remarkable effort that its member states made to give their commitment a semi-permanent status – to lock themselves in so as to make it difficult to exit.

The desire to overcome the dynamics of anarchy also gave rise to an agenda for economic co-binding, particularly in Europe. The European union movement explicitly sought to achieve economic interdependence between Germany and her neighbors in order to make strategic military competition much more costly and difficult to undertake. The first fruit of this program, the European Coal and Steel Community, effectively pooled these heavy industries that had been essential for war-making. In its administration of the Marshall Plan, the United States sought to encourage the creation of joint economic organizations in order to create economic interdependencies that crossed over the traditional lines of hostilities between European states.[11] The United States also supported the creation of political institutions of European union, so as to bind the European states together and foreclose a return to the syndromes of anarchy.[12] American supporters of European reconstruction, as well as European advocates of the European community, explicitly sought to create European institutions that were more like the United States than the traditional Westphalian states in anarchy.

The result of this security co-binding among Western liberal states was the creation of a political order that successfully mitigated anarchy within the West in ways that neorealist theory fails to appreciate. Although these institutions created by binding practices significantly altered the anarchical relations within the Atlantic world, they fell far short of creating a hierarchy. Because Waltzian neorealism conceives of order as either hierarchical or anarchical, it lacks the ability to grasp institutions between hierarchy and anarchy that constitute the structure of the liberal order.

Penetrated Hegemony

The second major realist explanation for the Western political order is American hegemony. Hegemony theorists, tracing their roots from Thucydides through to E. H. Carr, claim that order arises from concentrations of power, and when concentrated power is absent disorder marks politics, both domestic and international. In international systems, concentrations of power produce hegemony, which is conceived as a system organized around asymmetrical power relations.[13] Hegemonic theorists argue that Western order is the product of American preponderance, which was at its zenith in the immediate post-World War II years when the major security and economic rules and institutions were established. In this image of the West, order is maintained because the United States has the capacity and the will to compel and coerce, to establish and maintain rules, and to provide inducements and rewards to its client states in Europe and East Asia.

Both balance of power and hegemonic theories are conventionally viewed as versions of neorealism, but their relationship is much more problematic. In fact, these two versions of neorealist theory have quite contradictory images of order in world politics – one emphasizing that order comes from concentrations of power and the other emphasizing that concentrations of power produce balancing resistance. Thus balance of power theory poses a fundamental question to hegemonic theory: why do subordinate states within a hegemonic system not balance against the hegemon?[14] To answer this question one must look at the ways in which stable hegemonic orders depart from the simple image provided by hegemonic theory.

The American-centered Western order exhibits far more reciprocity and legitimacy than an order based solely on superordinate and subordinate relations. American hegemony has a distinctively liberal cast because it has been more consensual, cooperative, and integrative than it has been coercive. The distinctive features of this system – particularly its transparency, the diffusion of power into many hands, and the multiple points of access to policy-making – have enabled Western European and Japanese allies to participate in policy-making for the overall system.[15] As a result, American hegemony has been highly legitimate and is an "empire by invitation."[16]

To understand this system it is necessary to incorporate two factors neglected by realists: the structure of the American state and the prevalence of transnational relations. When a liberal state is hegemonic, the subordinate actors in the system have a variety of channels and mechanisms for registering their interests with the hegemon. Transnational relations are the vehicles by which subordinate actors in the system represent their interests to the hegemonic power and the vehicle through which consensus between the hegemon and lesser powers is achieved. Taken together, liberal state openness and transnational relations create an ongoing political process within the hegemonic system without which the system would be undermined by balancing or become coercive.

A distinctive feature of the American state is its decentralized structure, which provides numerous points of access to competing groups, both domestic and foreign. Because the decision-making process of the American liberal state is so transparent, secondary powers are not subject to surprises.[17] The fundamental character of the American liberal state is that it is elaborately articulated and accessible to groups and forces emerging from civil societies. The size, diversity, and federal character of the American political system also provide many points of influence and access. The American polity has many of the features associated with international politics – such as decentralization and multiple power centers – and therefore is particularly well prepared to incorporate pressures and influences from liberal societies outside itself.[18] In sum, the open domestic structure of the United States is not simply an anomalous or solely domestic phenomenon, but is integral to the operation of the Western system.

Transnational relations are a second integral component of the liberal hegemonic system, whose role and significance have not been grasped by either realist or liberal theorists. Realists view transnational relations as derivative of hegemonic power and thus of secondary importance. Hegemony provides a framework within which such interactions can flourish and the growth of transnational relations in the post-World War II era is a consequence of American hegemony.[19] Conversely, liberal theorists, who pay a great deal of attention to transnational relations, see them as the beginnings of a system that is expected to eventually displace the state and locate political power in non-state entities such as multinational corporations, international organizations, and networks of transnational and transgovernmental experts.[20]

Far from being ancillary or derivative, transnational relations are a vital component of the operation of this system.[21] This system provides transparency, access, representation, and communication and consensus-building mechanisms. Because of the receptiveness of the liberal state and the existence of transnational relations, subordinate states achieve effective representation. Furthermore, transnational connections between the actors in a hegemonic system constitute a complex communication system that is continuously shaping preferences and thus moderating the divergence of interests among actors in the system.[22] Transnational networks also serve to forge a consensus and lobby policy-makers throughout the system. In hegemonic systems infused with transnational relations, the legitimacy of the asymmetrical relationships is enhanced. Such processes endow the relations with a degree of acceptability in the eyes of subordinate powers. This in turn reduces the tendency for subordinate powers to resist and, correspondingly, diminishes the need for the hegemon to exercise coercion.[23] Such legitimacy endows hegemonic systems with a greater degree of stability and resilience than what the realist hegemonic model expects. Because of the accessible state structure and transnational state processes, the arrows of influence are not in one direction – from the center to the periphery – as in the hegemonic model, but rather run in both directions, producing a fundamentally reciprocal political order.

The relationship between the United States and Japan is less extensively institutionalized than Atlantic relations; however it also exhibits similar features.[24] Japanese corporate representatives have extensively accessed the Washington policy-making process and have been able to influence American decision-making in areas that affect Japanese interests, particularly with regard to trade policy.[25] This Japanese access has not been reciprocated, but this asymmetry helps compensate for the subordinate role of Japan as an ally. From the Japanese perspective, this access and influence help Japan cope with the enormous power the United States has over Japan, and thus adds legitimacy and stability to the relationship. Viewed from the perspective of the American state, this Japanese access is a weakness; viewed from the perspective of the American system, it is a strength.

Semi-Sovereignty and Partial Great Powers

A third major structural feature of the Western liberal order that distinguishes it from the realist image of states in anarchy is the distinctive status of Germany and Japan as semi-sovereign and partial great powers. Contrary to realist expectations, Germany and Japan both have "peace constitutions" that were initially imposed by the United States and the Western allies after World War II, but which have come to be embraced by the German and Japanese publics as acceptable and even desirable features of their political systems. The structure of these states is highly eccentric for realist models, but these are integral and not incidental features of the Western political order.

Realist theories assume that the nature of the units making up the international system are sovereign and, to the extent they have sufficient capacity, they are great powers. Sovereignty as understood by realists is Westphalian sovereignty, and this means that states are accorded a set of rights and assume a set of responsibilities, the most important of which is the mutual recognition of each other's autonomy and juridical equality.[26] Moreover, Westphalian sovereignty is understood by realists to be one of the primary means by which the system of anarchical states is institutionalized, thus reinforcing the primacy of the state, the absence of hierarchy characteristic of anarchy, and providing a degree of regularity to anarchy.[27]

Central to realist theory is also the concept of the Great Power, the exclusive set of states that have sufficient capacity to secure themselves but also to exercise influence over surrounding smaller states and to affect the entire system. Integral to the realist notion of the great power is that such states possess a full range of instruments of statecraft, most importantly a robust military establishment with which to make good their claims to great power status and to influence the system.[28] Together, Westphalian sovereignty and the great power are enduring features of the realist vision of anarchical society.

Two of the major states in the Western system, Germany and Japan, do not follow the expected realist pattern, but rather are semi-sovereign and partial great powers. It is widely noted that since World War II, Germany and Japan have been "semi-sovereign" states.[29] Such a label is partly misleading, but it is also essential to capture their distinctive and eccentric character and roles. As the reconstruction after 1945 progressed, Germany and Japan both sought to be accorded the full panoply of rights and responsibilities of a Westphalian sovereign, and the United States and the other Western states were forthcoming with this recognition as part of their reconstruction and reintegration into the international system. However, it is still appropriate to characterize these states as fundamentally semi-sovereign because in return for sovereign recognition they accepted a role in international relations that was self-constrained in major ways. They were able to gain juridical sovereignty only because they were willing to eschew the full range of great power roles and activities.

At the heart of this odd configuration of juridical sovereignty and effective semi-sovereignty have been two levels of structure: strong self-imposed constitutional constraints and the integration of Germany and Japan in wider political, security, and economic institutions. German and Japanese domestic political structures that were created during occupation and reconstruction featured parliamentary democracy, federalism, and an independent judiciary – and thus they were much more similar to the liberal American state than the traditional and closed autocratic state.[30] These domestic structures facilitate binding linkages, transnational interaction, and political integration. These structures of constraint and the practice of semi-sovereignty were anchored in a strong domestic consensus that traditional autocracy and imperialism had catastrophic consequences that had to be avoided at all costs.[31]

The most important way in which Germany and Japan are eccentric states to the realist model is that they are not playing the traditional role of great powers. Their partial great power status is defined by the discrepancy between their power potential and power mobilization and between the breadth of foreign policy interests and the underdevelopment of their policy instruments. As a product of the American and Western occupations of Germany and Japan, both countries created "peace constitutions" that wrote into their basic law a foreign policy orientation that was radically at variance with the requirements of great power status and activities. Most important was that these constitutions committed these states to purely defensive military orientations. A powerful expression of this self-restraint is that both Germany and Japan have voluntarily forgone the acquisition of nuclear weapons – the military instrument that more than any other has defined great powers during the last half century. In the postwar period, the international strategic environment has not allowed them to retreat into isolation or maintain neutrality. But their defensive military postures have not been autonomous, but rather have been elaborately and extensively integrated into multilateral arrangements. In addition to explicitly eschewing great power postures, German and Japanese constitutions contain a strong mandate for an activist foreign policy directed at maintaining international peace and building international institutions.

Although both Germany and Japan are semi-sovereign and partial great powers, there are important differences between them. Their regional contexts have imposed very different constraints and opportunities. Germany, sharing long contested land borders with many countries, has pursued its unique postwar role by integrating itself much more intensively militarily and economically with its neighbors. In contrast, insular Japan was alone in the Far East as a postwar liberal power and therefore its strategic binding with the rest of the system has been through the bilateral US–Japanese alliance. Furthermore, the Western reconstruction of Germany along liberal lines was much more intensive, while the early demands of the Cold War led the United States to less comprehensively reconfigure Japan. Partially as a result, German domestic political structures became more liberal and decentralized than Japan, where strong state capacity remained, particularly in the economic domain. Overall, German integration into the Western political order is much more complete than Japanese integration, in both multilateral economic and security systems. One expression of this difference is that German rearmament has been more extensive than Japanese because Germany is more thoroughly bound into the Western order than Japan.

The existence of Germany and Japan as semi-sovereign and partial great powers constitutes a fundamental anomaly for realist theory. The features of these states are not, however, incidental but are integral to the Western political order. The widely held realist expectation that Germany and Japan will revert back to great power status poses a test for these competing theories: should this pattern eccentric to realism persist, the explanatory utility of realism will have been compromised. Conversely, should Germany and Japan return to the normal realist pattern, the Western political order is not likely to endure – and if it does, the theory of structural liberalism will be called into question.

Economic Openness

It is widely recognized that a major feature of the Western order is the prevalence of capitalist economies and international institutions dedicated to economic openness. Neorealist theories offer two powerful explanations for the Western liberal economic order, one stressing American hegemony and the other Western alliance within bipolarity. Liberals also offer many explanations, including the rise of "embedded liberalism" among the advanced industrial nations. While offering important insights, these theories are insufficient and miss two crucial dimensions of the liberal economic order. First, advanced capitalism creates such high prospects for absolute gains that states attempt to mitigate anarchy between themselves so as to avoid the need to pursue relative gains. Second, liberal states have pursued economic openness for political ends, using free trade as an instrument to alter and maintain the preferences and features of other states that are politically and strategically congenial.

One powerful realist explanation for the prevalence of open economies in the Western order is hegemonic stability theory.[32] These realists argue that open international orders are created and sustained by the concentration of power in one state. Hegemonic powers establish and enforce rules, provide exchange currency, absorb exports, and wield incentives and inducements to encourage other states to remain open. Hegemonic stability theorists argue that economic openness in the nineteenth century was made possible by British hegemony and that when British power waned in the first decades of the twentieth century, the open trading system broke down. After World War II, the United States, then at the peak of its relative power, provided the leadership to establish Western liberal economic institutions, thereby catalyzing another era of economic openness and high growth.[33] Hegemonic stability theorists maintain that the relative economic decline of the United States threatens to undermine these arrangements. Because of bipolarity and American leadership in the Cold War, the effects of American relative decline have not been fully registered, but the expectation is that system will decay after the Cold War.

Another realist argument is that free trade has resulted from bipolarity and the Western strategic alliance.[34] In this view, allied states are less concerned with relative gains considerations than unallied states. Allied states are not as sensitive to relative shifts in economic advance that might result from free trade. Similarly, realist theorists argue that military allies see relative gains by each other as adding to the overall strength of the alliance. With the decline of bipolarity and the diminished importance of strategic alliances after the Cold War, the expectation of these realist theories is that the free trade order will come under increasing stress.

Liberals also advance powerful arguments about the sources of open economies. In particular, the "embedded liberalism" argument holds that liberal states in the twentieth century have committed themselves to ambitious goals of social welfare and economic stability, which in turn require them to pursue foreign economic policies that maintain a congenial international environment for the realization of these goals.[35] This argument situates the preference for open economic policies in the domestic structures of advanced industrial societies. As long as Western welfare states retain their commitment to high employment and social welfare, the theory expects that they will remain committed to liberal foreign economic policies.[36]

These realist and liberal arguments contain important insights, but they neglect two important sources of Western economic openness. Neorealists rightly insist that states in anarchy must be more concerned with relative than with absolute gains, and therefore are willing to forgo the absolute gains that often derive from economic exchange out of fear that their relative position will suffer.[37] The relative and absolute gains argument is typically seen as a powerful reason why states will not accept economic openness. In reality, however, it suggests a powerful explanation for why states will take steps to mitigate anarchy. In a world of advanced industrial capitalist states, the absolute gains to be derived from economic openness are so substantial that states have the strong incentive to abridge anarchy so that they do not have to be preoccupied with relative gains considerations at the expense of absolute gains. The assumption of the neorealist argument is that the only alternative to anarchy is hierarchy, but in fact liberal states have developed co-binding institutions and practices that make it possible to moderate anarchy without producing hierarchy. The extensive institutions that liberal states have built can be explained as the mechanisms by which they have sought to avoid the need to forgo absolute gains in order to pursue relative gains.

Three other features of advanced industrial capitalism also have significant implications for the politics of relative and absolute gains. First, modern industrial economies are characterized by great complexity and this means that states attempting to calculate the relative gains consequences of any particular policy face a high degree of uncertainty. In highly dynamic markets with large numbers of sophisticated, fast-moving, and autonomous corporate actors, it is very difficult to anticipate the distribution of gains and losses. Second, the rate of change in advanced industrial capitalism is so great that the distribution of relative gains and losses is likely to fluctuate between countries fairly rapidly. Thus, even if one country can foresee that it will be a loser in a particular period, it can assume that it will experience a different outcome in successive iterations.[38] Finally, modern industrial capitalist societies are multi-sectoral, and different sectors in one country may be simultaneously declining and rising as a result of international openness, making it difficult for governments to calculate their aggregate relative gains and losses. The multi-sectoral character of these societies helps insure that the pattern of relative gains and losses will be highly variegated, making it unlikely that any one state will be a loser or winner across the board.[39]

Western states also have political reasons to maintain an open economic order: free trade can spread and strengthen liberal democracy. The expansion of capitalism that free trade stimulates tends to alter the preferences and character of other states in a liberal and democratic direction, thus producing a more strategically and politically hospitable system. The collapse of the world economy in the Great Depression and the political turmoil it produced contributed to the retreat of democracy and liberalism in the 1930s, the rise of fascist and imperialist states, the emergence of rival economic blocs, and ultimately World War II. In reaction to these upheavals, the principal architects of the post-World War II liberal order employed economic openness as a strategy to avoid regional blocs, trade wars, illiberal regimes, and ruinous imperial rivalry.[40.] The architects of the liberal system perceived that a world populated by liberal states would be much more compatible with American interests and the survival of democracy and capitalism in the United States.[41] This proposition suggests that liberal economic order is not fundamentally dependent on bipolarity and American hegemony, but rather has a powerful independent source that is unlikely to be affected by the end of the Cold War.

Civic Identity

The fifth dimension of the Western political order is a common civic identity. Although difficult to quantify, what Montesquieu called "spirit" is an essential component of any political order. The West's "spirit" – common norms, public mores, and political identities – gives this political order cohesiveness and solidarity. Throughout the Western world, there is an overwhelming consensus in favor of political democracy, market economics, ethnic toleration, and personal freedom. The political spectrum throughout the West looks increasingly like the narrow "liberal" one that Louis Hartz once identified as distinctively American.[42] Compared to the diversity that characterized Europe as recently as the 1930s, the convergence of political practices and identities within the countries of the West is an important feature whose causes and consequences require explanation.

Realist approaches to international theory largely assume that the separate state units have distinct national identities. Realists emphasize that national identity provides states with legitimacy and serves as a basis for the mobilization of resources against outside threats. For realism, the experience of interstate war serves as an important source of national identity and loyalty because it provides the most potent and emotive symbolism of heroism, battlefield sacrifice, and collective memory of opposition and triumph.[43] Military organizations provide one of the most powerful means of socializing individuals into patriotism and veterans organizations constitute a major interest group that reinforces the primacy of the nation-state. For realism, these sociological processes are a crucial link between international anarchy and interstate war and the prevalence of the nation-state as a unit in the international system.

No enduring political order can exist without a substantial sense of community and shared identity. Political identity and community and political structure are mutually dependent. Structures that work and endure do so because they are congruent with identities and forms of community that provide them with legitimacy. Conversely, structures and institutions create and reinforce identities and community through processes of socialization and assimilation. These important sociological dimensions of political orders have been neglected by both neorealist and neoliberal theories, which take the preferences of the actors as given and examine only the interaction between interests and structure. As a result, they miss the identity and community dimensions of political order – both the national and the liberal civic alternatives.

An essential component of the Western political order is a widespread civic identity that is distinct from national, ethnic, and religious identities. At the core of the Western civic identity is a consensus around a set of norms and principles, most importantly political democracy, constitutional government, individual rights, private property-based economic systems, and toleration of diversity in non-civic areas of ethnicity and religion. Throughout the West, the dominant form of political identity is based on a set of abstract and juridical rights and responsibilities which coexist with private and semi-public ethnic and religious associations. Just as warring states and nationalism reinforce each other, so too do Western civic identity and Western political structures and institutions reinforce each other.

The West's common civic identity is intimately associated with capitalism, and its business and commodity cultures. As Susan Strange argues, capitalism has generated a distinctive "business civilization."[44] Across the advanced industrial world, capitalism has produced a culture of market rationality that permeates all aspects of life. The intensity and volume of market transactions across the industrial capitalist world provides a strong incentive for individual behaviors and corporate practices to converge. One strong manifestation of this convergence is the widespread use of English as the language of the marketplace. Likewise, the universality of business attire across the industrial capitalist world signifies this common business culture.

Another cultural dimension of the Western order is the commonality of commodities and consumption practices. Through the advanced industrial world, mass-produced and market commodities have produced a universal vernacular culture that reaches into every aspect of daily existence. The symbolic content of day-to-day life throughout the West is centered not upon religious or national iconography, but upon the images of commercial advertising. The ubiquitously displayed images of the good life are thoroughly consumerist. The demands of mass marketing and advertising place a premium on reaching the largest number of purchasers, and so it contributes to the homogenization of identities and the avoidance of polarizing ethnic or religious or racial traits. Further defining popular culture throughout the West is mass entertainment, particularly television, movies, music, and athletic events. Because of increased incomes and cheap transportation, international tourism has become a mass phenomenon. The cumulative effect of this symbolic and popular culture and interaction is to create similar lifestyles and values throughout the West.[45]

Another contributor to the commonality of identities in the West is the widespread circulation of elites and educational exchange. The advanced industrial countries contain many transnational networks based on professional and avocational specialization. Enabled by cheap air transportation and telecommunications, scientific, technological, medical, artistic, athletic, and public policy networks draw membership from across the Western world and have frequent conferences and events. Also significant is the great increase in the volume of international education activities, most notably the increasingly transnational character of the study bodies in elite universities and particularly graduate professional schools. These developments have produced a business, political, cultural, and technical elite with similar educational backgrounds and extensive networks of personal friendships and contacts. The cumulative weight of these international homogenizing and interacting forces has been to create an increasingly common identity and culture – a powerful sense that "we" constitutes more than the traditional community of the nation-state.

As civic and capitalist identities have strengthened, ethnic and national identity has declined. Although it is still customary to speak of the West as being constituted by nation-states, the political identity of Westerners is no longer exclusively centered on nationalism. The West has evolved a distinctive solution to the problem of nationalism and ethnicity that is vital to its operation and inadequately recognized by realists. The Western synthesis has two related features. First, ethnic and national identity has been muted and diluted to the point where it tends to be semi-private in character. Although not as homogeneous as anticipated by cosmopolitan philosophers of the Enlightenment, the identities of Westerners are largely secular and modern, thus allowing for many different loyalties and sensibilities – no one of which predominates. Second, an ethic of toleration is a strong and essential part of Western political culture. This ethic permits – and even celebrates – a highly pluralist society in which muted differences coexist, intermingle, and cross-fertilize each other. Unlike the chauvinism and parochialism of pre-modern and non-Western societies, an ethic of toleration, diversity, and indifference infuses the industrial democracies.

Many realists forecast that nationalist and ethnic identity will reassert itself in Western Europe in the wake of the Cold War, fueling conflict and destroying liberal democratic society. The virulence of ethnic conflict in the Balkans and elsewhere in former communist lands has revived the specter of the worst of Europe's past. The increase in anti-immigrant violence in Western Europe, particularly in Germany, demonstrates that the West is not immune to a new epidemic of ethnic violence and national war. The opponents of liberal pluralism are a loud but small minority of the alienated and economically dislocated. Their voices are not, however, a cause for a crisis of self-confidence. The ethos of the West remains overwhelmingly tolerant and receptive to diversity. Indeed, the anti-foreigner violence and ethnic ferment have been most revealing in the magnitude of the condemnation they have evoked. Measured by the standards of the past – even the recent past of the 1930s – these episodes are marginal and highlight the strong majorities committed to a liberal civic order.

Contrary to the dominant neorealist and neoliberal theories, identity and community are important components of political order. Identities are not primordial or immutable, but are the product of social, economic, and political forces operating in specific historical contexts. The liberal political order is strengthened by and in turn strengthens the distinctive liberal civic identity. The continued viability and expansion of capitalism, made possible by liberal multilateral institutions, sustains the business, commodity, and transnational cultures that in turn make it more politically feasible to sustain these institutions. Similarly, the success of security co-binding practices in preserving peace among liberal states reinforces political community by allowing memories of war, traditionally generative of conflicting national identities, to fade into an increasingly remote past. While the Cold War and the construction of a "free world" identity contributed to political solidarity and helped marginalize memories of international conflict among these countries (just as bipolarity contributed to Western institutional development), there are reasons to believe that the sources of civic identity are not likely to be diminished by the end of the Cold War.

Conclusion

A principal implication of our argument for international relations theory is that realist theories of balance of power, hegemony, sovereignty, and nationalism fail to capture the core dynamics of the liberal international order. This order has five distinctive and important components that together constitute structural liberalism: security co-binding, penetrated hegemony, semi-sovereignty and partial great powers, economic openness, and civic identity and community. The overall liberal political order is a complex composite in which these elements interact and mutually reinforce each other. It is the overall pattern of these elements and their interaction that constitute the structure of the liberal political order; the whole is greater than the sum of the parts. Any understanding of the liberal order that fails to bring in all of these components will fail to capture its structural character.

As realists point out, American hegemony and the bipolar balance helped give form and cohesion to this order. But because American hegemony is penetrated, it is more mutual and reciprocal than in realist formulations. Likewise, co-binding institutions and practices are a distinctive and independent response to the problem of anarchy among liberal states and not something derivative of bipolar balancing. Overall, the democratic industrial world exhibits patterns of political order that lie between traditional images of domestic and international politics, thus creating an unusual and distinctive subsystem in world politics.

Although there is good reason to believe that this liberal order has a very robust character, the fact that neither realism nor liberalism captures it very well is revealing of their theoretical limitations but also troubling in its implications for the maintenance of this system. Because of the Cold War, it is understandable that realpolitik approaches overshadowed liberal one in policy discourse and practice as well as in academic international relations theory. The hegemonic status of realism has marginalized and displaced the earlier American approaches to international affairs that were more pragmatic and more liberal. The realist characterization of liberalism as idealist and utopian belies its "realistic" sophistication and the extent to which the postwar order was created as a response to the earlier failures of both Wilsonian internationalism and the extreme realism of the interwar period (and its economic blocs, mercantilism, hypernationalism, and imperialism). With the end of the Cold War, the persistence of realism as a dominant approach to international affairs has real consequence because of its limited understanding of the Western political order and its inability to provide policy tools for operating within it. Policy agendas derived from realism could also become self-fulfilling prophecies and gradually undermine the Western order, particularly if those agendas include the conversion of Germany and Japan back into "normal" great powers. With the end of the Cold War, it is necessary to recover the theory and practice of structural liberalism so as to chart policy within the Western order.

Liberal theory has also failed to adequately grasp the liberal international system. The preoccupation of many liberals with building global institutions with universal scope, such as the United Nations, has ironically diverted their attention from understanding and building the liberal order within the West. Similarly, liberal international relations theory is not well situated to understand the Western order because of its lack of cumulation and sense of itself as a long tradition with significant historical accomplishments. Liberal theory's conceptual focus on process over structure and "micro" over "macro" also contributes to its inappropriate theoretical gauge. Also contributing to liberalism's limitations are the deference that it gives realism on security issues and its related focus on "low politics" rather than "high politics." Liberal theory is very heterogeneous and it does capture various components of the liberal international order, such as the democratic peace, but it fails to appreciate its distinctive history, architecture, and structure. Given the success of the liberal international subsystem and its centrality within the larger world system, a liberal international relations theory refocused on structure can lay claim to at least equality with realism.

If structural liberalism does capture the logic of the Western political order, then this suggests that the solidarity, cohesion, and cooperation of these countries will outlast the rise and fall of external threats. At the same time, no political order arises purely spontaneously and no political order endures without practices and programs based on an accurate understanding of its nature. In the post-Cold War era, the absence of bipolarity and the waning of American hegemony does remove forces that have contributed to the liberal order. Therefore, to sustain this order it is worthwhile to think about what might constitute a more self-conscious and robust liberal statecraft. A central task of such a liberal statecraft is the formulation of an agenda of principles and policies that serve to strengthen, deepen, and codify the liberal political order.

Notes

1   See Kenneth Waltz, *Theory of International Politics* (Reading, Mass.: Addison-Wesley, 1979). For extensions and debates, see Robert O. Keohane, ed., *Neorealism and its Critics* (New York: Columbia University Press, 1986).
2   John. J Mearsheimer, "Back to the Future: Instability of Europe after the Cold War," *International Security* 15 (Summer 1990): 5–57; and Conor Cruise O'Brien, "The Future of the West," *The National Interest* 30 (Winter 1992/3): 3–10.
3   See Robert Gilpin, *War and Change in World Politics* (New York: Cambridge University Press, 1981).
4   See G. John Ikenberry, "Liberal hegemony: The Logic and Future of America's Postwar Order," in John A. Hall and T. V. Paul, eds., *International Order and the Future of World Politics* (Cambridge: Cambridge University Press, 1999); and Ikenberry, "Rethinking the Origins of American Hegemony," *Political Science Quarterly* 104 (Fall 1989): 375–400.
5   For a survey of liberal theories, see Mark W. Zacher and Richard A. Matthew, "Liberal International Theory: Common Threads, Divergent Strands," in Charles W. Kegley, Jr., ed., *Controversies in International Relations Theory: Realism and the Neoliberal Challenge* (New York: St Martin's Press, 1995).
6   Waltz, *Theory of International Politics*; and Stephen Walt, *The Origins of Alliances* (Ithaca, NY: Cornell University Press, 1987).
7   See Daniel Deudney, "The Philadelphian System: Sovereignty, Arms Control, and Balance of Power in the American States-Union, 1787–1861," *International Organization* 49: 2 (Spring 1995); and Deudney, "Binding Sovereigns: Authority, Structure, and Geopolitics in Philadelphian Systems," in Thomas Biersteker and Cynthia Weber, eds., *State Sovereignty as Social Construct* (New York: Cambridge University Press, 1996).
8   See Thomas J. Knock, *To End All Wars: Woodrow Wilson and the Quest for a New World Order* (New York: Oxford University Press, 1992).
9   Mary Hampton, "NATO at the Creation: US Foreign Policy, West Germany and the Wilsonian Impulse," *Security Studies* 4: 3 (Spring 1995): 610–56; Geir Lundstadt, *The American "Empire"* (Oxford: Oxford University Press, 1990); David P. Calleo, *Beyond American Hegemony: The Future of the Western Alliance* (New York: Basic Books, 1988), ch. 1.

10 John Duffield, *Power Rules* (Stanford, Calif.: Stanford University Press, 1995).

11 Michael Hogan, *The Marshall Plan: America, Britain, and the Reconstruction of Western Europe, 1947–1952* (New York: Cambridge University Press, 1987).

12 Alberta Sbragia, "Thinking about European Future: The Uses of Comparison," in Sbragia, ed., *Euro-Politics: Institutions and Policymaking in the "New" European Community* (Washington, DC: Brookings, 1992).

13 See Gilpin, *War and Change in World Politics*; also Gilpin, *The Political Economy of International Relations* (Princeton, NJ: Princeton University Press, 1987), esp. pp. 72–80.

14 For a realist argument that secondary states will balance against American hegemony, see Christopher Layne, "The Unipolar Illusion," *International Security* 17: 4 (Spring 1993).

15 Some realists have faulted the United States for lacking a centralized and autonomous capacity to make and implement foreign policy, but it is precisely the absence of these features that have made possible the reciprocal and consensual exercise of American power.

16 Geir Lundstad, "Empire by Invitation? The United States and Western Europe, 1945–1952," in Charles Maier, ed., *The Cold War in Europe: Era of a Divided Continent* (New York: Wiener, 1991), pp. 143–68.

17 The incomplete nature of Japanese liberalism and the difficulty that transnational forces have in influencing the Japanese policy process suggest that Japanese hegemony would be more resisted and more coercive.

18 These characteristics of the American state have been described by many scholars. David B. Truman, *The Governmental Process* (New York: Alfred Knopf, 1952); Robert A. Dahl, *Who Governs?* (New Haven, Conn.: Yale University Press, 1961); and Theodore J. Lowi, *The End of Liberalism: Ideology, Policy, and the Crisis of Public Authority* (New York: Norton, 1969).

19 See Samuel P. Huntington, "Transnational Organizations in World Politics," *World Politics* 25 (April 1973); and Robert Gilpin, *US Power and the Multinational Corporation* (New York: Basic Books, 1975).

20 See, for example, Wolfgang Handreider, "Dissolving International Politics: Reflections on the Nation-State," *American Political Science Review* 72: 4 (1978): 1276–87; and James Rosenau, "The State in an Era of Cascading Politics: Wavering Concept, Widening Competence, Withering Colossus?" in James Caparaso, ed., *The Elusive State: International and Comparative Perspectives* (Newbury Park, Calif.: Sage, 1989), pp. 17–48.

21 For an exception, see Susan Strange, "Toward a Theory of Transnational Empire," in Ernst-Otto Czempiel and James N. Rosenau, eds., *Global Changes and Theoretical Challenges: Approaches to World Politics for the 1990s* (Lexington, Mass.: Lexington Books, 1989), pp. 161–76.

22 On the connection between domestic structures and transnational relations, see Thomas Risse-Kappen, ed., *Bringing Transnational Relations Back In: Non-State Actors, Domestic Structures and International Institutions* (New York: Cambridge University Press, 1995).

23 See G. John Ikenberry and Charles Kupchan, "Socialization and Hegemonic Power," *International Organization* 44: 3 (Summer 1990): 283–315.

24 See Peter J. Katzenstein and Yutaka Tsujinaka, " 'Bullying,' 'Buying,' and 'Binding': US–Japanese Transnational Relations and Domestic Structures," in Risse-Kappen, ed., *Bringing Transnational Relations Back In*, pp. 79–111.

25 Pat Choate, *Agents of Influence: How Japan Manipulates America's Political and Economic System* (New York: Touchstone Books, 1990).

26 See Michael Ross Fowler and Julie Marie Bunck, *Law, Power, and the Sovereign State: The Evolution and Application of the Concept of Sovereignty* (University Park, Penn.: Penn State University Press, 1995).

27 See Hedley Bull, *The Anarchical Society* (New York: Columbia University Press, 1997); Barry Buzan, "From International System to International Society: Structural Realism and Regime Theory meet the English School," *International Organization* 47: 3 (Summer 1993): 327–52.

28 See Leopold von Ranke, "The Great Powers," in Theodore von Laue, ed., *The Writings of Leopold von Ranke* (Princeton: Princeton University Press, 1963); Jack Levy, *War in the Modern Great Power System, 1495–1975* (Lexington: The University Press of Kentucky, 1983); and Martin White, *Power Politics*, edited by Hedley Bull and Carsten Holbraad (Manchester: Manchester University Press, 1978).

29 See Peter J. Katzenstein, *Policy and Politics in West Germany: The Growth of a Semi-Sovereign State* (Philadelphia: Temple University Press, 1987).

30 On American and Western efforts to liberalize postwar German and Japanese political institutions, see John Montgomery, *Forced to Be Free: The Artificial Revolution in Germany and Japan* (Chicago: University of Chicago Press, 1957); Robert E. Ward and Sakamoto Yoshikazu, eds., *Democratizing Japan: The Allied Occupation* (University of Hawaii Press, 1987); and Tony Smith, *America's Mission: The United States and the Worldwide Struggle for Democracy in the Twentieth Century* (Princeton, NJ: Princeton University Press, 1994), ch. 6.

31 See Ian Buruma, *The Wages of Guilt: Memories of War in Germany and Japan* (New York: Meridian, 1995).

32 Robert Gilpin, "The Politics of Transnational Economic Relations," *International Organization* 25 (Summer 1971); Charles P. Kindleberger, *The World in Depression* (Berkeley, Calif.: University of California Press, 1973); Stephen Krasner, "State Power and the Structure of International Trade," *World Politics* 28 (April 1976): 317–47.

33 See Gilpin, "Economic Interdependence and National Security in Historical Perspective," in Klaus Knorr and Frank Trager, eds., *Economic Issues and National Security* (Lawrence, Kan.: Regents Press of Kansas, 1977), pp. 19–66.

34 For variations of this argument, see Joanne Gowa, *Allies, Adversaries, and International Trade* (Princeton, NJ: Princeton University Press, 1994); and Edward D. Mansfield, *Power, Trade, and War* (Princeton, NJ: Princeton University Press, 1994).

35   See John Gerard Ruggie, "International Regimes, Transactions, and Change: Embedded Liberalism in the Postwar Economic Order," in Stephen D. Krasner, ed., *International Regimes* (Ithaca, NY: Cornell University Press, 1983).

36   Conversely, if states abandon their commitment to the welfare state then this motivation for their support of a liberal economic system would decline. Or structural changes in the international economy might be less congenial to domestic welfare commitments, in which case states would also pull back from the pursuit of open foreign economic policies. In either case, the liberal order would become "disembedded" and much less robust.

37   For systematic discussion of this logic, see Joseph Grieco, "Anarchy and the Limits of Cooperation: A Realist Critique of Neoliberal Institutionalism," *International Organization* 42 (1988): 485–507.

38   An example of this phenomenon is the high-technology sectors. In the late 1980s, Germany and Japan were leading the United States in many areas, but more recently this pattern has been reversed.

39   This is a variation on the argument made by Snidal, that multiple actors (in this case sectors and firms rather than states) complicate the simple calculation of relative gains and therefore mitigate its influence over policy. See Duncan Snidal, "International Cooperation Among Relative Gain Maximizers," *International Studies Quarterly* 35: 4 (December 1991): 387–402. The sector focus also yields mixed results in Michael Mastanduno, "Do Relative Gains Matter? America's Response to Japanese Industrial Policy," *International Security* 16 (Summer 1991): 73–113.

40   See Robert Pollard, *Economic Security and the Origins of the Cold War, 1945–1950* (New York: Columbia University Press, 1985).

41   See Ikenberry, "Liberal Hegemony."

42   Louis Hartz, *The Liberal Tradition in America* (New York: Harcourt Brace, 1955).

43   George Mosse, *The Nationalization of the Masses* (Ithaca, NY: Cornell University Press, 1991).

44   See Susan Strange, *States and Markets* (New York: Blackwell, 1988).

45   For an analysis of global cultural formations, see Mike Featherstone, ed., *Global Culture* (Newbury Park: Sage, 1990).

4

Constitutional Politics in International Relations

Introduction

It is widely agreed that domestic and international politics are rooted in very different types of order. Domestic politics is the realm of shared identity, stable institutions, and legitimate authority, while international politics is, as one realist scholar recently put it, a "brutal arena where states look for opportunities to take advantage of each other, and therefore have little reason to trust each other" (Mearsheimer 1994/5: 9). In the most influential formulation, the two realms have fundamentally different structures – one based on hierarchy and the other on anarchy (Waltz 1979).

But this core realist insight is deeply flawed. Both domestic and international order can take many different forms. In some countries, politics can be extremely ruthless and coercive, while some areas of international politics are remarkably consensual and institutionalized. Indeed, the most useful insight might be that both realms of politics – domestic and international – face similar problems in the creation and maintenance of order, and the solutions that emerge are also often quite similar.[1]

The similarity of domestic and international order can best be seen at historical moments when the basic organization of political order is up for grabs. Within countries this tends to come at "founding" moments, such as after independence, revolution, or civil war. At these junctures, the "founders" seek to entrench the principles and laws of the country, to lock into place the enduring principles by which the polity is organized. Constitutions or fundamental laws are established to set basic limits on the exercise of power and the scope of politics. In effect, order formation takes the form of constitution building.

Internationally, these moments tend to come after major wars – as the leading states attempt to rebuild order. The Westphalia settlement of 1648, according to one historian, established within Europe for the first time "what may fairly be described as an international constitution, which gave to all its adherents the right of intervention to enforce its engagements" (Hill 1925: 602). Gordon Craig and Alexander George argue that the Vienna settlement of 1815 was, in effect, an effort to craft a "constitution" for great power relations (1983: 31). The Versailles treaty of 1919 was seen by many, most notably Woodrow Wilson, as a constitutional agreement among states. The peace settlement that followed World War II was scattered across many institutions and agreements, but the highly institutionalized security, political, and economic order that emerged also had glimmerings of a constitutional-type settlement. To be sure, there are no constitutions as such in international relations. But moments do exist when states have sought to recast international relations and create binding principles and institutions.

A state that wins a major war faces a set of choices not unlike those of a new ruling elite in the aftermath of civil war or independence. It has acquired a preponderance of power, but the political order in which it operates is unformed and uncertain. Like the ruling elite, a dominant postwar state has a choice – it can use its commanding material capacities to win conflicts over the distribution of gains; or, knowing that its power position will eventually decline and that there are costs to enforcing its way within the order, it can move toward a constitutional settlement. In this situation, there are incentives for the leading state to agree to limit its power – to insert itself into a constitutional order – in exchange for the acquiescence and compliant participation of secondary states in the postwar order. Wherever there are newly consolidated power blocs in either domestic or international politics – that is, highly asymmetrical power relations in a strategic environment where the basic character of order is in transition – the logic of constitutionalism is relevant.

Fundamentally, constitutional orders reduce the implications of "winning" in politics. Limits are set on what a party or state can do if it gains an advantage at a particular moment – for example, by winning an election or gaining disproportionately from economic exchange. In other words, *constitutions limit the returns to power.* Limits are set on what actors can do with momentary advantages. Losers realize that their losses are limited and temporary – to accept those losses is not to risk everything nor will it give the winners a permanent advantage.

This article makes four arguments. First, the character of international order can best be grasped after major wars. The old order has broken down, newly powerful states have emerged, and the rules and organization of order are unformed. At these moments, newly powerful states have incentives to create a durable and legitimate order, and this entails gaining the willing acceptance and participation of less powerful, secondary states. To do so, leading states must engage in *strategic restraint* – conveying to weaker states that there are limits and restraints on the arbitrary exercise of state power. Compliance and participation of secondary states hinges on resolving the threats of domination and abandonment by newly powerful states.

Second, since 1815, the leading postwar states (Britain after the Napoleonic wars and the United States after the two world wars) have with increasing extensiveness and sophistication employed co-binding institutions to restrain power and overcome fears of domination and abandonment. It is these co-binding institutions that have given the succession of postwar orders constitutional-like characteristics. The basic constitutional bargain is simple – strong states agree to insert themselves in co-binding institutions in exchange for the participation and acquiescence of weaker states. The leading state agrees to limits on its power – that is, it agrees to operate within an institutionalized political process according to a set of rules and principles – in exchange for the agreement by secondary groups or states to be willing participants in the order.

Third, the incentives to move to a constitutional-like settlement are tied to the domestic character of the states involved, particularly the leading state. Secondary states will be reluctant to enter into constitutional arrangements without credible assurances that the leading state will not exit the agreement and exploit or dominate the weaker states. The domestic structures of the contracting states matter – states with similar domestic polities will be better able to convey assurances than states with divergent polities; and more importantly, democratic states will be more willing and able to enter into co-binding institutions and thereby reassure the other potential partners to the postwar settlement than non-democracies. Democratic polities have unusual capacities to reassure each other and overcome fears of domination and abandonment.

Fourth, the breakdown of order is itself important in triggering constitutional politics. Constitutions are a "solution set" for problems of political order that are only available every so often – indeed, they are a solution set precisely because they are not always readily available to political actors. A fundamental breakdown of political order appears to be a necessary condition. At these moments, the possibilities are not simply alternative political orders but also the absence of order itself. At the same time, a variety of circumstantial factors also matters in determining if and how constitutional settlements emerge. The most important are those that deal with the nature of the "historical breakpoint" – the degree of breakdown in the old order, the nature of the "victory" won by the leading states, the concentration of power in the hands of the victorious states, and the ideas and lessons embraced by the states engaged in the postwar settlement.

The argument will proceed in four steps. First, I lay out the patterns and puzzles associated with postwar settlements and historical moments of order formation. Second, I present a model of constitutional order-building in international relations which specifies the incentives and conditions that shape and constrain its pursuit. Third, I discuss the domestic structural conditions that provide opportunities for states to convey credible commitment. Finally, I discuss historical cases and episodes that allow us to assess the relevance of constitutionalism in international relations.

Postwar Settlements and the Problem of Order

Order formation in international relations has tended to come at dramatic and episodic moments – typically after great wars. These shifts in the system are what Robert Gilpin calls "systemic change," moments when the governing rules and institutions are remade to suit the interests of the newly powerful states or hegemon.[2] The irregular and episodic pattern of international order formation is itself an important observation about the nature of change. The importance of war, breakdown, and reconstruction in relations among states speaks to a central aspect of international change – that history is, as Peter Katzenstein argues, a "sequence of irregular big bangs" (1989: 296). History is marked by infrequent discontinuities that rearrange world politics.

The major postwar settlements were all historical big bangs – Westphalia in 1648, Utrecht in 1712, Vienna in 1815. After World War I, a dramatic effort was made to build a new international order, but it ended in bitter failure. The United States advanced the most far-reaching proposals, but its leaders were unable to generate sufficient domestic support to ratify the agreement. After World War II, there was again an ambitious attempt to construct a postwar order, much of it very self-conscious of the earlier failure, but there was also – eventually – a successful agreement. Institutions were created that served to reopen the world economy and unite the industrial democracies in a security alliance.

It is useful to think about the politics of order formation in international relations as a class of events that shares characteristics with the politics of order formation within domestic systems. The great postwar settlements have parallels with domestic order formation that follows in the wake of internal political upheaval – upheaval such as social revolutions, civil wars, and national independence. If a new "systemic" order is not simply the result of the exercise of power – an order built on coercion – then we need to know how basic rules and institutions get established with some minimal degree of legitimacy and mutual consent.

The postwar settlements of 1648, 1712, 1815, 1919, and 1945 may all have been major reordering moments, but the specific character of the orders they produced evolved over the centuries.[3] The settlements grew increasingly global in scope. Westphalia was primarily a continental European settlement, while Utrecht saw the beginning of Britain's involvement in shaping the European state system. In the twentieth century, the settlements were truly global. The peace agreements also expanded in scope and reach. They dealt with a widening range of security, territorial, economic, and functional issues. The settlements that emerged also became increasingly interventionistic – entailing greater involvement in the internal structures and administration of the defeated states, culminating in 1945 with the occupation and reconstruction of Germany and Japan (Opie et al. 1951: 2–5).

The settlements also evolved in terms of the ideas and mechanisms that the leading states brought to bear on order creation. At each postwar juncture, the leading states offered distinctive solutions to the problem of order. In one sense, the evolution of ideas and mechanisms were from the simple to the complex. The Westphalia settlement was organized around autonomy and mutual recognition – the enshrinement of the norms of state sovereignty. At Vienna, the notions of balance and the great power management of the order were more sophisticated than those of Utrecht. Likewise, at Versailles and after World War II, the conceptions of order were much more developed, increasingly emphasizing the role of multilateral institutions, joint management of the international economy, and the pursuit of a wide set of socioeconomic goals. Most importantly, the settlements increasingly sought to institutionalize cooperation – to go beyond reinforcing state autonomy and reconstructing the balance of power by binding states to each other in mutually constraining institutions. With the rise of these co-binding institutions, the settlements increasingly came to resemble constitutional-like orders. Why this is so is a great theoretical and historical puzzle.

Constitutional Logics

The overriding incentive faced by the victorious state after a major war is to construct a postwar order that is legitimate and durable. That is, there are reasons for the leading state to attempt to convert its favorable postwar power position into a durable political order that commands the allegiance of the other states within it. To achieve a legitimate order means to secure agreement among the relevant states on the basic rules and principles of political order. A legitimate political order is one where its members willingly participate and agree with the overall orientation of the system. They abide by its rules and principles because they accept them as desirable – they embrace them as their own.[4]

This incentive to create a legitimate order can make movement toward a constitutional political order appealing. A constitutional political order has three basic characteristics.[5] First, there is a shared agreement over the basic principles and rules of order. Participation and consent are based on this shared agreement on basic principles. There is a meeting of minds about what the "rules of the game" will be within the political order, and these "rules of the game" will contribute to the operation of a stable and non-coercive order – that is, a functioning political order that participants anticipate will continue into the future.[6] Participants will pursue their own interests, but they will do so within agreed rules and institutions.

Second, rules and institutions are established that set binding and authoritative limits on the exercise of power. Unbridled power does not rule within the polity. Constitutions are a form of legal constraint on politics, manifest as a declaration of principles that specify rights, protections, and basic rules. Constraints on power are also insured through institutional devices and procedures – such as the separation of powers and checks and balances. The end result is that holders of power must exercise that power within an institutionalized political process. The political order's rules and institutions are to a significant extent intractable – and through their design, entrenchment, and principled specificity, limits on power are established.

Finally, in a constitutional order, these rules and institutions are in a fundamental sense entrenched in the wider political system and not easily altered. Constitutional struggles happen only rarely, and once they are settled, politics is expected to take place within these parameters. The expectation is of infrequent historical junctures of constitutional change and settlement – political crisis triggers struggle and debate within a society; a set of constitutional principles and rules are crystallized; within this new constitutional framework day-to-day politics takes place until the next constitutional opening.[7] In other words, there is a notion of political "path dependency" in arguments about constitutions and constitutional change.[8]

Most importantly, constitutional agreements reduce the implications of "winning" in international relations. They do so in two ways. First, they set limits on what a state that gains disproportionately within the order can do with those gains. These institutional agreements serve to reduce the stakes of uneven gains. Second, constitutions serve to reduce the "returns to power," which means that they reduce the possibilities that a state can turn short-term gains into a long-term power advantage (Przeworski 1991: 36). In both these ways, constitutions set limits on what states can do with momentary advantages. Losers realize that their losses are limited and temporary – to accept those losses is not to risk everything, nor will it give the winner a permanent advantage.[9]

Strategic restraint and power conservation

There are a variety of reasons why states in a commanding power position after a major war might want to secure a constitutional settlement. The basic incentive, however, is rather simple – the victorious state has an interest in conserving its power. The leading state takes advantage of its privileged postwar position to secure a set of legitimate and durable rules and institutions that will preserve and extend its advantages into the future. The leading state engages in strategic restraint – it gives up some of its unilateral discretion to use its asymmetric power position to force favorable outcomes in exchange for the acquiescence and compliance of secondary states organized around agreed upon principles and institutional processes.

Constitutional settlements conserve power in two ways. First, there is an *institutional investment* motive for constitutional order. The leading state can take advantage of its momentarily superordinate position and use it to create rules and institutions that will serve its interests in the years after its power position declines in relative terms. It gives up some discretion and autonomy in the use of its power capacities to secure specific gains in exchange for a durable and predictable political order that safeguards its interests in the future.

This institutional investment motive for constitutional order is based on several assumptions. First, it is assumed that the power position of the victorious state is ultimately in relative decline over the medium to long term. As the leading state makes choices about how to use its power after the war, it knows that its commanding position is not permanent. Thus, everything else being equal, it will be in a more constrained and diminished position tomorrow than it is today.[10] Second, the leading postwar state can make a choice between using its power capabilities to gain momentary advantages in particular distributional struggles or it can use those capabilities to invest in institutions that will persist into the future.[11] The implication is that there is a trade-off between these choices, and each choice will produce a different rate of return to the leading state over the short and long term.[12] Finally, institution building is a form of investment because rules and institutions are sticky. Unless there is a substantial shift in state power and interests, postwar institutions are likely to persist and continue to shape and constrain state action even after the power that created them has declined.[13]

Second, constitutional settlements conserve power by lowering the *enforcement costs* for maintaining order within the system. The constant use of power capabilities – and the coercion and inducements it implies – to secure specific interests and continuously resolve conflicts is costly (Ikenberry and Kupchan 1990). It is less costly over the long term to create an order where secondary states embrace its rules and principles on their own. It is far more effective over the long term to shape the interests and orientations of other states rather than directly shape their actions through coercion and inducements.[14]

The leading state lowers its enforcement costs in a constitutional order by giving weaker states a stake in the system and gaining their overall support. As Lisa Martin argues, "a hegemon can expect fewer challenges to an institution in which smaller states have a say in joint decisions than to a unilaterally imposed arrangement" (1993: 110). In effect, a constitutional settlement is one where the leading state agrees to extend decision-making access and rights to secondary states in exchange for their acquiescence in the order's rules and institutions. The resulting legitimacy of the order reduces the chance that secondary states will seek to overturn or continually challenge the overall order. Margaret Levi argues that a similar incentive exists for power-holders in domestic systems – institutionalized bargaining is less risky for the dominant actor than the constant expenditure of resources to quell resistance: "Coercion is expensive, and its use often precipitates resentments that can fuel the flames of opposition. Thus, rulers will seek to create compliance that is quasi-voluntary" (1988: 32). A constitutional settlement reduces the necessity of the costly expenditure of resources by the leading state on bargaining, monitoring, and enforcement.

Institutional and substantive agreements

To understand the logic of constitutionalism, it is useful to make a distinction between institutional and substantive agreements. One type of bargaining is over distributive outcomes, where states struggle over the distribution of benefits in specific relationships (Krasner 1991). The other type of bargaining is "institutional bargaining," which Oran Young calls "efforts on the part of autonomous actors to reach agreement among themselves on the terms of constitutional contracts or interlocking sets of rights and rules that are expected to govern their subsequent interactions" (1991:

Table 4.1   Substantive agreements versus institutional agreements

Advantages of short-term substantive agreements	Advantages of longer-term institutional agreements
Achievement of immediate gains: • uncertainty over future gains from institutional agreements • gains can be put to work immediately	Conservation of state power: • gains continue after power declines • lower enforcement costs for hegemony

282). The first type of agreement is a substantive agreement with outcomes that determine the actual distribution of material benefits between the states. The second type is an institutional agreement that specifies the principles, rules, and parameters within which particular bargains are conducted over outcomes.[15]

For the leading postwar state to offer a constitutional settlement to other states does not mean it is seeking agreement or conceding on specific issues. Constitutional agreements specify the rules of the game – that is, the parameters within which states will compete and settle disputes over specific issues. States may have widely different expectations about the settlement of various distributional conflicts. A constitutional agreement specifies the principles and mechanisms through which those conflicts will be settled.

If the leading postwar state seeks a constitutional settlement, it is in effect offering to operate within a defined set of rules and institutions. It is agreeing to conduct relations within an institutionalized political process. The calculation made by the leading state is that while it is compromising on the formal or institutional settlement, within those newly created institutions, it will still be able to press its advantage.

Thus when a leading postwar state makes a choice between ways of allocating its power assets, between substantive and institutional bargaining, it is faced with alternative attractions and limitations, and these are summarized in table 4.1.

The use of power assets for short-term gains is attractive in that gains are more certain and they can be put to work immediately. On the other hand, if institutional agreements can be secured, they are a remarkable power saving arrangement. They can potentially lock in agreements well into the future, providing an ongoing stream of benefits, even after the state's power position has declined. They can also reduce the otherwise ongoing need to use power resources to secure compliance and favorable outcomes.

The possibility of an institutional settlement stems from the ability to achieve agreement on institutional arrangements even if the underlying substantive interests remain widely divergent and antagonistic. It is the capacity of institutions to shape and limit outcomes that makes institutional compromise possible. For the powerful state, institutions are attractive because they can effectively rule out some outcomes that would harm its fundamental limits, and constrain other states well into the future.[16] Under the right conditions, these attractions can outweigh the loss of some autonomy and limits of the arbitrary use of power. For weaker states, the institutional compromise also rules out some outcomes that it fears – such as domination or abandonment by stronger states. Institutions are not "neutral" with respect to the interests of states; they do not make all outcomes equally possible. Agreement to abide by the new institutional rules comes from an understanding that within this framework, the arrangements will allow them to defend and protect their interests – at least enough to make it a more attractive option than the risky alternative.

Power constraint strategies

Constitutions are institutional mechanisms for the control of power within a political order. But it is useful to see constitutional constraints as part of a wider continuum of techniques and arrangements that states can employ to constrain and disperse power within the international system.[17] These include the promotion of state autonomy, the division of territory to disperse power, the creation of counter-balancing alliances, and the creation of co-binding institutions. This spectrum of power control strategies is summarized in table 4.2.

The most basic strategy is to reinforce state sovereignty. If states are given legal independence and political primacy within the order, this undercuts the aggrandizement of power by imperial and religious groupings. Power is controlled through the fragmentation of political units into sovereign states. This decentralization of power is reinforced through the codification of state sovereignty in international public law. This was the most important objective of the Westphalia settlement – conferring ultimate sovereign autonomy to territorial states, subordinate to no other type of authority, such as universal monarchy. The rights and sovereign autonomy of states were divorced from particular religions and the Westphalia settlement extended international law by putting republican and monarchical states on an equal footing (Gross 1948). The treaties of Osnabruck and Munster fixed by written instrument the political status of individual states, affirming the principle of territorial sovereignty, both in religious and political matters.[18]

Table 4.2   Power constraint strategies

Technique	Logic
Reinforce state autonomy political units	Fragmentation of political units Undercut religious and imperial groupings
Territorial/power distribution	Disperse power capability into multiple units Restrain power aggrandizement
Counter-balancing alliances	Check power aggrandizement through blocking coalitions of states
Institutional co-binding	Tie potentially threatening states together in alliances and mutually constraining institutions
Supranational integration	Share sovereignty with overarching political institutions/authorities

A second power control technique is the breaking up or separation of territorial units so as to disperse power capabilities. The aim is to make sure that no state possesses sufficient territorial assets to dominate the other states in the order. When territorial boundaries are open for redrawing, such as in the aftermath of war, the opportunity to employ this strategy emerges. At postwar peace conferences, the map of political order is literally on the table. Defeated states have few options to resist this territorial redrafting exercise, and the collapse of failed hegemonic states, such as France after 1712 and 1815 and Germany after the world wars, opens up vast territorial domains to negotiation. In some cases, such as after the wars of the Spanish succession, the postwar territorial negotiations are explicitly concerned with the fragmentation and distribution of territory so as to disperse power potential, and in other cases the break-up of huge territorial powers has been pursued in the name of self-determination, such as after World War I. But the aim is the same – to constrain power aggrandizement by fragmenting and distributing territorial units

The third strategy of power control is the most familiar – the balance of power. Here states develop arrangements that allow them to temporarily aggregate their power in alliance to offset and counter-balance threatening powers in the international system, and this balancing behavior facilitates international stability (Claude 1962: 3–93; Gulick 1967; Haas 1953; Sheehan 1996; Waltz 1979; Wight 1966). The specific mechanisms and processes of power balance can vary widely, and theories of balance of power reflect this diversity.[19] The working of balance may be more or less explicit as a principle of order and alliance groupings may be more or less formal and institutionalized. But the essential logic is the same – the aggrandizement of power is checked by countervailing power.

The fourth strategy is institutional co-binding. Here states respond to potential threats and strategic rivalries by linking states together in mutually constraining institutions. Institutions can have this impact because of their potential "binding" and "lock-in" effects. States might ordinarily seek to preserve their options, to cooperate with other states but to leave open the option of disengaging. But co-binding states do exactly the opposite – they build long-term security, political, and economic commitments that are difficult to retract. They "lock-in" their commitments and relationships, to the extent that this can be done by sovereign states. Examples of binding mechanisms include treaties, interlocking organizations, joint management responsibilities, agreed upon standards and principles of relations, and so forth. These mechanisms raise the "costs of exit" and create "voice opportunities," thereby providing mechanisms to mitigate or resolve the conflict.

Institutional binding can itself vary in terms of its intensiveness. Paul Schroeder argues that the alliance that formed the Concert of Europe was an early manifestation of this co-binding logic. In this and other subsequent cases, alliances have been created as *pacta de contrahendo* – pacts of restraint (Schroeder 1975). They have served as mechanisms for states to manage and restrain their partners within the alliance. "Frequently the desire to exercise such control over an ally's policy," Schroeder argues, "was the main reason that one power, or both, entered into the alliance" (1975: 230). Alliances can take the form of binding treaties that allow states to keep a hand in the security policy of their partners.[20]

Co-binding can also be manifest in other types of institutions that lock states together in joint decision-making, enmeshing states in deeply rooted forms of institutionalized cooperation. The practice of institutional co-binding only make sense if international institutions or regimes can have an independent ordering impact on the actions of states.[21] The assumption is that institutions are sticky – that they can take on a life and logic of their own, shaping and constraining even the states that create them. When states employ institutional binding as a strategy, they are essentially agreeing to mutually constrain themselves. They give up some autonomy and discretion, but they get more predictability in other states. Institutional co-binding is possible only because institutions can specify what it is that states are expected to do and make it difficult and costly for states to do otherwise.[22]

A final strategy is formal supranational integration, where the formal legal and institutional obligations between states within the union are essentially indistinguishable from internal legal and political institutions. Some analysts argue that the European Union is approaching this situation, and European lawyers and judges have begun talking about the EU as a "constitutional" polity (Manicini 1991; Stein 1981; Weiler 1991).

This continuum is defined by the degree of institutionalized cooperation that defines and constrains the exercise of power. In one sense, the strategies are all techniques that seek to balance power. As Carl Friedrich has argued, "the substitution of . . . an international organization for an international balancer is, in a sense, merely a specific instance of the general feature of all constitutions; a constitution seeks to balance various governmental powers and organizes a balance of interests . . . in the community" (1950: 86). But in another sense, when the international order does employ institutional co-binding practices, it is substituting balance-of-power controls with principled constraints on the exercise of power. The logic of balance is to check power with power; the logic of institutional co-binding is to restrain power through the establishment of an institutionalized political process.

The constitutional bargain

A constitutional settlement is only possible when the leading state calculates its interests in a farsighted manner by responding to incentives that emerge in a postwar environment. But once established, the constitutional order will itself create incentives for states to act in ways that reinforce the constitutional settlement – that is, it creates positive feedback effects on the states that are party to the settlement, which will in turn strengthen the order's rules and institutions.

In agreeing to a constitutional order, states are making a mutual commitment to operate within a given set of institutions and rules – creating a political process that makes certain that the various states within the order will remain linked and engaged with each other. This creates greater certainty about the future, which in turn allows longer-term calculations and investments in deepening relations. If a state knows that relations with other states within the order will not break apart, incentives grow to invest in the relationship. Put more sharply, if two states know that competition between them will remain contained within an institutionalized political process and not lead to war or the threat of war, they will more readily agree to cooperate and engage in relations. Less secure states – worried about their autonomy and relative position – will tend to refrain from such joint investments and relations.[23] In this sense, it is the relative certainty of stable and contained relations between states – made possible by the binding character of constitutional agreement – that creates incentives to cooperate, and this in turn reinforces the constitutional agreement.

The danger faced by secondary states is that they will be dominated or abandoned by the hegemonic or leading state. Weaker states must be assured that the leading state will not break out of its institutional restraints and exploit momentary advantages.[24] The implications of failure to secure guarantees and convey credible commitment are potentially huge. If constitutional agreements fail, the consequences are potentially dire for secondary states, and as a result the agreements will quickly unravel and states will move to provide for their security and advance their interests in other ways. As neorealists argue, anarchy sharply constrains the willingness of states to make and keep agreements (Waltz 1979). Fear of cheating, problems of relative gains, threats to political autonomy – all these possibilities constrain the willingness of states to make binding agreements.

But if commitments are credible in regard to the limits to which the leading state can dominate the weaker states within the order, the constitutional order can be very attractive to secondary states. A constitutional settlement involves the creation of a political process by which states make joint decisions and settle disputes. This institutionalized political process provides mechanisms by which the weaker states can exercise their "voice" in their relations with the dominant state.[25] The calculation is that by operating within joint institutions, weaker states have opportunities to shape and constrain the actions of the leading state in ways that accommodate the interests of the weaker states.

Explaining Constitutional Variations

Although there are incentives for states in a dominant position after major wars to pursue a constitutional settlement, the strength of the incentive will vary with postwar circumstances.[26] These circumstances include the character of the breakdown after the war and level of uncertainty that confronts the leading states, the postwar configuration of power, and the types of states that are party to the agreement. Importantly, the willingness of states to pursue a constitutional settlement will hinge on their ability to convey assurances and commitments, and this in turn depends heavily on the character of the states themselves. Democratic states are usually willing and able to move toward constitutional-type orders.

Risks and uncertainty

A circumstance that will bear on the willingness of states to forge a constitutional settlement deals with the level of uncertainty over the specific distribution of gains that the various parties will yield under the settlement. The distinction was made earlier between institutional and substantive agreements – institutional agreements dealing with the rules of the game and substantive agreements involving the outcomes of struggles over distributive gains. The more uncertainty there is over the implications of the institutional settlement for the distribution of gains, the more likely it is that a constitutional settlement can be reached. This is true for several reasons.

To begin with, the more uncertainty there is over the distribution of benefits, the more likely it is that bargaining over settlement rules and institutions will be conducted according to considerations of principle and fairness. Operating under a "veil of uncertainty," where it is difficult for states to determine how specific institutional arrangements will affect their interests over time, states will seek to develop rules and institutions that are fair in that "patterns of outcomes generated under such arrangements will be broadly acceptable, regardless of where the participant might be located in such outcomes" (Brennan and Buchanan 1985: 30). Such agreements are more likely to be legitimate and durable over time because they do not hinge on a particular distribution of benefits to participating states. The various states have bought into the institutional agreement with the view that they can live with the settlement regardless of their eventual position within the newly created postwar order. Agreement is not based on an expectation of a specific distribution and flow of benefits.

The scope of the institutional agreement will also matter. The greater the scope – that is, the more issues that are under negotiation and covered in the agreement – the more difficult it will be to determine in advance the specific distribution of gains between states, and this increased uncertainty (as argued earlier) increases the possibility for institutional agreement. Moreover, the greater the scope – with a wide multiplicity of issues, arrangements, and transactions – the greater the incentives to reach a settlement on the general principles and not on every specific issue. This is a political efficiency incentive – to resolve matters at the level of principle and rules of political process, arrangements which can in turn guide the resolution of the many specific issues and controversies. This incentive to make a settlement at the level of principle and general rules reinforces the disjunction between institutional and substantive agreements.

Such considerations underscore the importance of how the historical juncture that triggers order-building presents itself – particularly the character and extent of war and system breakdown. The more complete the system breakdown, the more fundamental or basic will be the discussion of institutional arrangements. It makes negotiations over basic principles and norms of order more necessary (the default option of not reaching some agreement is less available). There will be more basic discussion of institutions and less incremental assessment of how institutions are in practice serving to distribute benefits. Also more issues will be involved. This will increase the uncertainty – it will be more difficult for states to calculate the specific distribution of benefits that are shaped by the rules and institutions. And as we have seen, the greater uncertainty there is over how the rules and institutions will impact on specific states, the more likely that decisions will be made based on general principle and considerations of fairness, and this in turn will contribute to the creation of an order with greater legitimacy and durability.

Similarity of states and constitutional commitment

The ability of states to convey reassurances and commitments in a constitutional settlement will hinge on the character of the polities of the participating states. To begin, when the participating states have similar types of domestic political orders they are more likely to agree on a settlement. This is true for two reasons. First, when states have similar polities, they are more likely to have similar goals and preferences in regard to the type of order to be created after the war. This increases that convergence of interests in a particular organization of postwar order and reduces the level of potential conflict. Second, when states have similar polities, each will have a set of domestic structures that shapes and constrains policy in similar ways – and this creates more confidence in what states will or will not do (or can and cannot do). As a result, the level of confidence in the mutual commitments of these states will rise.

States with similar polities are more likely to have similar preferences about how the international order should be organized than states with divergent polities. Because of this, they are likely to seek and support the construction of similar types of rules and institutions. This in turn helps ensure that agreements can be reached and conflicts will not emerge over the basic terms of order – and confidence in the maintenance of the order's rules and institutions rises.

The assumption behind this claim is that the goals and preferences that states have about international order are rooted, at least in part, in their domestic political structures. This is true for several reasons. First, states differ in their organizational characteristics, and these differences can provide advantages or disadvantages in various types of international order. Autocratic states, with closed domestic political orders, are more likely to operate successfully in a bilateral and centralized system than in a decentralized and multilateral system (Ruggie 1993). Democratic states, with open and decentralized polities, are better equipped to operate in postwar orders that are similarly organized. States will want postwar rules and institutions in which they can operate successfully – where there is an effective operational fit between domestic structure and international order.

Second, different types of international order will strengthen and weaken different types of states. States will not just seek a postwar order in which they can operate effectively, but also one that reinforces their domestic polity in desired ways. Third World states in the 1970s, for example, wanted to create an anti-liberal international order with international economic regimes that would serve to strengthen the position of government elites in relation to society (Krasner 1985). Regulative regimes, more so than market regimes, would reinforce the position of government elites, providing them with resources and power that these vulnerable elites desired. Likewise, democratic polities and autocratic/authoritarian states will have their respective polity principles reinforced by different types of security orders. Everything else being equal, balance-of-power orders are more congenial to closed and centralized polities than to open, decentralized democracies.

Behind these considerations is a deeper claim about the connection between domestic and international orders – that states seek to find a "fit" between the two orders in a way that strengthens the legitimacy of their domestic polities. The claim is that where states have an opportunity, they will seek to create international rules and institutions that are consistent with domestic principles of political order.[27] One aspect of this argument deals with the use of force – states will attempt to create international rules about intervention and the use of military force that are consistent with the internal standards. It is difficult to uphold highly circumscribed limits on the state's coercive authority at home and a more unlimited writ abroad. Another aspect deals more generally with the internal character of political authority. Polities can be distinguished between those that privilege the "nation" and civil society and others that privilege the "state." Each variety will seek international rules and institutions that reinforce its reigning principles of political authority (Barkin and Cronin 1994). Finally, the principles of domestic legitimacy relate to the state's role in providing for the social welfare and economic security of its citizens. There may be practical reasons why a state may want a particular set of international rules and institutions to facilitate its capacity to make good its obligations. But precisely because of this, states will seek an order that reflects the basic principles and rules of state involvement in the society and economy (Ikenberry and Kupchan 1990).

What each of these lines of argument suggests is that international standards of legitimacy are ultimately guided by the prevailing internal standards of political legitimacy. The conclusion follows that where states have similar sorts of "polity principles," they are more likely to find agreement over principles of international order.

These considerations bear on the problem of reassurance and commitment. Similar types of states not only will have similar preferences about the organization of postwar order, they also will able to convey to each other some measure of assurance that they will abide by the agreements that are reached. States can be confident – up to some point – about the durability of the commitments made by other states if those commitments appear to be rooted in that state's domestic political order. It is precisely because preferences over the character of the organization of international order are rooted in domestic political structures that states can calculate the risks of constitutional failure.[28]

If state preferences on the rules and institutions of postwar order are in fact rooted – at least in part – in domestic political structure, several conclusions follow. First, it provides another reason why agreement over the general rules and principles of order may be easier to achieve than agreement on specific distributive issues. It was argued earlier that "institutional" agreements are easier to conclude than "substantive" agreements because they are agreements about rules and process and not about the resolution of specific distributive conflicts. What is added here is that these are also the types of agreement over which credible commitment is most demonstrable. Second, the domestic structural sources of preferences on international order also lead us to expect a great deal of attention by states seeking a postwar settlement to questions of domestic regime character. States are more likely to seek constitutional settlements with states that have similar polities and such settlements are more likely to be successful.

Democracy and constitutional agreement

Beyond these considerations, democratic states are more effective in reassuring other states about their commitments than non-democracies and, as a result, democracies are more readily able to create constitutional settlements. Democracies – that is, open and decentralized polities with competitive parties – have a variety of characteristics that are relevant to reducing uncertainty and conveying commitment. These characteristics are political transparency, accessibility, and policy viscosity.

Democracies have higher levels of political transparency than non-democracies, and this allows other states to make more exact determinations of the state's commitment to rules and agreements. Political transparency refers to the openness and visibility of the polity, and democracies have a variety of characteristics that promote such transparency. The most crucial characteristic is the decentralization of power and decision-making. Decision-making is dispersed, which means that more people and a more elaborate process are involved in decision-making – and as a result, more of the business of politics must be conducted in the open. Reinforcing this situation are the norms and expectations of democratic politics. Elected officials are ultimately accountable to voters and therefore the expectation is that the public will observe – if not directly participate in – policy-making. Secrecy is seen to be the exception and not the norm. Finally, the competitive party system also generates information about the state's policy intentions and commitments. The vetting process of national elections increases the chances that leaders will be known entities who embrace well-hewn policy orientations (Deudney and Ikenberry 1994). Political competition is a punishment and reward system that creates incentives for leaders to be open and accountable. The electoral system creates incentives for each party to expose inconsistencies and credibility gaps in the policy commitments of the other party.[29] Because of these competitive party dynamics and the transparency of the decision-making process, other states are less subject to surprises than non-democracies – and this increases the confidence that others will have in the state's commitments.

The openness and decentralization of democratic states also provides opportunities for other states to directly consult and make representations, thus increasing their willingness to make co-binding commitments.[30] The multiple points of access allow other states to make direct assessments of policy commitments and to lobby on behalf of their interests. The array of officials and offices that have a hand in policy are all potential access points. In some instances, elaborate consultative mechanisms may exist to facilitate consultation and representation; in others, it may be less direct and formal, with governments working through private representatives and agents (Ikenberry 1997). Democratic polities provide opportunities for access by other states, which can increase levels of information about policy intentions and commitments – and it can also provide opportunities for foreign governments to press their interests within the policy-making process. As a result, the credibility of commitments rises.

Finally, democratic states have greater institutional checks on abrupt policy shifts than non-democratic states, and this "policy viscosity" serves to reduce policy surprises (Deudney and Ikenberry 1994; Ikenberry 1997; Mastanduno 1996). One type of check is simply that policy in a decentralized pluralistic democracy must usually pass through a series of veto points. It is very difficult for any official within the state to unilaterally change policy in a radically new direction. Policy-making is essentially a process of coalition building, and this makes it less likely that one individual can command policy unilaterally and move it abruptly in ways that are threatening to other states. Likewise, the competitive electoral process also exerts an ongoing pressure on the overall direction of policy. Successful leaders must build majority coalitions of voters and this creates an incentive to reflect the positions of the "median voter" (Cowhey 1993). The structure of electoral politics ensures that the range of policies will be – at least over the long term – within the center of the political spectrum.

As a result, democracies are able to convey greater credibility in their commitments than non-democracies. Their openness and transparency allows greater opportunities to determine the character and durability of policies. Their accessibility allows other governments to not just gather information but also to directly deliver information and actively participate at least on the fringes of policy-making. The competitive party system also provides a mechanism that exerts a pull on policy, creating an ongoing incentive for policy to be situated in the center of the political spectrum. None of these factors guarantees that democratic polities will always make good on their commitments, but they do reduce the uncertainty about abrupt and untoward shifts in policy emerging.

Historical Cases and Comparisons

The postwar settlements all show signs of constitutional politics, although in different ways and extents. The leading states in the postwar settlements of 1815, 1919, and 1945 were all concerned with the principles of order and the desirability of a mutually acceptable – that is to say, legitimate – postwar order. Also, these agreements tended to be increasingly institutional agreements; that is, they dealt with process and the formal aspects of consultation and decision-making. The Vienna settlement was infused with agreements about how territorial adjustments and other security arrangements would be processed (Holsti 1991: ch. 6). The notion was that if there are procedures available to settle disputes, it reduces the possibility that more extreme forms of interstate conflict will be necessary. Creating a political process helps shape expectations.

The settlement among the industrial democracies after 1945 looks even more like a constitutional order. The Western countries made systematic efforts to anchor their joint commitments in principled and binding institutional mechanisms – giving them an almost distinctive "domestic" character. The Western governments "locked in" their commitments and relationships, to the extent that this can be done by sovereign states. This is constitutionalism in the sense that these governments attempted to construct a political order based on commonly embraced norms and principles along with institutional mechanisms for resolving conflicts and reaching specific agreements.

The structural characteristics of the United States – its liberal democratic polity – were crucial in helping the postwar Western states overcome the problem of credible commitment. The open and decentralized character of the American political system provided opportunities for other states to exercise their "voice" in the operation of the American hegemonic order, thereby reassuring these states that their interests could be actively advanced and processes of conflict resolution would exist. In this sense, the American postwar order was a "penetrated hegemony," an extended system that blurred domestic and international politics as it created an elaborate transnational and transgovernmental political system with the United States at its center.

There are actually several ways in which America's penetrated hegemony serves to reinforce the credibility of the United States' commitment to operating within an institutionalized political order. The first is simply the transparency of the system, which reduces surprises and allays worries by partners that the United States might make abrupt changes in policy. This transparency comes from the fact that policy-making in a large, decentralized democracy involves many players and an extended and relatively visible political process. But it is not only that it is an open and decentralized system; it is also one with competing political parties and an independent press – features that serve to expose the underlying integrity and viability of major policy commitments (Fearon 1994). The open and competitive process may produce mixed and ambiguous policies at times, but the transparency of the process at least allows other states to make more accurate calculations about the likely direction of American foreign policy, which lowers levels of uncertainty and provides a measure of reassurance – which, everything else being equal, provides greater opportunities to cooperate.

Another way in which the penetrated hegemonic order provides reassurances to partners is that the American system invites (or at least provides opportunities for) the participation of outsiders. The fragmented and penetrated American system allows and invites the proliferation of a vast network of transnational and transgovernmental relations with Europe, Japan, and other parts of the industrial world. Diffuse and dense networks of governmental, corporate, and private associations tie the system together.

The United States is the primary site for the pulling and hauling of trans-Atlantic and trans-Pacific politics. Europeans and Japanese do not have elected officials in Washington – but they do have representatives.[31] Although this access to the American political process is not fully reciprocated abroad, the openness and extensive decentralization of the American liberal system assures other states that they have routine access to the decision-making processes of the United States.

A final way in which reassurance was mutually conveyed was in the institutions themselves, which provided "lock-in" and "binding" constraints on the United States and its partners, thereby mitigating fears of domination or abandonment. The Western countries made systematic efforts to anchor their joint commitments in principled and binding institutional mechanisms. Governments might ordinarily seek to preserve their options, to cooperate with other states but to leave open the option of disengaging. What the United States and the other Western states did after the war was exactly the opposite – they built long-term economic, political, and security commitments that were difficult to retract. They "locked in" their commitments and relationships, to the extent that this can be done by sovereign states.

The Bretton Woods economic and monetary accords exhibit the institutional binding logic. These were the first accords to establish a permanent international institutional and legal framework to ensure economic cooperation between states. They were constructed as elaborate systems of rules and obligations with quasi-judicial procedures for adjudicating disputes (James 1995). In effect, the Western governments created an array of functionally organized transnational political systems. Moreover, the democratic character of the United States and the other Western countries facilitated the construction of these dense interstate connections. The permeability of domestic institutions provided congenial grounds for reciprocal and pluralistic "pulling and hauling" across the advanced industrial world.

It was here that the Cold War's security alliances provided additional institutional-binding opportunities. The old saying that NATO was created to "keep the Russians out, the Germans down, and the Americans in" is a statement about the importance of the alliance structures for locking in long-term commitments and expectations. The American–Japanese security alliance also had a similar "dual containment" character. These institutions not only served as alliances in the ordinary sense as organized efforts to balance against external threats, they also provided mechanisms and venues to build political relations, conduct business, and regulate conflict.[32]

The constitutional features of the Western order have been particularly important for Germany and Japan. Both countries were reintegrated into the advanced industrial world as "semi-sovereign" powers; that is, they accepted unprecedented constitutional limits on their military capacity and independence.[33] As such, they became unusually dependent on the array of Western regional and multilateral economic and security institutions. The Western political order in which they were embedded was integral to their stability and functioning. The Christian Democrat Walther Leisler Kiep argued in 1972 that "the German–American alliance . . . is not merely one aspect of modern German history, but a decisive element as a result of its preeminent place in our politics. In effect, it provides a second constitution for our country" (quoted in Schwartz 1995: 555). Western economic and security institutions provide Germany and Japan with a political bulwark of stability that far transcends their more immediate and practical purposes.

Overall, American hegemony is reluctant, penetrated, and highly institutionalized. All these characteristics have helped to facilitate a rather stable and durable political order. American strategic restraint after the war left the Europeans worried more about abandonment than domination, and they actively sought American institutionalized commitments to Europe. The American polity's transparency and permeability fostered an "extended" political order – reaching outward to the other industrial democracies – with most of its roads leading to Washington. Transnational and transgovernmental relations provide the channels. Multiple layers of economic, political, and security institutions bind these countries together in ways that reinforce the credibility of their mutual commitments. The United Stated remains the center of the system, but other states are highly integrated into it, and its legitimacy diminishes the need for the exercise of coercive power by the United States or for balancing responses from secondary states.

The Vienna settlement was not as extensive in its design or institutions as the settlements of 1919 or 1945. But the states themselves were not as readily able to convey the necessary credible commitment to go beyond its parameters. Arguably, however, the common domestic predicament of these states was crucial in inducing a negotiated institutional settlement. While the relevant states were not identical, they were all non-democracies in the sense that the rulers in each state felt incentives to reinforce their domestic position. It was this mutual predicament that helped provide a sense of common cause, reassurance, and legitimacy.[34] Likewise, the fact that the order itself was anchored in an organized balance of territory and power created a sufficiently secure fall-back option for the relevant states.

In effect, the states – because of their non-democratic character – were not able to give high levels of credible commitment, but the acceptable escape option allowed the states to go forward with the levels of reassurance that did exist.

The failure of 1919 had many causes, including the idiosyncratic ones associated with Woodrow Wilson. But there were deeper problems. One problem was that several of the core states, particularly France, were not really interested in a constitutional settlement. In the eyes of its leaders, France could not afford to make choices in favor of longer-term investments in institutions. The United States, which did feel this incentive, was not in a sufficiently commanding position to override this resistance. Both the diversity of states that were party to the settlement and the widely divergent strategic positions that the various states occupied mattered in the failure that followed.

Conclusion

This essay argues that the problem of order building in international relations is not unlike order building within countries. Where newly powerful states confront an undefined and unsettled political order, they face a choice – whether to use their material capabilities to win in myriad struggles over the distribution of gains or seek a more general settlement over principles and norms of order. The historical evidence indicates that leading states do prefer to operate within a legitimate and durable political order. But the creation of such an order has many requirements beyond the general incentive that both leading and secondary states may have in its creation. It is here that the historical circumstances that attend the postwar settlement matter – the way the war was won, the resulting distribution of power, the character of the states that are party to the settlement, and the ideas and lessons embraced by the leading states.

In effect, the constitutional logic will be most fully felt when the breakdown is huge, the power concentration is great, and the leading states are open and democratic. Where the breakdown in the old order is extensive, several imperatives follow – the option of "no agreement" is essentially unacceptable to all parties; and the wide scope of issues (security, economic, etc.) up for settlement reinforces that need for principled agreements on political process. Where the concentration of power is great, the incentives for and ability to implement a constitutional settlement rise. In the 1945 settlement, the United States had a commanding position – it was the only country that emerged from the war with more material capabilities than it started with, and this power position was itself magnified by the completeness and unconditionality of victory over Germany and Japan.

Finally, the (perhaps historically accidental) fact that the United States was a large and open democracy provided a decisive mechanism for building constitutional order in the West. Even before the Cold War created additional reasons to cooperate, the Western countries signaled an intention to bind themselves together in ways that were unprecedented. The transparency and accessibility of the United States provided a measure of confidence in its commitments to a reciprocal, multilateral, and open postwar political order.

The 1945 settlement among the Western countries would surely not have taken a constitutional character if the states had not been democracies. The willingness to engage in intensive institutional binding is only comprehensible in terms of the unusual ability of democratic states to convey credible commitment. In particular, the open and decentralized American state was critical in the construction of institutional mechanisms that allowed secondary states access to consultation and decision-making in exchange for their acquiescence. The Cold War helped create an added measure of solidarity between the Western democracies, but the institutional agreements preceded bipolarity and appear to be outlasting the end of it as well (Ikenberry 1996).

The ordering of domestic and international politics often occurs in the aftermath of great upheaval and conflict. There is reason to think that similar processes are at work in the creation of order after the drama is over. The imperatives of securing reciprocal consent are felt by wielders of power regardless of the realms in which they operate. Order formation and constitution building are general processes that encompass the affairs of states – both domestic and international.

Notes

I would like to thank Inwon Choue, Daniel Deudney, Judith Goldstein, Joe Grieco, Charles Kupchan, David Lake, Michael Mastanduno, Joe Lepgold, Duncan Snidal, participants at seminars at Cornell University and Georgetown University, and three anonymous referees for their helpful comments.

1 Others have made this observation, see Lake 1996 and Milner 1991.
2 Gilpin 1981: 41–4. This type of change is contrasted with "systems change," which refers to change in the basic character of the actors within the global system; and it is contrasted with "interaction change," which refers to change in the political, economic, and other processes among actors.
3 For an impressive survey, see Holsti 1991.

4   Legitimate orders are marked by acceptance by participating members of the basic norms and principles of the order, but this need not involve the incorporation of all the institutional features of constitutionalism. See Beetham 1991.

5   These aspects of constitutionalism suggest that there is a spectrum to constitutional orderings and that specific historical orders will vary in the degree to which they exhibit these constitutional characteristics.

6   Lord Bolingbroke defined it thus in 1733: "By constitution we mean, whenever we speak with an exactness, that assemblage of laws, institutions and customs, derived from certain fixed principles of reason, directed to certain fixed objects of public good, that comprise the general system, according to which the community hath agreed to be governed" (quoted in McIlwain 1940: 5).

7   As Jon Elster argues, constitutionalism stands for "the rare moments in a nation's history when deep, principled discussion transcends the logrolling and horse-trading of everyday majority politics, the object of these debates being the principles which are to constrain future majority decisions" (1988: 6).

8   This logic of constitutional politics is advanced by Bruce Ackerman, who embraces a "dualist" theory of constitutional development and makes a basic distinction between "higher" and "normal" lawmaking in American political development (see Ackerman 1991).

9   There is considerable disagreement among theorists over the sources of constitutional authority, particularly among instrumental views and deeper, goal and value views. Some theorists stress the specific legal and judicial mechanisms that protect rights and create limitations on power. In this view, constitutions are a form of legal constraint on politics, manifest as a declaration of principles that specify rights, protections, and basic rules. In this way the constitution provides a sort of "last word" on the essential principles and rules of political order – but legal principles and rules that can be applied, interpreted, and extended (Elster 1988). The argument made by some that the European Union is becoming a constitutional order stresses the spread of European judicial principles and practices, serving to create a Europe governed by a "specified interstate governmental structure defined by a constitutional charter and constitutional principles" (Weiler 1991: 2407). Others stress the institutional architecture of constitutional orders, creating limits on power through the many institutional devices and procedures that they specify. Theories of institutional balance, separation, oversight, and judicial review have an intellectual lineage that can be traced from Aristotle to Locke and Montesquieu. Constitutions create limits through institutional design. Finally, others argue that constitutional authority is really a reflection of (and therefore dependent on) the wider, shared consensus on political order within the polity. The stable functioning of a constitution requires a consensus on basic principles and rules. It is the diffuse authority of common values and political goals that creates the constraint on power.

In this essay, I am stressing the way in which power is restrained through co-binding institutions. In this sense, constitutionalism depends heavily on the role of international institutions as shaping, constraining, and connecting mechanisms between states. It is precisely because institutions can in various ways bind (particularly democratic) states together, constrain state actions, and create complicated and demanding political processes that participating states can overcome worries about the arbitrary and untoward exercise of power.

10 The dominant state's relative power decline may result simply from the bounce back of the defeated states, whose weakness is temporarily magnified by the devastation of war, and/or from the longer-term processes of rise and decline of the leading powers and gradual shifts in the distribution of power.

11 The classic statement of these state choices is Arnold Wolfers' distinction between "possession" and "mileau" foreign policy goals (1962: 73–4).

12 In effect, the leading state enters the postwar period sitting on a declining power asset base. A constitutional settlement allows that state to conserve its asset base by creating rules and institutions that will extend the stream of benefits and advantages into the future beyond what would otherwise be the case.

13 The claim is that institutions can have an independent ordering impact on their environment even after the disappearance or decline of the actors that created them. See March and Olsen 1989. Regarding international regimes, see Krasner 1982 and Young 1989.

14 This is true even if the leading state has to use more power resources at the outset to get agreement on basic rules and institutions and even if it has to compromise (to some extent) so as to get agreement on the character of those rules and institutions.

15 For a useful discussion of the distinction between substantive and institutional agreements, see Przeworski 1988: 64–70.

16 Adam Przeworski makes this point: "Agreements about institutions are possible, even if the political forces involved have conflicting interests and visions because institutions shape the opportunities of realizing specific interests and the groups involved understand that institutions have this effect" (1988: 70)

17 For a typology of regimes and constitutional agreements, see Stone 1994.

18 There is a lively historical and theoretical debate about how significant the Westphalia settlement really was as a constructed, institutional, and defining political moment. For an important skeptical view, see Krasner 1993.

19 Organski, for example, identifies six methods by which states might attempt to maintain the balance of power – to arm, seize territory, establish buffer zones, form alliances, intervene in the internal affairs of other nations, or divide and conquer (1968: 267).

20 For an important statement of the logic of security co-binding, see Deudney 1995, 1996.

21   In other words, the assumption is that under some circumstances, institutions can be more than simply "solutions" for states seeking to reduce uncertainty and alter transaction costs. For a discussion of this more limited, "rationalistic" understanding of institutions, see Keohane 1988 and Snidal 1996.

22   This view accords with our general view of what institutions are and do. As Lorenzo Ornaghi argues, "the role of institutions in politics is to give the rules of the game, in that, by reducing the uncertain and unforeseeable character of interpersonal relations, insurance is mutually provided" (1990: 27).

23   Robert Powell (1991) argues that where the threat of war is absent, states are more likely to calculate their interests in terms of absolute gains. Constitutional commitments are, in effect, joint commitments to conduct relations without the threat or resort to war.

24   The general problem of credible commitment and its importance to constitutional development and the rule of law is explored in North 1993, Weingast 1997, and Weingast and North 1989.

25   For a discussion of "voice opportunities" as an explanation for European union, see Grieco 1995. The classic formulation of this logic is Hirschman 1970.

26   In effect, the question being posed here is: what are the conditions under which a leading postwar state will act in a farsighted manner, giving up short-term gains and coercive management of the postwar order in favor of a legitimate and institutionalized order?

27   On this basic claim about the interrelationship of domestic and international political legitimacy, see Wight 1977.

28   The assumption behind this claim is that domestic political orders have a shaping and constraining impact on what states want to do and can do. This in turn provides some measure of confidence that states will carry out the agreements that they reach. For a discussion of the impact of domestic structures on state policy, see Evangelista 1997.

29   For a survey of arguments in this area, see Gaubatz 1996.

30   In this sense, information about intentions and commitments flows in both directions. Democracies expose themselves more fully to other states than non-democracies, and their accessible institutions also allow them to absorb more information on the policies and motivations of other states.

31   For the transnational political process channeled through the Atlantic security institutions, see Risse-Kappen 1995. On the US–Japanese side, see Katzenstein and Tsujinaka 1996.

32   The argument that an alliance can serve to manage and stabilize relations among its partners is made by Schroeder 1975.

33   On the notion of semi-sovereignty, see Katzenstein 1987. For a discussion of Japanese semi-sovereignty and the postwar peace constitution, see Tamamoto 1995.

34   This is a conventional perspective on the Vienna settlement. See Kissinger 1957.

References

Ackerman, Bruce (1991) *We the People: Foundations* (Cambridge, Mass.: Belknap Press).

Barkin, J. Samuel and Bruce Cronin (1994) "The State and the Nation: Changing Norms and the Rules of Sovereignty in International Relations," *International Organization* 48(1): 107–30.

Beetham, David (1991) *The Legitimation of Power* (London: Macmillan).

Brennan, Geoffrey and James M. Buchanan (1985) *The Reason of Rules: Constitutional Political Economy* (Cambridge: Cambridge University Press).

Claude, Inis, Jr (1962) *Power and International Relations* (New York: Random House).

Cowhey, Peter F. (1993) "Elect Locally – Order Globally: Domestic Politics and Multilateral Cooperation," in John Ruggie, ed., *Multilateralism Matters: The Theory and Praxis of an Institutional Form* (New York: Columbia University Press).

Craig, Gordon and Alexander George (1983) *Force and Statecraft* (New York: Oxford University Press).

Deudney, Daniel (1995) "The Philadelphia System: Sovereignty, Arms Control, and Balance of Power in the American States-Union, 1787–1861," *International Organization* 49(2): 191–228.

Deudney, Daniel (1996) "Binding Sovereigns: Authority, Structure, and Geopolitics in Philadelphia Systems," in Thomas Biersteiker and Cynthia Weber, eds., *State Sovereignty as Social Construct* (New York: Cambridge University Press), pp. 190–239.

Deudney, Daniel and G. John Ikenberry (1994) "Democratic Competence: The Performance of Democracy in Great Power Balancing," mimeo, The University of Pennsylvania.

Elster, Jon (1988) "Introduction," in Jon Elster and Rune Slagstad, eds., *Constitutionalism and Democracy* (New York: Cambridge University Press), pp. 1–17.

Evangelista, Mathew (1997) "Domestic Structure and International Change," in Michael Doyle and G. John Ikenberry, eds., *New Thinking in International Relations Theory* (Boulder: Westview Press), pp. 202–28.

Fearon, James (1994) "Domestic Political Audiences and the Escalation of International Disputes," *American Political Science Review* 88(3): 577–92.

Friedrich, Carl J. (1950) *Constitutional Government and Democracy* (Boston: Ginn).

Gaubatz, Kurt Taylor (1996) "Democratic States and Commitment in International Relations," *International Organization* 50(1): 109–39.

Gilpin, Robert (1981) *War and Change in World Politics* (New York: Cambridge University Press).

Grieco, Joseph (1995) "The Maastricht Treaty, Economic and Monetary Union, and the Neo-Realist Research Programme," *Review of International Studies* 21: 21–40.

Gross, Leo (1948) "The Peace of Westphalia, 1648–1948," *American Journal of International Law* 42: 20–41.

Gulick, Edward V. (1967) *Europe's Classical Balance of Power* (New York: Norton).

Haas, Ernst (1953) "The Balance of Power: Prescription, Concept or Propaganda," *World Politics* 15(3): 370–98.

Hill, David Jayne (1925) *A History of Diplomacy in the International Development of Europe*, vol. II (New York: Longmans, Green, and Co.).

Hirschman, Albert (1970) *Exit, Voice and Loyalty – Responses to Decline in Firms, Organizations, and States* (Cambridge, Mass.: Harvard University Press).

Holsti, Kalevi J. (1991) *Peace and War: Armed Conflict and International Order, 1648–1989* (Cambridge: Cambridge University Press).

Ikenberry, G. John (1996) "the Myth of Postwar Chaos," *Foreign Affairs* 75(3): 79–91. (Reproduced in ch. 6 of this volume as "The Myth of Post-Cold War Chaos".)

Ikenberry, G. John (1997) "Liberal Hegemony: Explaining the Persistence of the American Postwar Order," mimeo, The University of Pennsylvania.

Ikenberry, G. John and Charles A. Kupchan (1990) "Socialization and Hegemonic Power," *International Organization* 44(3): 283–315. (Reproduced in ch. 2 of this volume.)

James, Harold (1995) *International Monetary Cooperation Since Bretton Woods* (New York: Oxford University Press).

Katzenstein, Peter J. (1987) *Policy and Politics in West Germany: The Growth of A Semi-Sovereign State* (Philadelphia: Temple University Press).

Katzenstein, Peter J. (1989) "International Relations Theory and the Analysis of Change," in Ernst-Otto Czempiel and James N. Rosenau, eds., *Global Changes and Theoretical Challenges* (Lexington, Mass.: Lexington Books), pp. 291–304.

Katzenstein, Peter J. and Yutaka Tsujinaka (1996) "'Bullying,' 'Buying,' and 'Binding': US–Japanese Transnational Relations and Domestic Structures," in Thomas Risse-Kappen, ed., *Bringing Transnational Relations Back In* (London: Cambridge University Press), pp. 79–111.

Keohane, Robert (1988) "International Institutions: Two Approaches," *International Studies Quarterly* 32: 379–96.

Kissinger, Henry A. (1957) *A World Restored: Metternich, Castlereagh and the Problems of Peace, 1812–1822* (New York: Houghton Mifflin).

Krasner, Stephen D. (1982) *International Regimes* (Ithaca: Cornell University Press).

Krasner, Stephen D. (1985) *Structural Conflict: The Third World Against Global Liberalism* (Berkeley: University of California Press).

Krasner, Stephen D. (1991) "Global Communications and National Power: Life on the Pareto Frontier," *World Politics* 43(3): 336–66.

Krasner, Stephen D. (1993) "Westphalia and All That," in Judith Goldstein and Robert Keohane, eds., *Ideas and Foreign Policy: Beliefs, Institutions, and Political Change* (Ithaca: Cornell University Press), pp. 235–64.

Lake, David (1996) "Anarchy, Hierarchy, and the Variety of International Theory," *International Organization* 50(1): 1–34.

Levi, Margaret (1988) *Of Rule and Revenue* (Berkeley: University of California Press).

McIlwain, Charles Howard (1940) *Constitutionalism and the Changing World* (Cambridge, Mass.: Harvard University Press).

Manicini, Frederico G. (1991) "The Making of a Constitution for Europe," in Robert Keohane and Stanley Hoffmann, eds., *The New European Community* (Boulder, Colo.: Westview Press), pp. 177–94.

March, James G. and Johan P. Olsen (1989) *Discovering Institutions: The Organizational Basis of Politics* (New York: Free Press).

Martin, Lisa (1993) "The Rational State Choice of Multilateralism," in John Gerard Ruggie, ed., *Multilateralism Matters: The Theory and Praxis of an Institutional Form* (New York: Columbia University Press).

Mastanduno, Michael (1996) "The United States Political System and International Leadership: A 'Decidedly Inferior' Form of Government," in G. John Ikenberry, ed., *American Foreign Policy: Theoretical Essays* (New York: HarperCollins), pp. 328–48.

Mearsheimer, John (1994/5) "The False Promise of International Institutions," *International Security* 19(3): 5–49.

Milner, Helen (1991) "The Assumption of Anarchy in International Relations Theory: A Critique," *Review of International Studies* 17(1): 67–85.

North, Douglass C. (1993) "Institutions and Credible Commitment," *Journal of Institutional and Theoretical Economics* 149(1): 11–23.

Opie, Redvers, Joseph W. Ballantine, Paul Birdsall, Jeanette E. Muther, and Clarence E. Thurber (1951) *The Search for Peace Settlements* (Washington, DC: The Brookings Institution).

Organski, A. F. K. (1968) *World Politics*, 2nd edn. (New York: Knopf).

Ornaghi, Lorenzo (1990) "Economic Structure and Political Institutions: A Theoretical Framework," in Mauro Baranzini and Roberto Scazzieri, eds., *The Economic Theory of Structure and Change* (Cambridge: Cambridge University Press), pp. 23–44.

Powell, Robert (1991) "Absolute and Relative Gains in International Relations Theory," *American Political Science Review* 85(4): 1303–20.

Przeworski, Adam (1988) "Democracy as a Contingent Outcome of Conflicts," in Jon Elster and Rune Slagstad, eds., *Constitutionalism and Democracy* (New York: Cambridge University Press), pp. 59–80.

Przeworski, Adam (1991) *Democracy and the Market* (New York: Cambridge University Press).

Risse-Kappen, Thomas (1995) *Cooperation Among Democracies: The European Influence on US Foreign Policy* (Princeton: Princeton University Press).

Ruggie, John (1993) "Multilateralism: The Anatomy of an Institution," in John Ruggie, ed., *Multilateralism Matters: The Theory and Praxis of an Institutional Form* (New York: Columbia University Press), pp. 3–47.

Schroeder, Paul W. (1975) "Alliances, 1815–1945: Weapons of Power and Tools of Management," in Klaus Knorr, ed., *Historical Dimensions of National Security Problems* (Lawrence, Kan.: University Press of Kansas), pp. 227–62.

Schwartz, Thomas A. (1995) "The United States and Germany after 1945: Alliances, Transnational Relations, and the Legacy of the Cold War," *Diplomatic History* 19(4): 549–68.

Sheehan, Michael (1996) *The Balance of Power: History and Theory* (London: Routledge).

Snidal, Duncan (1996) "Political Economy and International Institutions," *International Review of Law and Economics* 16: 121–37.

Stein, Eric (1981) "Lawyers, Judges, and the Making of a Transnational Constitution," *American Journal of International Law* 75(1): 1–27.

Stone, Alec (1994) "What is a Supranational Constitution? An Essay in International Relations Theory," *The Review of Politics* 56(3): 441–74.

Tamamoto, Masaru (1995) "Reflections on Japan's Postwar State," *Daedalus* 125(2): 1–22.

Waltz, Kenneth (1979) *Theory of International Politics* (Reading, Mass.: Addison-Wesley).

Weiler, Joseph (1991) "The Transformation of Europe," *Yale Law Journal* 100: 2403–83.

Weingast, Barry (1997) "The Political Foundations of Democracy and the Rule of Law," *American Political Science Review* 91(2): 245–63.

Weingast, Barry and Douglass C. North (1989) "Constitutions and Commitment: The Evolution of Institutions Governing Public Choice in Seventeenth Century England," *Journal of Economic History* 44: 803–32.

Wight, Martin (1966) "The Balance of Power," in H. Butterfield and M. Wight, eds., *Diplomatic Investigations* (Cambridge, Mass.: Harvard University Press), pp. 149–75.

Wight, Martin (1977) *Systems of States* (London: Leicester University Press).

Wolfers, Arnold (1962) "The Goals of Foreign Policy," in A. Wolfers, ed., *Discord and Collaboration: Essays on International Politics* (Baltimore: Johns Hopkins University Press), pp. 67–80.

Young, Oran (1989) *International Cooperation: Building Regimes for Natural Resources and the Environment* (Ithaca: Cornell University Press).

Young, Oran (1991) "Political Leadership and Regime Formation: On the Development of Institutions in International Society," *International Organization* 45(3): 281–308.

5

American Power and the Empire of Capitalist Democracy

The United States is today a global superpower without historical precedent. It stands at the center of an expanding democratic-capitalist world order that is itself, 50 years after its creation, the dominant reality in world politics. Despite expectations that American hegemony would disappear and trigger the emergence of a new and unstable multipolar post-Cold War order, the opposite has in fact happened. American power has grown even greater in the decade since the collapse of the Soviet Union. Although American power is not uniformly welcome around the world, serious ideological challengers or geopolitical balancers are not to be found. Scholars who a decade ago were debating the prospect of cooperation and conflict in a post-hegemonic world are now debating the character and future of world politics within an American unipolar order.

The rise of American unipolarity is surprising. Many observers expected the end of the Cold War to usher in a new era of multipolarity. Some anticipated a return to the balance of power politics of the late nineteenth century. Others saw signs of regional blocs that would return the world to the instabilities of the 1930s. But the distribution of power took a dramatic turn in America's favor. The sudden collapse of the Soviet Union, the decline in ideological rivalry, lagging economic fortunes in Japan and continental Europe, growing disparities in military and technological expenditure, and America's booming economy all intensified power disparities in the 1990s.

The United States began the 1990s as the world's only superpower and it had a better decade that any of the other great powers. Between 1990 and 1998, the American economy grew 26 percent, while Europe grew 17 percent and Japan 7 percent. The United States has reduced its military spending at a slower rate than other countries. It has also been steadily distancing itself from other states in the range and sophistication of its military power.[1] The global reach and multifaceted character of American power separates the American unipolar moment from earlier eras of hegemonic dominance. "The United States of America today predominates on the economic level, the monetary level, on the technological level, and in the cultural area in the broadest sense of the word," observed French Foreign Minister Hubert Vedrine in a speech in Paris in early 1999. "It is not comparable, in terms of power and influence, to anything known in modern history."[2]

But disparities in material capabilities do not capture the full character of American unipolarity. The United States is a different type of hegemonic power. It is not just a powerful state that can throw its weight around – although it is that as well. The United States also dominates world politics by providing the language, ideas, and institutional frameworks around which much of the world turns. The extended institutional connections that link the United States to the other regions of the world provide a sort of primitive governance system. The United States is a central hub through which the world's important military, political, economic, scientific, and cultural connections pass. No other great power – France, Germany, the United Kingdom, Japan, or China – has a global political or security presence. The European Union has a population and economic weight equal to the United States but it does not have a global geopolitical or strategic reach. It cannot project military power or pursue a unified foreign policy toward, for example, China. Japan, which many thought a decade ago might emerge as the next great world power, is struggling under the weight of political gridlock and economic malaise. America's far-flung network of political partnerships and security commitments – together with the array of global and regional institutions – provide what passes for global governance.

To look at the current world order with realist eyes – focusing on anarchy and great power politics – misses the deeper structures of hierarchy and democratic community that prevail today. It is remarkable that 50 years after their defeat in World War II, Japan and Germany – now the second and third largest economies in the world – are still dependent on the American security commitment and station American military forces on their soil. If empires are coercive systems of domination, the American-centered world order is not an empire. If empires are inclusive systems of order organized around a dominant state – and its laws, economy, military, and political institutions – then the United States has indeed constructed a world democratic-capitalist empire.

The United States is not just a unipolar power. It is also the dominant state within a unipolar world order. This world order – perhaps best called the American system – is organized around American-led regional security alliances in Europe and Asia, open and multilateral economic relations, several layers of regional and global multilateral institutions, and shared commitments to democracy and open capitalist economies. It is an order built around American power and a convergence of interests between the United States and other advanced industrial democratic states. Shared values and interests help give shape to the American system, but it is also an engineered political order that is built around a series of political bargains between the United States and its European and Asian partners after World War II and renewed and expanded over the decades.

But how stable is this order? The answer depends on what the precise character of this order actually is. Some argue that behind the façade of democracy and institutional cooperation lies a predatory and imperial American state. Chalmers Johnson argues that the American "empire" is as coercive and exploitative as the Soviet empire and anticipates a backlash in which America's resentful junior partners will wreak their revenge and bring the entire imperial edifice down.[3] This is an echo of a revisionist tradition that sees American global dominance driven by expansionary and exploitative capitalists or a crusading national security state. American Cold War-era interventionism in Latin America and elsewhere around the world provides ample material to make this claim.[4] Some intellectuals in the West even suggest that an arrogant and overbearing America brought the terrorism of September 11, 2001, on itself.[5] Taking the opposite view, John Gaddis argues that the American empire is fundamentally different from the old Soviet empire. The habit of democracy and reciprocity has given American relations with Europe and Asia a more benign and legitimate cast.[6] Realists, such as Kenneth Waltz, argue that the American unipolar order is inherently unstable not because of any special malign American characteristics but because of the inherent insecurity that unequal power confers on weaker states. In anarchic orders, weaker states are threatened by extreme concentrations of power and will seek protection in counter-hegemonic groupings. The balance of power will reassert itself.[7] But the debate about whether there is a coming backlash begs the question: what is the character of American unipolar order as a political formation?

I argue that American unipolarity is an expansive and highly durable political order. It is not a transitional phase in international relations but is a political formation with its own character and logic. Nor is it a political formation that falls easily into a particular historical category – empire, superpower, hegemonic order. The American order is built on power – at least at its core. The extended system of American-led security protection in Europe, the Middle East, and Asia is an essential element of this order and it can only be sustained by dominant military capabilities, which in turn depends on continuing American economic and technological strength. But the American order is sustained by more than power, and therefore its political dynamics – and historical trajectory – are not intelligible from a narrow realist perspective.

The American unipolar order has deep foundations. It is unlikely that any other state or alternative political order will soon arise to replace it. Nor is the world likely to return to a more traditional multipolar world of great power politics. The reason is that the sources of American dominance – and the stability of the American-centered liberal capitalist world order – are remarkably multidimensional and mutually reinforcing. Critical features of the order make American power less threatening and there-fore reduce the incentives that other states have to distance themselves from or balance against the United States.

There are four major facets of the American order that make it robust and durable. One dimension is identified by realist theorists of hegemony, such as Robert Gilpin, who focus on power as the essential glue – power manifest in American security protection, market dominance, and the inter-national role of the dollar. A second dimension is found in the special cir-cumstances of American geography and historical staging. American power is offshore – geographically isolated from the other major powers – making that power less threatening and more useful in stabilizing regional relations. The United States also rose to power as an anti-colonial and post-imperial state with strategic interests that could be pursued by articulating universal principles of state relations. A third dimension of American unipolarity is the distinctive way in which democracy and international institutions have provided the United States with mechanisms to make itself less threatening to the rest of the world. The liberal character of American hegemony allows the United States unusual capacities to make commitments and restrain power. Finally, the deep forces of modernization and the distinctive prin-ciples of the American polity – civic nationalism and multicultural identity – also give the United States unusual influence and political congruence with world political development. The durability of the American order is not simply sustained by the exertion of American power – activity shaping and managing the world. Rather it is the country's deep alignment with global development processes – and the "project of modernity" – that gives the American system its durability and global reach.

This article will examine these facets of the American order. It will conclude by looking at the underlying political bargain that the United States has made with the rest of the world and discuss whether that bargain is coming unstuck or not. The American system has a long future if its leaders understand its logic and rules.

Balance of Power, Hegemony, and the American System

In explaining the character and future of American unipolarity, structural realism provides the most elegant and time-honored theory. International order is the result of balancing by states under conditions of anarchy to counter opposing power concentrations or threats. In this view, the rise of the American order was itself a creature of the Cold War and bipolar balancing. The Soviet threat provided the essential stimulant for American-led postwar order building in the non-communist world. But with the end of the bipolar threat, American preponderance is unsustainable: now it poses a danger to other states and balancing reactions are inevitable. Kenneth Waltz provides the logic of this realist expectation. The underlying condition of anarchy leads weaker states to resist and balance against the predominant state. Security – indeed survival – is the fundamental goal of states, and because states cannot ultimately rely on the commitments or guarantees of other states to insure their security, states will be very sensitive to their relative power position. When powerful states emerge, secondary states will seek protection in countervailing coalitions of weaker states. The alternatives risk domination. As Waltz argues: "Secondary states, if they are free to choose, flock to the weaker side; for it is the stronger side that threatens them. On the weaker side they are both more appreciated and safer, provided, of course, that the coalition they join achieves enough defensive or deterrent strength to dissuade adversaries from attacking."[8] Alliances emerge as temporary coalitions of states formed to counter the concentration of power. As the distribution of power shifts, coalitions will also shift. American unipolar power is manifestly unstable.

Yet it is remarkable that despite the sharp shifts in the distribution of power, the other great powers have not yet responded in a way anticipated by balance of power theory. Despite the disappearance of the Soviet threat, it is difficult to discern a significant decline in alliance solidarity between the United States and its European and Asian partners. "Rather than edging away from the United States, much less balancing against it, Germany and Japan have been determined to maintain the pattern of engagement that characterized the Cold War," argues Michael Mastanduno. "Neither China nor Russia, despite having some differences with the United States, has sought to organize a balancing coalition against it. Indeed, the main security concern for many countries in Europe and Asia is not how to distance from an all-too-powerful United States, but how to prevent the United States from drifting away."[9] Both NATO and the US–Japan alliance have recently reaffirmed and deepened their ties. Nor have wider realms of political and economic cooperation or accompanying multilateral relations declined in serious ways. Trade and investment have expanded across the Atlantic and Pacific and an increasingly dense web of intergovernmental and transnational relations connect these countries. Despite the most radical shifts in international power in half a century, the relations among the major states have remained remarkably stable and continuous.

For Waltz, the expectation of a return to a global balance of power requires patience. Realist theory clearly expects that "balances disturbed will one day be restored," but it cannot predict when national governments will respond to these structural pressures. In Waltz's structural realist view, unipolarity is the least durable of international configurations that inevitably will provoke actions and responses by the dominant and weaker states that will ultimately return the system to a more traditional balance of power order. A unipolar state is fundamentally unrestrained – and this makes its foreign policy less disciplined and more dangerous to other states. Resistance and counter-balancing will follow. Indeed, Waltz claims that one can observe "balancing tendencies already taking place."[10]

Aside from balance of power theory, a second realist theory holds that order is created and maintained by a hegemonic state which uses power capabilities to organize relations among states.[11] The preponderance of power by a state allows it to offer incentives – both positive and negative – to the other states to agree to ongoing participation within the hegemonic order. According to Gilpin, an international order is, at any particular moment in history, the reflection of the underlying distribution of power of states within the system. Over time, this distribution of power shifts, leading to conflicts and ruptures in the system, hegemonic war, and the eventual reorganization of order so as to reflect the new distribution of power capabilities. It is the rising hegemonic state or group of states, whose power position has been ratified by war, which defines the terms of the postwar settlement – and the character of the new order.

In the strong version, hegemonic order is built around direct and coercive domination of weaker and secondary states by the hegemon. The dominant state manipulates the world to its purposes. But actual hegemonic orders have tended to be more complex and less coercive. Gilpin depicts the British and American hegemonic orders as ones built around dominant military and economic capabilities but bolstered as well by mutually beneficial trade relations and shared liberal ideology. Indeed, he argues that hegemony without a commitment to liberalism is likely to lead to imperial systems, regional blocs, and the imposition of severe restrictions on lesser states.[12] Hegemonic orders can be relatively benevolent and non-coercive – organized around reciprocal, consensual, and institutionalized relations. The order is still organized around asymmetrical power relations, but the most overtly coercive character of domination is muted.

In a highly imperial hegemonic order, weaker and secondary states are simply unable to counter-balance. Domination itself prevents the escape to a balance of power system. In more benign and consensual hegemonic orders, where restraints on hegemonic power are sufficiently developed, it is the expected value of balancing that declines. Balancing is an option for weaker and secondary states, but the benign character and institutional limits on hegemonic power reduce the incentives to do so.

Following this observation, it is possible to identify three variants of hegemonic order. The first is based on coercive domination. Weaker and secondary states are not happy about their subordinate position and would actively seek to overturn the order if they were capable of doing so. But the prevailing power distribution provides insufficient capabilities for these states to challenge the dominant state. This is in effect an informal imperial order.[13] Power – and in the final instance coercive domination – keeps the order together.[14]

A second type of hegemonic order is held together by some minimal convergence of interests. The dominant state might provide "services" to subordinate states that these states find useful – and sufficiently useful to prevent them from actively seeking to overturn the order. In this order, the dominant state's security or economic assets can be used or employed in one way of another by weaker partner states – the leading state provides security protection or access to its market – and these opportunities for gain outweigh the dangers of domination or abandonment. America's extended security role in Western Europe, East Asia, and the Middle East, for example, is welcomed by states in these regions because it allows them to stabilize local rivalries. Finally, in a third variant, hegemonic order might even be more thoroughly institutionalized and infused with reciprocal processes of political interaction so that the hierarchy of the order is all but obscured. This is quasi-rule-based and open hegemony. In such a benevolent hegemonic formation, where there are real institutional restraints on the exercise of power, the resulting order begins to reflect less faithfully the underlying distribution of power. This is reflected in the American hegemonic order, where the web of institutional relations – security, political, and economic – that the United States spun after World War II and in later decades has transformed the sharp power disparities into a more principled and mutually acceptable order.

Security Alliances, Markets, and the Dollar

American power – military, political, economic – is the not-so-hidden hand that built and sustains the American system. The realist narrative is straightforward. The United States emerged from World War II as the leading global power and it proceeded to organize the postwar system in a way that accorded with its interests. In 1947, the British scholar Harold Laski wrote: "America bestrides the world like a colossus; neither Rome at the height of its powers nor Great Britain in the period of its economic supremacy enjoyed an influence so direct, so profound, so pervasive."[15] America's allies and the defeated axis states were battered and diminished by the war, whereas the United States grew more powerful through mobilization for war. The American government was more centralized and capable, and the economy and military were unprecedented in their power and still on an upward swing. America's position was also enhanced because the war had ratified the destruction of the old order of the 1930s, eliminated the alternative regional hegemonic ambitions of Germany and Japan, and diminished the viability of the British imperial order. The stage was set for the United States to shape the postwar order.

The extraordinary power disparities of the moment were not lost on American officials. George Kennan pointed to this reality in 1948: "We have about 50 percent of the world's wealth but only 6.3 percent of its population. . . . Our real task in the coming period is to devise a pattern of relationships which will permit us to maintain this position of disparity without positive detriment to our national security."[16] Kennan is expressing a quintessentially realist sentiment that the United States needed to construct a postwar order that would allow it to retain its power and advantages but do so in a clever enough way so as not to provoke resistance.

Two sorts of strategic objectives became attached to the exercise of American power in the 1940s. One dealt with the geoeconomic organization of the postwar order: the United States sought to build an order that would avoid the return to the antagonist regional blocs of the 1930s. The United States wanted to situate itself in an open order that would allow multilateral trade and resource access with the other regions of the world. America's other great ambition emerged later – countering Soviet communism by creating a worldwide system of alliance partnerships and pursuing containment.

During the 1930s, the United States saw its geopolitical operating space shrink as the other great powers began to construct closed and competing regional blocs. Germany pursued a series of bilateral trade agreements with Eastern European countries in order to consolidate an economic and political sphere of influence in the region. Japan pursued an even more overt campaign to create a Greater East Asian Co-Prosperity Sphere. In a less obvious or aggressive way, Britain also was pursuing a strategy of discriminatory economic cooperation with its Commonwealth partners – a non-territorial economic bloc built around the imperial preferential system.

By the end of the 1930s, the world was effectively carved up into relatively insular economic blocs – antagonistic groupings that American officials understood to be at least partly responsible for the onset of war.[17]

This is where American strategic thinkers began their debates in the 1930s. The question these thinkers pondered was whether the United States could remain as a great industrial power within the confines of the Western hemisphere. What were the minimum geographical requirements for the country's economic and military viability? For all practical purposes this question was answered by the time the United States entered the war. An American hemispheric bloc would not be sufficient; the United States must have security of markets and raw materials in Asia and Europe.[18] If the rimlands of Europe and Asia became dominated by one or several hostile imperial powers, the security implications for the United States would be catastrophic. To remain a great power, the United States must seek openness, access, and balance in Europe and Asia.

This view that America must have access to Asian and European markets and resources – and must therefore not let a potential adversary control the Eurasian landmass – was also embraced by postwar defense planners. As the war was coming to an end, defense officials began to see that America's security interests required the building of an elaborate system of forward bases in Asia and Europe. Hemispheric defense would be inadequate.[19] Defense officials also saw access to Asian and European raw materials – and the prevention of their control by a prospective enemy – as an American security interest. Melvin Leffler notes that "Stimson, Patterson, McCloy, and Assistant Secretary Howard C. Peterson agreed with Forrestal that long-term American prosperity required open markets, unhindered access to raw materials, and the rehabilitation of much – if not all – of Eurasia along liberal capitalist lines."[20] Indeed, the base systems were partly justified in terms of their impact on access to raw materials and the denial of such resources to an adversary. Some defense studies went further, and argued that postwar threats to Eurasian access and openness were more social and economic than military. It was economic turmoil and political upheaval that were the real threats to American security, as they invited the subversion of liberal democratic societies and Western-oriented governments. A CIA study concluded in mid-1947: "The greatest danger to the security of the United States is the possibility of economic collapse in Western Europe and the consequent accession to power of Communist elements."[21] Access to resources and markets, socioeconomic stability, political pluralism, and American security interests were all tied together.

By the late 1940s, the twin objectives of openness and containment came together. The building of security partnerships and open economic relations with Western Europe and East Asia were essential to fighting the Cold War, while the imperatives of the Cold War reinforced cooperation with America's partners and created domestic support for American leadership. Robert Gilpin argues that the Soviet threat was critical in fostering cohesion among the capitalist democracies and providing the political glue that held the world economy together. Over time, in his view, an elaborate American-led political order emerged that was built on two pillars: the US dollar and the American security umbrella. The American military guarantee to Europe and Asia provided a national-security rationale for Japan and the Western democracies to open their markets. Free trade helped cement the alliance, and in turn the alliance helped settle economic disputes. In Asia, the export-oriented development strategies of Japan and the smaller Asian tigers depended on America's willingness to accept their imports and live with huge trade deficits; alliances with Japan, South Korea, and other Southeast Asian countries made this politically tolerable.[22]

The importance of American power in postwar order building was most evident in the occupation and security binding of Germany and Japan. American troops began as occupiers of the two defeated axis states and never left. They eventually became protectors, but also a palpable symbol of America's superordinate position. Host agreements were negotiated that created a legal basis for the American military presence – effectively circumscribing Japanese and West German sovereignty. West German rearmament and restoration of its political sovereignty – made necessary in the early 1950s by a growing Cold War – could only be achieved by binding Germany to Europe, which in turn required a binding American security commitment to Europe. Complex and protracted negotiations ultimately created an integrated European military force within NATO and legal agreements over the character and limits of West German sovereignty and military power.[23] A reciprocal process of security binding lay at the heart of the emerging American system. John McCloy identified the "fundamental principle" of American policy in the early 1950s: that "whatever German contribution to defense is made may only take the form of a force which is an integral part of a larger international organization. . . . There is no real solution of the German problem inside Germany alone. There is a solution inside the European-Atlantic-World Community."[24]

Japan was also brought into the American security and economic orbit during the 1950s. The United States took the lead in helping Japan find new commercial relations and raw material sources in Southeast Asia to substitute for the loss of Chinese and Korean markets.[25] Japan and Germany were now twin junior partners of the United States – stripped of their military capacities and reorganized as engines of world economic growth. Containment in Asia would be based on the growth and integration of Japan in the wider non-communist Asian regional economy – what Secretary of State Dean Acheson called the "great crescent" in referring to the countries arrayed from Japan through Southeast Asia to India. Bruce Cumings captures the logic: "In East Asia, American planners envisioned a regional economy driven by revived Japanese industry, with assured continental access to markets and raw materials for its exports."[26] This strategy would link together threatened non-communist states along the crescent, create strong economic links between the United States and Japan, and lessen the importance of European colonial holdings in the area. The United States would actively aid Japan in re-establishing a regional economic sphere in Asia, allowing it to prosper and play a regional leadership role within the larger American postwar order. Japanese economic growth, the expansion of regional and world markets, and the fighting of the Cold War went together.

Behind the scene, America's hegemonic position was also backed by the reserve and transaction-currency role of the dollar. The dollar's special status gave the United States the rights of "seigniorage": it could print extra money to fight foreign wars, increase domestic spending, and go deeply into debt without fearing the pain that other states would experience. Other countries would have to adjust their currencies, which were linked to the dollar, when Washington pursued an inflationary course to meet its foreign and domestic policy agendas. Because of its dominance, the United States did not have to raise interest rates to defend its currency, taking pressure off its chronic trade imbalances. In the 1960s, French President Charles de Gaulle understood this hidden source of American hegemony all too well and complained bitterly. But most of America's Cold War allies were willing to hold dollars for fear that a currency collapse might lead the United States to withdraw its forces overseas and retreat into isolationism.

In this postwar bargain, American security protection, its domestic market, and the dollar bound the allies together and created the institutional supports of the stable political order and open world economy. Because the US economy dwarfed other industrial countries, it did not need to worry about controlling the distribution of gains from trade between itself and its allies. The United States provided its partners with security guarantees and access to American markets, technology, and supplies within an open world economy, In return, East Asian and European allies would become stable partners who would provide diplomatic, economic, and logistical support for the United States as it led the wider American-centered, non-communist postwar order.

Geography and Historical Staging

The geographic setting and historical timing of America's rise in power have also shaped the way American primacy has been manifest. The United States is the only great power that is not neighbored by other great powers. This geographical remoteness made the power ascent of the United States less threatening to the rest of the world and it reinforced the disinclination of American leaders to directly dominate or manage great power relations. In the twentieth century, the United States became the world's pre-eminent power, but the location and historical entry point of that power helped shaped how this arrival was greeted.

In the 1870s, the United States surpassed Britain as the largest and most advanced economy, but because of its geographical remoteness this development – and its continued growth – did not destabilize great power relations. America's era of territorial expansion took place without directly threatening other major states. The European powers had stakes in the New World but not fundamental interests, or even – at least by the mid-nineteenth century – a direct presence. The United States purchased territory from France rather than acquiring it by conquest. Indigenous peoples were the main losers in the American pursuit of manifest destiny. Later in the nineteenth century, the United States became the leading industrial power without triggering new interstate rivalries. Germany, of course, was not as geographically lucky and the expansion and unification of Germany unleashed nationalist rivalries, territorial ambitions, arms races, and ultimately world war.[27] More generally, power transitions – with rising powers overtaking status quo powers – are dangerous and conflict-prone moments in world history.[28] As European great powers grew in strength, they tended to trigger security dilemma-driven conflict and balancing reactions in their regional neighborhood. But America's remoteness lessened the destabilizing impact of its transition to global pre-eminence.

The open spaces of the New World also meant that American political and economic advancement could take place – at least until 1914 – without the development of a war-making strong state.[29] The United States became a world power though the gradual expansion of its industry and economy rather than by the orchestration or command of the central government. American power was latent – rooted in an expanding civil society, productive economy, and stable constitutional democracy. Even on the eve of the European war in 1914, the United States had a tiny standing army and little capacity to mobilize or project military force. This made the United States less able to directly maneuver among or deter the other great powers, but it also made the United States less threatening. American power was submerged within its society and removed from the territorial battlegrounds of the other great powers, thereby allowing it to grow unimpeded and unchecked.

When the United States was drawn into European power struggles, it did so primarily as an offshore balancer.[30] This was an echo of Britain's continental strategy which for several centuries was based on aloofness from European power struggles, intervening at critical moments to tip and restore the balance among the other states.[31] This offshore balancing role was played out by the United States in the two world wars. America entered each war relatively late and tipped the balance in favor of the allies. After World War II, the United States emerged as an equally important presence in Europe, Asia, and the Middle East as an offshore military force that each region found useful in solving its local security dilemmas. In Europe, the reintegration of West Germany into the West was only possible with the American security commitment. The Franco-German settlement was explicitly and necessarily embedded in an American-guaranteed Atlantic settlement. In Joseph Joffe's apt phrase, the United States became "Europe's pacifier."[32] In East Asia, the American security pact with Japan also solved regional security dilemmas by creating restraints on the resurgence of Japanese military power. In the Middle East a similar dynamic drew the United States into an active role in mediating between Israel and the Arab states. In each region, American power is seen less as a source of domination and more as a useful tool.

Because the United States is geographically remote, abandonment rather than domination has been seen as the greater risk by many states. As a result, the United States has found itself constantly courted by governments in Europe, Asia, and elsewhere. When Winston Churchill advanced ideas about postwar order, he was concerned above all in finding a way to tie the United States to Europe.[33] British Foreign Minister Ernest Bevin had similar thoughts when he heard Secretary of State George Marshall's celebrated speech in June 1947 announcing aid for Europe:

> The first thought that came into his mind was not that this gave a prospect of American economic help for Europe. He saw that, and grasped the chance with both hands; but first came the realization that his chief fear had been banished for good. The Americans were not going to do as they had done after the first World War and retreat into their hemisphere. . . . The keystone of Bevin's foreign policy had swung into place.[34]

As Geir Lundestad has observed, the expanding American political order in the half century after World War II has been in important respects an "empire by invitation."[35] The remarkable global reach of American postwar hegemony has been at least in part driven by the efforts of European and

Asian governments to harness American power, render that power more predictable, and use it to overcome their own regional insecurities. The result has been a durable system of America-centered economic and security partnerships.

Finally, the historical timing of America's rise in power also left a mark. The United States came relatively late to the great power arena, after the colonial and imperial eras had run their course. This meant that the pursuit of America's strategic interests was not primarily based on territorial control but on championing more principled ways of organizing great power relations. The world had already been carved up by Japan and the European states. As a late-developing great power, the United States needed openness and access to the regions of the world rather than recognition of its territorial claims. The American issuance of its Open Door policy toward China reflected this orientation. Woodrow Wilson's championing at Versailles of democracy and self-determination and FDR's support of decolonialization several decades later were also statements of American strategic interests issued as principled appeals.[36] American officials were never fully consistent in wielding such principled claims about order and they were often a source of conflict with the other major states. But the overall effect of this alignment of American geostrategic interests with enlightened normative principles of order reinforced the image of the United States as a relatively non-coercive and non-imperial hegemonic power.

Institutions, Democracy, and Strategic Restraint

The American unipolar order is also organized around democratic polities and a complex web of intergovernmental institutions – and these features of the American system alter and mute the way in which hegemonic power is manifest. One version of this argument is the democratic peace thesis: open democratic polities are less able or willing to use power in an arbitrary and indiscriminate manner against other democracies.[37] The calculations of smaller and weaker states as they confront a democratic hegemon are altered. Fundamentally, power asymmetries are less threatening or destabilizing when they exist between democracies. This might be so for several reasons. Open polities make the exercise of power more visible and easy to anticipate. Accountable governments make the exercise of power more predictable and institutionalized. Democracies are more accessible from the outside than non-democracies. Leaders who rise through the ranks within democratic countries are more inclined to participate in the "give and take" with other democratic leaders than those who rise up in autocratic and authoritarian states.

In these various ways, European and Asian countries are more willing to cooperate with America because hegemonic power is wielded by a democracy. Processes of interaction between democracies make crude and manipulative exercise of power less likely or consequential. Institutions and norms of consultation and reciprocal influence are manifest in relations across the democratic world. As a result, asymmetries of power do not generate the sort of strategic insecurities and security dilemmas that would otherwise pervade such sharp disparities of power. These facets of democracy are stressed by John Gaddis: "Negotiation, compromise, and consensus-building came naturally to statesmen steeped in the uses of such practices at home: in this sense, the American political tradition served the country better than its realist critics – Kennan among them – believed it did."[38]

It is possible to identify several features of American-style hegemony that distinguish it from past hegemonic or imperial powers. Rooted in democratic culture and institutions, American hegemony is unusually reluctant, open, and highly institutionalized. The reluctant character of American hegemony is seen in the absence of a strong imperial impulse to directly dominate or manage weaker or secondary states within the order. One aspect of this reluctant hegemony has been manifest – ironically – in the very ambitiousness of America's order-building proposals in the twentieth century. The United States has frequently sought to reshape the world precisely so that it would not need to manage it. Woodrow Wilson championed a democratic revolution in Europe because a rising tide of democracy would ensure the working of the League of Nations and a peaceful functioning postwar order. When Wilson presented his Fourteen Points in January 1918, it looked as if the tide of European politics was moving in the liberal and social democratic direction. The revolution in Russia seemed to confirm the democratic revolution that was sweeping across the major industrial societies. The United States would lead the world to democracy, but it would not rule the world or provide traditional security commitments to Western Europe. An expanding community of democracies would govern itself.[39] To British and French leaders, Wilson seemed to be the very embodiment of the arrogant and pushy American leader – preaching to Europe to reform its politics but stopping short of making real and practical commitments to the security of the continent. But Wilson wanted to transform the world precisely so the United States would not need to rule it.

The same logic informed America's plans for the post-1945 world economy. It is revealing that the initial and most forcefully presented American view of postwar order was the State Department's proposal for a postwar system of free trade. This proposal did not only reflect an

American conviction about the virtues of open markets, but it also was a vision of order that would require very little direct American involvement or management.[40] The system would largely be self-regulating, leaving the United States to operate within it, but without the burdens of direct and ongoing supervision. This general characteristic was not lost on the Europeans, and it mattered as America's potential partners contemplated whether and how to cooperate with the United States. It meant that the Europeans would need to actively seek to court American involvement in Europe rather than resist it, and it provided some reassurance that the United States would operate within limits and not use its overwhelming power position simply to dominate.

Another aspect of this imperial reluctance is the American eagerness to construct a legitimate international order – that is, an order that is recognized as acceptable and desirable by the countries operating within it. This desire for legitimate order has led the United States to make extensive compromises in its foreign policy goals so as to achieve a mutually agreeable settlement. This orientation was reflected during World War II in the compromises that the United States made in accommodating European views about the postwar world economy. The British and the continental Europeans, worried about postwar depression and the protection of their fragile economies, were not eager to embrace America's stark proposals for an open world trading system, favouring a more regulated and compensatory system.[41] The United States did attempt to use its material resources to pressure and induce Britain and the other European countries to abandon bilateral and regional preferential agreements and accept the principles of a postwar economic system organized around a nondiscriminatory system of trade and payments.[42] The United States knew it held a commanding position and sought to use its power to give the postwar order a distinctive shape. But it also prized agreement over deadlock, and it ultimately moved a great distance away from its original proposals in setting up the various postwar institutions.[43]

Another aspect of the non-imperial American hegemonic orientation is manifest in the lack of a singular grand strategic vision to inform the construction of the American-led postwar order. There is an old quip that Great Britain acquired its Indian empire "in a fit of absence of mind." In important respects this is also true of America as it acquired a global order. There was as much inadvertence and unintended consequence as grand design. As the realist narrative presented earlier suggests, important aspects of the American order were engineered – particularly the security alliances – as part of postwar political bargains with Western Europe and Asia. At the same time, however, it is difficult to discern a singular vision or grand strategy in this order. Even after World War II, when the foundations of the American order were put in place, there were many different ideas and projects. Different bureaucracies and political groups, each with its own agenda, went about building a slice of the postwar order. There were the United Nations activists, the free trade groups, and the geopolitical strategists. The post-1945 order was cobbled together. The United States did strike a bargain with the rest of the world but it was largely implicit and manifest in a rolling process of piecemeal institutional agreements and security relationships.

A second major way in which the power asymmetries were made more acceptable to other countries was the liberal democratic structure of the American polity. The open and decentralized character of the American political system provided opportunities for other states to exercise their voice in the operation of hegemonic order, thereby reassuring these states that their interests could be actively advanced and processes of conflict resolution would exist. In this sense, the American postwar order was a "penetrated hegemony," an extended system that blurred domestic and international politics as it created an elaborate transnational and transgovernmental political system with the United States at the centre.[44]

There are several ways in which the penetrated hegemonic order provided ways for the United States to restrain and commit its power. To begin with, America's mature political institutions organized around the rule of law have made it a relatively predictable and cooperative hegemon. The pluralistic and regularized way in which American foreign and security policy is made reduces surprises and allows other states to build long-term, mutually beneficial relations. The governmental separation of powers creates a shared decision-making system that opens up the process and reduces the ability of any one leader to make abrupt or aggressive moves toward other states. An active press and competitive party system also provide a service to outside states by generating information about United States policy and determining its seriousness of purpose. The messiness of democracy can frustrate American diplomats and confuse foreign observers. But over the long term, democratic institutions produce more consistent and credible policies than autocratic or authoritarian states.

The institutional opportunities for foreign officials to actively work within the American system – exercising voice opportunities – also reduces worries about American power.[45] The fragmented and penetrated American system allows and invites the proliferation of a vast network of transnational and transgovernmental relations with Europe, Japan, and other parts of the world. Diffuse and dense networks of governmental, corporate, and private associations tie the system together. The United States is the primary site for the pulling and hauling of trans-Atlantic and trans-Pacific politics. European and Asian governments do not have elected officials in Washington but they do have representatives.[46] Although this access to the American political process is not fully reciprocated abroad, the openness and extensive decentralization of the American liberal system assures other states that they have routine access to the decision-making processes of the United States.

A final way in which the United States overcame fears of domination was through binding itself institutionally to other states. Security binding means establishing formal institutional links between countries that are potential adversaries, thereby reducing the incentives for each state to balance against the other.[47] Rather than responding to a potential strategic rival by organizing a counter-balancing alliance against it, the threatening state is invited to participate within a joint security association or alliance. By binding to each other, surprises are reduced and expectations of stable future relations dampen the security dilemmas that trigger worst-case preparations, arms races, and dangerous strategic rivalry. Also, by creating institutional connections between potential rivals, channels of communication are established which provide opportunities to actively influence the other's evolving security policy. When states employ institutional binding as a strategy, they are essentially agreeing to mutually constrain themselves. In effect, institutions specify what it is that states are expected to do and they make it difficult and costly for states to do otherwise. In binding itself to its weaker partners, the leading state is giving up some policy autonomy and discretion but gains the non-coerced cooperation of the other states by making itself less threatening.

The United States and its allies built the postwar order around binding institutions. They built long-term political and security commitments – the alliance system itself most importantly – that were difficult to retract. NATO and the US–Japan security treaties were the most important binding institutions in the American system. The old saying that NATO was created to "keep the Russians out, the Germans down, and the Americans in" is a statement about the importance of the alliance structures for locking in long-term commitments and expectations. The American-Japanese security pact has had a similar "dual containment" character. These institutions have not only served as alliances in the ordinary sense as organized efforts to balance against external threats, they also provided mechanisms and venues to build political relations, conduct business, and regulate conflict.[48] The binding logic of NATO allowed France and the other Western partners to acquiesce in Germany's military rearmament during the Cold War. Even today, the United States and its European and Japanese partners ward off rivalry and balancing among themselves by maintaining their security alliances. It is the binding logic – more so than the response to external threats – that makes these institutions attractive today.

American-led economic and security institutions provide Germany and Japan with a political bulwark of stability that far transcends their more immediate and practical purposes. Germany has had more opportunities to bind itself to Western Europe and the Atlantic order than Japan has had opportunities in East Asia. The European Community – and later European Union – and the NATO alliance have given Germany a layer of institutions with which to bind itself to neighbors and thereby reduce security dilemma instabilities. Indeed, the Christian Democrat Walther Leisler Kiep argued in 1972 that "the German–American alliance . . . is not merely one aspect of modern German history, but a decisive element as a result of its pre-eminent place in our politics. In effect, it provides a second constitution for our country."[49] Japan – because of geography, history, and politics – does not have as many regional institutional options. The US–Japan alliance is currently the only serious institution with which Japan can signal restraint and commitment. As a result, the bilateral alliance has become even more indispensable to Japan and the region.[50]

Modernization and Civic Nationalism

American power has been rendered more acceptable to the rest of the world because the United States "project" is congruent with the deeper forces of modernization. The point here is not that the United States has pushed other states to embrace its goals and purposes but that all states are operating within a transforming global system – driven by modernization, industrialization, and social mobilization. The synchronicity between the rise of the United States as a liberal global power and the system-wide imperatives of modernization create a sort of functional "fit" between the United States and the wider world order. If the United States were attempting to project state socialist economic ideas or autocratic political values, its fit with the deep forces of modernization would be poor. Its purposes would be resisted around the world and trigger resistance to American power. But the deep congruence between the American model and the functional demands of modernization both boost the power of the United States and make its relationship with the rest of the world more harmonious.

Modernization is a slippery notion that is difficult to specify, but it generally refers to the processes whereby historically evolved institutions are adapted to the changing demands and opportunities created by ongoing scientific, technological, and industrial revolutions.[51] These processes had their origins in the societies of Western Europe but in the last two centuries they have extended to societies in other regions and have resulted in a worldwide transformation in human relations. Some accounts have been concerned primarily with political modernization, while others have focused on societal changes that accompany industrialization.[52] Theorists of industrial modernism have focused specifically on industrial society and emphasized variations and contingencies in the ability of societies to adapt and take advantage of unfolding advances in science, technology, and industrialism.[53]

Industrialization is a constantly evolving process and the social and political characteristics within countries that it encourages and rewards – and that promote or impede industrial advancement – change over time and as countries move through developmental stages. In this sense, the fit between a polity and modernization is never absolute or permanent, as the changing virtues and liabilities of the Japanese developmental state make clear.[54] Industrialism in advanced societies tends to feature highly educated workforces, rapid flows of information, and progressively more specialized and complex systems of social and industrial organization. These features of industrial society – sometimes called late industrialism – tend to foster a citizenry that is heterogenous, well educated, and difficult to coerce.[55] From this perspective it is possible to see why various state socialist and authoritarian countries – including the Soviet Union – ran into trouble as the twentieth century proceeded. The old command order impeded industrial modernization while, at the same time, industrial modernization undercut the old command order.[56] In contrast, the American polity has tended to have a relatively good fit with the demands and opportunities of industrial modernization. European and Asian forms of capitalist democracy have also exhibited features that seem in various ways to be quite congruent with the leading edge of advanced industrial development.[57] The success of the American model is partly due to the fact that it used its postwar power to build an international order that worked to the benefit of the American style of industrial capitalism. But the success of the American model – and the enhanced global influence and appeal that the United States has experienced in recent decades – is also due to the deep congruence between the logic of modernization and the American system.

The functionality between the United States polity and wider evolutionary developments in the international system can also be traced to the American political identity – which is rooted in civic nationalism and multiculturalism. The basic distinction between civil and ethnic nationalism is useful in locating this feature. Civic nationalism is group identity that is composed of commitments to the nation's political creed. Race, religion, gender, language, or ethnicity are not relevant in defining a citizen's rights and inclusion within the polity. Shared belief in the country's principles and values embedded in the rule of law is the organizing basis for political order, and citizens are understood to be equal and rights-bearing individuals. Ethnic nationalism, in contrast, maintains that individuals' rights and participation within the polity are inherited – based on ethnic or racial ties.[58]

Civic national identity has four sorts of implications for the orientation – and acceptability – of American hegemonic order. First, civic identity has tended to encourage the American projection outward of domestic principles of inclusive and rule-based international political organization. The American national identity is not based on ethnic or religious particularism but on a more general set of agreed-upon and normatively appealing principles. Ethnic and religious identities and disputes are pushed downward into civil society and removed from the political arena. When the United States gets involved in political conflicts around the world, it tends to look for the establishment of agreed-upon political principles and rules to guide the rebuilding of order. Likewise, when the United States promotes rule-based solutions to problems, it is strengthening the normative and principled basis for the exercise of its own power – and thereby making disparities in power more acceptable.

Second, because civic nationalism is shared with other Western states it tends to be a source of cohesion and cooperation. Throughout the industrial democratic world, the dominant form of political identity is based on a set of abstract and juridical rights and responsibilities which coexist with private ethnic and religious associations. Just as warring states and nationalism tend to reinforce each other, so too do Western civic identity and cooperative political relations reinforce each other. Political order – domestic and international – is strengthened when there exists a substantial sense of community and shared identity. It matters that the leaders of today's advanced industrial states are not seeking to legitimate their power by making racial or imperialist appeals. Civic nationalism, rooted in shared commitment to democracy and the rule of law – provides a widely embraced identity across most of the American hegemonic order. At the same time, potentially divisive identity conflicts – rooted in antagonistic ethnic or religious or class divisions – are dampened by relegating them to secondary status within civil society.[59]

Third, the multicultural character of the American political identity also reinforces internationalist – and ultimately multilateral – foreign policy. John Ruggie notes that culture wars continue in the United States between a pluralistic and multicultural identity and nativist and parochial alternatives, but that the core identity is still "cosmopolitan liberal" – an identity that tends to support instrumental multilateralism. "[T]he evocative significance of multilateral world order principles – a bias against exclusive bilateralist alliances, the rejection of discriminatory economic blocs, and facilitating means to bridge gaps of ethos, race, and religion – should resonate still for the American public, insofar as they continue to reflect its own sense of national identity."[60] American society is increasingly heterogenous in race, ethnicity, and religion. This tends to reinforce an activist and inclusive foreign policy orientation and a bias in favor of rule-based and multilateral approaches to the organization of hegemonic power.[61]

Finally, American civic identity has tended to give the United States an unusual ability to absorb and integrate immigrants within a stable yet diverse political system. This integrative capacity will grow in importance. The mature industrial democracies are all experiencing a decline in their birth rates and a gradual population ageing. In the decades ahead, many of these countries – most notably Japan and Italy – will see their populations actually shrink, with a smaller workforce unable to support an ageing demographic bubble. Immigration is increasingly a necessary aspect of economic growth. If Japan and other industrial societies are to maintain their population size and social security provisions, they will need to open the door wide to immigration – but these imperatives are fiercely resisted.[62] The American willingness and ability to accept immigrants – putting it on the receiving end of the brain drain – already gives it an edge in knowledge and service industries. These advantages will only grow in the future and keep the United States at the dynamic center of the world economy. Multinational and multiethnic empires of the nineteenth century ultimately failed and were broken apart in the twentieth century. Built on a civic national base, the United States has pioneered a new form of multicultural and multiethnic political order that appears to be stable and increasingly functional with the demands of global modernization.

Conclusion

The world has seen many great powers rise up to dominate the international system. Charles V, Louis XIV, Napoleon I, Wilhelmine, and Nazi Germany – each became a hegemonic threat to Europe and triggered a backlash that rearranged the geopolitical landscape. Today it is the United States that looms above all other states and the question that many observers pose is: will the United States suffer a similar fate? "There is one ideology left standing, liberal democratic capitalism, and one institution with universal reach, the United States," observes Fareed Zakaria. "If the past is any guide, America's primacy will provoke growing resistance."[63] Resistance has in fact appeared and may be growing. But it is remarkable that despite the sharp shifts in the distribution of power, the other great powers have not yet responded in a way anticipated by balance of power theory.

This essay argues that American power – and the American unipolar order – is different and less threatening to other states than that which is envisaged in theoretical and historical claims about the balance of power. A variety of features associated with American hegemony – rooted in geography, history, ideology, democracy, institutional structures, and modernization itself – make it different from past great powers. These characteristics of American power mute and restrain that power and alter the risk calculations of weaker and secondary states. It also matters that these restraining characteristics are deeply rooted in the American polity. American power is reluctant, open, and highly institutionalized. It is also situated offshore from the other great powers, which spares it from regional antagonisms and rivalries. American power is also able to deploy its power to solve problems for other states – particularly regional security dilemmas – and this weakens the incentives other states might have to engage in counter-balancing.

The United States used its power in the 1940s and afterwards to build a world order. An entire system of alliances, multilateral institutions, and entangling relations have emerged, such that it is possible to talk about American unipolarity as a distinctive political formation. *Pax Americana* is not just a powerful country throwing its weight around. It is a political formation with its own logic and laws of motion. It is an order that was created and sustained by American power but it is also not simply a reflection of that power. Indeed, it is the ability of this order to mute the impact of power symmetries that give it its durability. The deep congruence between the internal American political system – and its civic and multicultural identity – and the long-term project of modernity also gives the unipolar order robustness. The United States remains at the core of this order, but it is an order that now has a life of its own.

Notes

The author would like to thank Christopher Jones, Jonathan Kirshner, and participants at a Cornell University Government Department seminar for helpful comments on an earlier draft of this essay.

1   Calculated from OECD statistics (July 1999 web edition). GDP measures are calculated at 1990 prices and exchange rates. Reflecting the sharp disparities in military power – and its likely continuation well into the future – 80 percent of world defense research and development takes place in the United States. For this and other empirical indicators of American unipolar power, see William Wohlforth, "The Stability of a Unipolar World," *International Security* (Summer 1999).

2   Quoted in Craig R. Whitney, "NATO at 50: With Nations at Odds, Is It a Misalliance?" *New York Times*, February 15, 1999, p. A7.

3   Chalmers Johnson, *Blowback: The Costs and Consequences of American Empire* (New York: Metropolitan Books, 2000).

4   See, for example, Noam Chomsky, *Turning the Tide: US Intervention in Latin America and the Struggle for Peace* (Boston, Mass.: South End Books, 1986).

5   See, for example, Steven Erlanger, "In Europe, Some Say the Attacks Stemmed from American Failings," *The New York Times*, September 22, 2001; and Elaine Sciolino, "Who Hates the US? Who Loves It?" *The New York Times*, September 23, 2001.

6   John Lewis Gaddis, *We Now Know: Rethinking Cold War History* (New York: Oxford University Press, 1997), ch. 2.

7   Kenneth Waltz, "Structural Realism after the Cold War," *International Security* (Summer 2000).

8   Waltz, *Theory of International Politics* (New York: Random House, 1979), p. x. See also Waltz, "The Emerging Structure of International Politics," *International Security* 18: 2 (1993); and Waltz, "Structural Realism after the Cold War."

9   Michael Mastanduno, "Preserving the Unipolar Moment: Realist Theorise and US Grand Strategy after the Cold War," *International Security* 21: 4 (1997): 58.

10 Waltz, "Structural Realism after the Cold War."

11 See Robert Gilpin, *War and Change in World Politics* (Cambridge: Cambridge University Press, 1981).

12 See Gilpin, "Economic Interdependence and National Security in Historical Perspective," in Klaus Knorr and Frank Trager, eds., *Economic Issues and National Security* (Lawrence, Kan.: Regents Press of Kansas, 1977), pp. 19–66.

13 For discussion of empires – their sources of order and variation – see Michael Doyle, *Empires* (Ithaca, NY: Cornell University Press, 1986); Alexander Motyl, *Revolutions, Nations, Empires: Conceptual Limits and Theoretical Possibilities* (New York: Columbia University Press, 1999); S. N. Eisenstadt, *The Political Systems of Empires: The Rise and Fall of the Historical Bureaucratic Societies* (New York: Free Press, 1969); and Karen Dawisha and Bruce Parrott, *The Disintegration and Reconstruction of Empires* (Armonk: M. E. Sharpe, 1966). For a discussion of European empire and reactions to it, see Philip D. Curtin, *The World and the West: The European Challenge and the Overseas Response in the Age of Empire* (New York: Cambridge University Press, 2000). For a broad historical survey of types of international orders in historical and comparative perspective, see Barry Buzan and Richard Little, *International Systems in World History: Remaking the Study of International Relations* (New York: Oxford University Press, 2000).

14 In a variation of this view, William Wohlforth argues that it is the sheer preponderance of American power that prevents a return to traditional patterns of balance. The power disparity is such that a countervailing coalition

is not possible. "No other major power is in a position to follow any policy that depends for its success on prevailing against the United States in a war or an extended rivalry," Wohlforth argues. "None is likely to take any step that might invite the focused enmity of the United States" ("The Stability of a Unipolar World," p. x).

15 Harold J. Laski, "America – 1947," *Nation* 165 (December 13, 1947): 641.

16 "Memorandum by the Director of the Policy Planning Staff [Kennan] to the Secretary of State and Under Secretary of State [Lovett]," February 24, 1948, *Foreign Relations of the United States* (1948), vol. 1, p. 524.

17 For arguments that the great mid-century struggle was between an open capitalist order and various regional, autarkic challengers, see Bruce Cumings, "The Seventy Years' Crisis and the Logic of Trilateralism in the New World Order," *World Policy Journal* (Spring 1991); and Charles Maier, "The Two Postwar Eras and the Conditions for Stability in Twentieth-Century Western Europe," in Maier, *In Search of Stability: Explorations in Historical Political Economy* (New York: Cambridge University Press, 1987).

18 The culmination of this debate and the most forceful statement of the new consensus was presented in Nicholas John Spykman's *America's Strategy in the World: The United States and the Balance of Power* (New York: HarcourtBrace, 1942).

19 See Melvyn P. Leffler, "The American Conception of National Security and the Beginning of the Cold War, 1945–48," *American Historical Review* 48 (1984): 349–56.

20 Ibid. p. 358.

21 CIA, "Review of the World Situation as It Relates to the Security of the United States," September 26, 1947. Quoted in Leffler, "The American Conception of National Security", p. 364.

22 Robert Gilpin, *The Challenge of Global Capitalism: The World Economy in the 21st Century* (Princeton, NJ: Princeton University Press, 2000), ch. 2.

23 A treaty governing the relationship between the new German state and Britain, France, and the United States was signed in 1952, and specified ongoing "rights and responsibilities" of the three powers. "Convention on Relations between the Three Powers and the Federal Republic of Germany, 26 May, 1952, as modified by the Paris Accords of October 1954," reprinted in Department of State, *Documents on Germany, 1944–1985* (Washington, DC: Department of State, 1986), pp. 425–30. See also Paul B. Stares, *Allied Rights and Legal Restraints on German Military Power* (Washington, DC: Brookings Institution, 1990). Later, when speculation arose in the 1950s that a German Social Democratic leader might be elected and request the Americans to leave, an Eisenhower official quipped that if this were to happen the United States would respond by doubling the size of its forces in Germany. See Mark Trachtenburg, *A Constructed Peace: The Making of the European Settlement, 1945–1963* (Princeton, NJ: Princeton University Press, 2000).

24 Quoted in Thomas Schwartz, *America's Germany: John J. McCloy and the Federal Republic of Germany* (Cambridge, Mass.: Harvard University Press, 1991), p. 228.

25   Michael Schaller, "Securing the Great Crescent: Occupied Japan and the Origins of Containment in Southeast Asia," *Journal of American History* 69 (September 1982): 392–414.

26   Bruce Cumings, "Japan's Position in the World System," in Andrew Gordon, ed., *Postwar Japan as History* (Berkeley, Calif.: University of California Press), p. 38.

27   A. J. P. Taylor, *The Course of German History* (London: Hamish Hamilton, 1945).

28   On power transitions and hegemonic wars, see Gilpin, *War and Change in World Politics.*

29   On divergent European and American state building experiences, see Samuel Huntington, *Political Order in Changing Societies* (New Haven, Conn.: Yale University Press, 1968); Charles Tilly, "Reflections on the History of European State-Making," in Tilly, ed., *The Formation of National States in Western Europe* (Princeton, NJ: Princeton University Press, 1975), pp. 3–83; Charles Tilly, *Coercion, Capital, and European States, AD 990–1990* (Oxford: Blackwell, 1990); and Michael Mann, *The Sources of Social Power,* vol. 2: *The Rise of Classes and Nation-States, 1760–1914* (Cambridge: Cambridge University Press, 1993).

30   On the notion of offshore balancing, see Christopher Layne, "From Preponderance to Offshore Balancing," *International Security* 22: 1 (1997).

31   See Paul Kennedy, *The Rise and Fall of the Great Powers: Economic Change and Military Conflict from 1500 to 2000* (New York: Vintage Books, 1989).

32   Joseph Joffe, "Europe's American Pacifier," *Foreign Policy* 54 (1984): 64–82. See also Robert Art, "Why Western Europe Needs the United States and NATO," *Political Science Quarterly* 111 (1996): 1–39.

33   See G. John Ikenberry, *After Victory: Institutions, Strategic Restraint, and the Rebuilding of Order After Major Wars* (Princeton, NJ: Princeton University Press, 2000), ch. 6.

34   Sir Oliver Franks, in *Listener,* June 14, 1956. Quoted in John W. Wheeler-Bennett and Anthony Nicholls, *The Semblance of Peace: The Political Settlement after the Second World War* (London: Macmillan, 1972), p. 573.

35   Geir Lundestad, "Empire by Invitation? The United States and Western Europe, 1945–1952," *The Journal of Peace Research* 23 (September 1986): 263–77. See also Charles Maier, "Alliance and Autonomy: European Identity and US Foreign Policy Objectives in the Truman Years," in Michael J. Lacey, ed., *The Truman Presidency* (New York: Cambridge University Press, 1989), pp. 273–98; and David Reynolds, "America's Europe, Europe's America: Image, Influence, and Interaction, 1933–1958," *Diplomatic History* 20 (Fall 1996).

36   See Tony Smith, *America's Mission: The United States and the Worldwide Struggle for Democracy in the Twentieth Century* (Princeton, NJ: Princeton University Press, 1994).

37   See Bruce Russett and John Oneal, *Triangulating Peace: Democracy, Interdependence, and International Organizations* (New York: Norton, 2001).

38   Gaddis, *We Now Know*, p. 50.

39   This argument is made in Ikenberry, *After Victory*, ch. 5.

40   Ikenberry, "Rethinking the Origins of American Hegemony," *Political Science Quarterly* 104 (1989): 375–400.

41   The strongest claims about American and European differences over postwar political economy are made by Fred Block, *The Origins of International Economic Disorder* (Berkeley, Calif.: University of California Press, 1977).

42   The 1946 British loan deal was perhaps the most overt effort by the Truman administration to tie American postwar aid to specific policy concessions by allied governments. This was the failed Anglo-American Financial Agreement, which obliged the British to make sterling convertible in exchange for American assistance. See Richard Gardner, *Sterling–Dollar Diplomacy* (New York: McGraw Hill, 1969); and Alfred E. Eckes, Jr., *A Search for Solvency: Bretton Woods and the International Monetary System, 1944–1971* (Austin, Tex.: University of Texas Press, 1971).

43   G. John Ikenberry, "A World Economy Restored: Expert Consensus and the Anglo-American Postwar Settlement," *International Organization* 46 (1991/2): 289–321.

44   See Daniel Deudney and G. John Ikenberry, "The Sources and Character of Liberal International Order," *Review of International Studies* 25: 2 (1999): 179–96.

45   The notion of "voice opportunities," drawn for Albert Hirschman's distinction between exit and voice, is discussed in Joseph Grieco, "The Maastricht Treaty, Economic and Monetary Union and the Neo-Realist Research Programme," *Review of International Studies* 21 (1995): 21–40.

46   Thomas Risse finds a similar pattern in his study of American–European relations within NATO. See Risse-Kappen, *Cooperation among Democracies* (Princeton, NJ: Princeton University Press, 1994). For patterns in US–Japanese relations, see Peter J. Katzenstein and Yutaka Tsujinaka, " 'Bullying,' 'Buying,' and 'Binding': US–Japanese Transnational Relations and Domestic Structures," in Thomas Risse-Kappen, ed., *Bringing Transnational Relations Back In* (Cambridge: Cambridge University Press, 1995).

47   See Paul Schroeder, "Alliances, 1815–1945: Weapons to Power and Tools of Management," in Klaus Knorr, ed., *Historical Dimensions of National Security Problems* (Lawrence: University of Kansas Press, 1976), pp. 227–62.

48   On security binding, see ibid. On more recent formulations, see Joseph M. Grieco, "State Interests and Institutional Rule Trajectories: A Neorealist Interpretation of the Maastricht Treaty and European Economic and Monetary Union," *Security Studies* 5: 3 (1996); and Daniel Deudney, "The Philadelphian System: Sovereignty, Arms Control, and Balance of Power in the American States-Union," *International Organization* 49 (Spring 1995): 191–228.

49   Quoted in Thomas Schwartz, "The United States and Germany after 1945: Alliances, Transnational Relations, and the Legacy of the Cold War," *Diplomatic History* 19: 4 (1995): 555.

50   For a discussion on this basic difference between Japan and Germany, see
     Erica R. Gould and Stephen D. Krasner, "Germany and Japan: Binding
     versus Autonomy," in Wolfgang Streeck and Kozo Yamamura, eds., *The End
     of Diversity? Prospects for German and Japanese Capitalism* (Ithaca, NY:
     Cornell University Press, 2003).

51   See C. E. Black, *The Dynamics of Modernization: A Study in Comparative
     History* (New York: Harper and Row, 1966); and Edward L. Morse, *Mod-
     ernization and the Transformation of International Relations* (New York:
     Free Press, 1976). For a survey of modernization ideas, see Krishan Kumar,
     *Prophecy and Progress: The Sociology of Industrial and Post-Industrial
     Society* (New York: Penguin Books, 1978).

52   Huntington, *Political Order in Changing Societies*; and Ralf Dahrendorf,
     Class and Class Conflict in Industrial Society (Stanford, Calif.: Stanford
     University Press, 1959).

53   See Raymond Aron, *The Industrial Society: Three Essays on Ideology and
     Development* (New York: Clarion Books, 1966); Leon Lindberg, ed., *Politics
     and the Future of Industrial Society* (New York: David McKay, 1976); and
     Clark Kerr, *The Future of Industrial Societies: Covergence or Continuing
     Diversity?* (Cambridge, Mass.: Harvard University Press, 1983).

54   See Meredith Woo-Cumings, ed., *The Developmental State* (Ithaca, NY:
     Cornell University Press, 1999).

55   See Daniel Dell, *The Coming of Post-Industrial Society* (New York: Basic
     Books, 1973).

56   See Daniel Deudney and G. John Ikenberry, "Soviet Reform and the End of
     the Cold War: Explaining Large-Scale Historical Change," *Review of Inter-
     national Studies* 17 (1991): 225–50.

57   For a discussion of the variety of advanced industrial democratic forms, see
     Herbert Kitschelt, Peter Lange, Gary Marks, and John D. Stephens, "Con-
     vergence and Divergence in Advanced Capitalist Democracies," in Kitschelt
     et al., eds., *Continuity and Change in Contemporary Capitalism*
     (Cambridge: Cambridge University Press, 1999).

58   This distinction is made by Anthony D. Smith, *The Ethnic Origins of Nations*
     (Oxford: Blackwell, 1986). For an important reconceptualization of national-
     ism – emphasizing the strategic use of national identity by elites – see
     Michael Hechter, *Containing Nationalism* (Oxford: Oxford University Press,
     2000).

59   See Daniel Deudney and G. John Ikenberry, "The Nature and Sources of
     Liberal International Order," *Review of International Studies* 25: 2 (1999).

60   John Gerard Ruggie, *Winning the Peace: America and World Order in the
     New Era* (New York: Columbia University Press, 1996), p. 170.

61   On the ways in which American ethnic groups encourage foreign policy
     activism, see Tony Smith, *Foreign Attachments: The Power of Ethnic Groups
     in the Making of American Foreign Policy* (Cambridge, Mass.: Harvard
     University Press, 2000).

62   See Christian Joppke, *Immigration and the Nation-State* (New York: Oxford
     University Press, 1999).

63   Fareed Zakaria, "The Empire Strikes Out," *New York Times Magazine*, April 18, 1999, p. 99. For views along these lines, see Peter W. Rodman, "The World's Resentment: Anti-Americanism as a Global Phenomenon," *The National Interest* 60 (Summer 2000): 33–41; and Samuel Huntington, "The Lonely Superpower," *Foreign Affairs* 78: 2 (March/April 1999): 35–49.

Part II

Unipolarity and Multilateralism

6

The Myth of Post-Cold War Chaos

The 1945 Order Lives On

A great deal of ink has been shed in recent years describing various versions of the post-Cold War order. These attempts have all failed, because there is no such creature. The world order created in the 1940s is still with us, and in many ways stronger than ever. The challenge for American foreign policy is not to imagine and build a new world order but to reclaim and renew an old one – an innovative and durable order that has been hugely successful and largely unheralded.

The end of the Cold War, the common wisdom holds, was a historical watershed. The collapse of communism brought the collapse of the order that took shape after World War II. While foreign policy theorists and officials scramble to design new grand strategies, the United States is rudderless on uncharted seas.

The common wisdom is wrong. What ended with the Cold War was bipolarity, the nuclear stalemate, and decades of containment of the Soviet Union – seemingly the most dramatic and consequential features of the postwar era. But the world order created in the middle to late 1940s endures, more extensive and in some respects more robust than during its Cold War years. Its basic principles, which deal with organization and relations among the Western liberal democracies, are alive and well.

These less celebrated, less heroic, but more fundamental principles and policies – the real international order – include the commitment to an open world economy and its multilateral management, and the stabilization of socioeconomic welfare. And the political vision behind the order was as important as the anticipated economic gains. The major industrial democracies took it upon themselves to "domesticate" their dealings through a dense web of multilateral institutions, intergovernmental relations, and joint management of the Western and world political economies. Security and stability in the West were seen as intrinsically tied to an array of institutions – the United Nations and its agencies and the General Agreement on Tariffs and Trade (GATT) only some among many – that bound the democracies together, constrained conflict, and facilitated political community. Embracing common liberal democratic norms and operating within interlocking multilateral institutions, the United States, Western Europe, and, later, Japan built an enduring postwar order.

The end of the Cold War has been so disorienting because it ended the containment order – 40 years of policies and bureaucratic missions and an entire intellectual orientation. But the watershed of postwar order predated hostilities with the Soviet Union. The turning point was not a Cold War milestone such as the announcement of the Truman Doctrine in 1947 or the creation of the Atlantic Alliance in 1948–9. It might have come as early as 1941, when Roosevelt and Churchill issued the Atlantic Charter declaring the liberal principles that were to guide the postwar settlement. The process became irreversible in 1944, when representatives at the Bretton Woods conference laid down the core principles and mechanisms of the postwar Western economic order and those at Dumbarton Oaks gave the political aspect of the vision concrete form in their proposals for a United Nations. The Cold War may have reinforced the liberal democratic order, by hastening the reintegration of Germany and Japan and bringing the United States much more directly into the management of the system. But it did not call it forth.

In world historical terms, the end of the Cold War is an overrated event. Former Secretary of State James A. Baker III observes in his 1995 memoir, *The Politics of Diplomacy,* "In three and a half years [from the late 1980s to the early 1990s] . . . the very nature of the international system as we know it was transformed." To be sure, large parts of the non-Western world are undergoing a tremendous and difficult transformation. A great human drama is playing itself out in the former communist states, and the future there hangs in the balance. But the system the United States led the way in creating after World War II has not collapsed; on the contrary, it remains the core of world order. The task today is not to discover or define some mythic new order, but to reclaim the policies, commitments, and strategies of the old.

A Tale of Two Doctrines

World War II produced two postwar settlements. One, a reaction to deteriorating relations with the Soviet Union, led to the containment order, which was based on the balance of power, nuclear deterrence, and political and ideological competition. The other, a reaction to the economic rivalry and political turmoil of the 1930s and the resulting world war, can be called the liberal democratic order. It culminated in a wide range of new institutions and relations among the Western industrial democracies, built around economic openness, political reciprocity, and multilateral management of an American-led liberal political system.

Distinct political visions and intellectual rationales animated the two settlements, and at key moments the American president gave voice to each. On March 12, 1947, President Truman delivered his celebrated speech before Congress announcing aid to Greece and Turkey, wrapping it in an American commitment to support the cause of freedom worldwide. The declaration of the Truman Doctrine was a founding moment of the containment order, rallying Americans to a new great struggle, this one against what was thought to be Soviet communism's quest for world domination. A "fateful hour" had struck, Truman said, and the people of the world "must choose between two alternate ways of life." If the United States failed to exercise leadership, he warned, "we may endanger the peace of the world."

It is often forgotten that six days before, Truman had delivered an equally sweeping speech at Baylor University. On this occasion he spoke of the lessons the world must learn from the disasters of the 1930s. "As each battle of the economic war of the Thirties was fought, the inevitable tragic result became more and more apparent," said Truman. "From the tariff policy of Hawley and Smoot, the world went on to Ottawa and the system of imperial preferences, from Ottawa to the kind of elaborate and detailed restrictions adopted by Nazi Germany." Truman reaffirmed America's commitment to "economic peace," which would involve tariff reductions and rules and institutions of trade and investment. When economic differences arose, he said, "the interests of all will be considered, and a fair and just solution will be found." Conflicts would be captured and tamed in a cage of multilateral rules, standards, safeguards, and procedures for dispute resolution. According to Truman, "This is the way of a civilized community."

But it was the containment order that impressed itself on the popular imagination. In celebrated American accounts of the early years after World War II, intrepid officials struggled to make sense of Soviet military power and geopolitical intentions. A few "wise men" fashioned a reasoned and coherent response to the global challenge of Soviet communism, and their containment strategy gave clarity and purpose to several decades of American foreign policy. Over those decades, sprawling bureaucratic and military organizations were built around containment. The bipolar division of the world, nuclear weapons of growing size and sophistication, the ongoing clash of two expansive ideologies – all these gave life to and reinforced the centrality of the containment order.

By comparison, the thinking behind the liberal democratic order was more diffuse. The liberal democratic agenda was less obviously a grand strategy designed to advance American security interests, and it was inevitably viewed during the Cold War as secondary, a preoccupation of economists and businessmen. The policies and institutions that supported free trade among the advanced industrial societies seemed the stuff of low politics. But the liberal democratic agenda was actually built on a robust yet sophisticated set of ideas about American security interests, the causes of war and depression, and a desirable postwar political order. Although containment overshadowed it, the postwar liberal democratic order was more deeply rooted in the American experience and an understanding of history, economics, and the sources of political stability.

The proper foundations of political order have preoccupied American thinkers from the nation's founding onward, and innovative institutions and practices were developed in response to independence, continental expansion, civil war, economic depression, and world war. The liberal ideal was held high: open and decentralized political institutions could limit and diffuse conflict while integrating diverse peoples and interests. Moreover, a stable and legitimate political order was assured by its grounding in the Constitution, which specified rights, guarantees, and an institutionalized political process. When American officials began to contemplate postwar order, they were drawing on a wellspring of ideas, experiments, and historical lessons, and sifting these with an abiding liberal belief in the possibility of peaceful and mutually beneficial international relations.

The most basic conviction underlying the postwar liberal agenda was that the closed autarkic regions that had contributed to the worldwide depression and split the globe into competing blocs before the war must be broken up and replaced by an open, nondiscriminatory economic system. Peace and security, proponents had decided, were impossible in the face of exclusive economic regions. The challengers of liberal multilateralism, however, occupied almost every corner of the advanced industrial world. Germany and Japan were the most overtly hostile; both had pursued a dangerous path that combined authoritarian capitalism with military dictatorship and coercive regional autarky. But the British

Commonwealth and its imperial preference system also challenged liberal multilateral order.

The hastily drafted Atlantic Charter was an American effort to ensure that Britain signed on to its liberal democratic war aims.[1] The joint statement of principles affirmed free trade, equal access to natural resources for all interested buyers, and international economic collaboration to advance labor standards, employment security, and social welfare. Roosevelt and Churchill declared before the world that they had learned the lessons of the interwar years – and those lessons were fundamentally about the proper organization of the Western political economy. America's enemies, its friends, and even America itself had to be reformed and integrated into the postwar economic system.

The Liberal Manifesto

The postwar liberal democratic order was designed to solve the internal problems of Western industrial capitalism. It was not intended to fight Soviet communism, nor was it simply a plan to get American business back on its feet after the war by opening up the world to trade and investment. It was a strategy to build Western solidarity through economic openness and joint political governance. Four principles pursued in the 1940s gave shape to this order.

The most obvious principle was economic openness, which would ideally take the form of a system of nondiscriminatory trade and investment. As American strategic thinkers of the 1930s watched the world economy collapse and the German and Japanese blocs emerge, they pondered whether the United States could remain a great industrial power within the confines of the Western hemisphere. What were the minimum geographical requirements for the country's economic and military viability? For all practical purposes they had their answer by the time the United States entered the war. An American hemispheric bloc would not be sufficient; the United States needed secure markets and supplies of raw materials in Asia and Europe. Experts in a Council on Foreign Relations study group reached a similar conclusion when considering the necessary size of the area on which the United States depended for economic vitality.

American thinking was that economic openness was an essential element of a stable and peaceful world political order. "Prosperous neighbors are the best neighbors," remarked Roosevelt administration Treasury official Harry Dexter White. But officials were convinced that American economic and security interests demanded it as well. Great liberal visionaries and hard-nosed geopolitical strategists could agree on the notion of open markets; it united American postwar planners and was the seminal idea informing the work of the Bretton Woods conference on postwar economic cooperation. In his farewell remarks to the conference, Secretary of the Treasury Henry Morgenthau asserted that the agreements creating the International Monetary Fund and the World Bank marked the end of economic nationalism, by which he meant not that countries would give up pursuit of their national interest but that trade blocs and economic spheres of influence would no longer be their vehicles.

The second principle was joint management of the Western political-economic order. The leading industrial democratic states must not only lower barriers to trade and the movement of capital, but must govern the system. This also was a lesson from the 1930s: institutions, rules, and active mutual management by governments were necessary to avoid unproductively competitive and conflictual economic practices. Americans believed such cooperation necessary in a world where national economies were increasingly at the mercy of developments abroad. The unwise or untoward policies of one country threatened contagion, undermining the stability of all. As Roosevelt said at the opening of Bretton Woods, "The economic health of every country is a proper matter of concern to all its neighbors, near and far."

The belief in cooperative economic management also drew inspiration from the government activism of Roosevelt's New Deal. The postwar Western system was organized at a high tide of optimism about the capability of experts, economic and technical knowledge, and government intervention. The rise of Keynesian economics in Europe in the 1930s had begun to encourage an activist role for the state in the economy and society. International economic governance was a natural and inevitable extension of the policies being tried in individual Western industrial societies.

A third principle of liberal democratic order held that the rules and institutions of the Western world economy must be organized to support domestic economic stability and social security. This new commitment was foreshadowed in the Atlantic Charter's call for postwar international collaboration to ensure employment stability and social welfare. It was a sign of the times that Churchill, a conservative Tory, could promise a historic expansion of the government's responsibility for the people's well-being. In their schemes for postwar economic order, both Britain and the United States sought a system that would aid and protect their nascent social and economic commitments. They wanted an open world economy, but one congenial to the emerging welfare state as well as business.

The discovery of a middle way between old political alternatives was a major innovation of the postwar Western economic order. British and American planners began their discussion in 1942 deadlocked, Britain's desire for full employment and economic stabilization after the war running up against the American desire for free trade. The breakthrough came in 1944 with the Bretton Woods agreements on monetary order, which secured a more or less open system of trade and payments while providing safeguards for domestic economic stability through the International Monetary Fund. The settlement was a synthesis that could attract a new coalition of conservative free traders and the liberal prophets of economic planning.

A final element of the liberal democratic system might be termed "constitutionalism" – meaning simply that the Western nations would make systematic efforts to anchor their joint commitments in principled and binding institutional mechanisms. In fact, this may be the order's most basic aspect, encompassing the other principles and policies and giving the whole its distinctive domestic character. Governments might ordinarily seek to keep their options open, cooperating with other states but retaining the possibility of disengagement. The United States and the other Western nations after the war did exactly the opposite. They built long-term economic, political, and security commitments that were difficult to retract, and locked in the relationships, to the extent that sovereign states can. Insofar as the participating governments attempted to construct a political order based on commonly embraced norms and principles along with institutional mechanisms for resolving conflicts and reaching specific agreements, they practiced constitutionalism.

Democracies are particularly capable of making constitutional commitments to each other. For self-regarding states to agree to pursue their interests within binding institutions, they must perceive in their partners a credible sense of commitment – an assurance that they will not exit at the least sign of disagreement. Because policy-making in democracies tends to be decentralized and open, the character of commitments can be more clearly determined and there are opportunities to lobby policy-makers in the other democracies. Democracies do not just sign agreements; they create political processes that reduce uncertainty and build confidence in mutual commitments.

A Constitution for the West

The constitutional political order was constructed in the West around economic, political, and security institutions. In the economic realm, the Bretton Woods accords were the first permanent international arrangements for cooperation between states. Rules and institutions were proposed to ensure a stable and expansionary world economy and an orderly exchange rate system. Many of the original agreements for a rule-based monetary order gave way to ad hoc arrangements based more on the American dollar, but the vision of jointly managed, multilateral order remained. The organization of postwar trade relations also had an uncertain start, but ultimately an elaborate system of rules and obligations was developed, with quasi-judicial procedures for adjudicating disputes. In effect, the Western governments created an array of transnational political arenas organized by function. The postwar years were filled with economic disputes, but they were largely contained within these arenas.

The constitutional vision informed the creation of the United Nations, which combined political, economic, and security aspirations. To be sure, the UN system preserved the sovereign rights of member states. Intent on avoiding the failures of the League of Nations, the architects of the new international body drafted a charter under which the great powers would retain their freedom of action. But despite its weak rules and obligations, the United Nations reflected American and European desires to insure against a relapse of American isolation, to establish principles and mechanisms of conflict resolution, and to mute conflicts between states within a semi-institutionalized political process.

Cold War security structures provided additional constitutional architecture. Lord Ismay's observation that NATO was created to keep the Russians out, the Germans down, and the Americans in encapsulates the alliance's importance in locking in long-term commitments and expectations. The American–Japanese security pact had a similar dual-containment character. These institutions not only served as alliances in the ordinary sense of organized efforts to balance external threats, but offered mechanisms and venues for building relations, conducting business, and regulating conflict. The recent French decision to rejoin NATO can be understood only in this light. If NATO were simply a balancing alliance, the organization would be in an advanced stage of decay. It is NATO's broader political function – binding the democracies together and reinforcing political community – that explains its remarkable durability.

The democratic character of the United States and its partners facilitated construction of these dense interstate connections. The decentralized and open character of domestic institutions encouraged political give-and-take across the advanced industrial world. Thus the Western liberal democratic order was not only defined by a set of institutions and agreements but made for a particular kind of politics – transnational, pluralistic, reciprocal, legitimate.

The constitutional features of the Western order have been especially important for Germany and Japan. Both countries were reintegrated into the advanced industrial world as semi-sovereign powers that had accepted unprecedented constitutional limits on their military capacity and independence. As such, they became unusually reliant on Western regional and multilateral economic and security institutions. The Western order in which they were embedded was integral to their stability and their very functioning. The Christian Democratic politician Walther Leisler Kiep argued in 1972 that "the German–American alliance . . . is not merely one aspect of modern German history, but a decisive element as a result of its preeminent place in our politics. In effect, it provides a second constitution for our country." Western economic and security institutions were and are for Germany and Japan a political bulwark that provides stability and transcends those institutions' more immediate purposes.

What Endures

For those who thought cooperation among the advanced industrial democracies was driven primarily by Cold War threats, the last few years must appear puzzling. Relations between the major Western countries have not broken down. Germany has not rearmed, nor has Japan. What the Cold War focus misses is an appreciation of the other, less heralded, postwar American project – the building of a liberal order in the West. Archaeologists remove one stratum only to discover an older one beneath; the end of the Cold War allows us to see a deeper and more enduring layer of the postwar political order that was largely obscured by the more dramatic struggles between East and West.

Fifty years after its founding, the Western liberal democratic world is robust, and its principles and policies remain the core of world order. The challenges to liberal multilateralism both from within and from outside the West have mainly disappeared. Although regional experiments abound, they are fundamentally different from the autarkic blocs of the 1930s. The forces of business and financial integration are moving the globe inexorably toward a more tightly interconnected system that ignores regional as well as national borders. Recent proposals for an Atlantic free trade agreement and a Transatlantic Treaty, whatever their economic merits, reflect the trend toward increased integration across regions. The successful conclusion of the Uruguay Round of international trade talks in 1994 and the launching of the World Trade Organization on January 1, 1995, testify to the vigor of liberal multilateral principles.

Some aspects of the vision of the 1940s have faded. The optimism about government activism and economic management that animated the New Deal and Keynesianism has been considerably tempered. Likewise, the rule-based, quasi-judicial functions of liberal multilateralism have eroded, particularly in monetary relations. Paradoxically, although the rules of cooperation have become less coherent, cooperation itself has increased. Formal rules governing the Western world economy have gradually been replaced by a convergence of thinking on economy policy. The consensus on the broad outlines of desirable domestic and international economic policies has both reflected and promoted increased economic growth and the incorporation of emerging economies into the system.

The problems the liberal democratic order confronts are mostly problems of success, foremost among them the need to integrate the newly developing and post-communist countries. Here one sees most clearly that the post-Cold War order is really a continuation and extension of the Western order forged during and after World War II. The difference is its increasingly global reach. The world has seen an explosion in the desire of countries and peoples to move toward democracy and capitalism. When the history of the late twentieth century is written, it will be the struggle for more open and democratic polities throughout the world that will mark the era, rather than the failure of communism.

Other challenges to the system are boiling up in its leading states. In its early years, rapid and widely shared economic growth buoyed the system, as working- and middle-class citizens across the advanced industrial world rode the crest of the boom. Today economic globalization is producing much greater inequality between the winners and the losers, the wealthy and the poor. How the subsequent dislocations, dashed expectations, and political grievances are dealt with – whether the benefits are shared and the system as a whole is seen as socially just – will affect the stability of the liberal world order more than regional conflict, however tragic, in places like the Balkans.

To be sure, the Cold War reinforced solidarity and a sense of common identity among the liberal democracies, so it would be a mistake to take these binding forces for granted now. Trade disputes, controversies over burden-sharing, and regional conflict will test the durability of the liberal order. Without a Cold War threat to unite their countries, leaders in the advanced democracies will have to work harder to manage the inevitable conflicts and fissures. An agenda of reform and renewal would be an intelligent move to protect 50 years of investment in stable and thriving relations. Policies, institutions, and political symbols can all be directed at reinforcing liberal order, just as they are in individual liberal polities. At the very least, Western leaders could spend much more time acknowledging and celebrating the political space they share.

It is fashionable to say that the United States after the Cold War faces its third try at forging a durable world order, at reinventing the basic rules of world politics, just as after both world wars. But this view is more rhetorically compelling than historically valid. The end of the Cold War was less the end of a world order than the collapse of the communist world into an expanding Western order. If that order is to be defended and strengthened, its historical roots and accomplishments must be reclaimed. The United States built and then managed the containment order for 40 years, but it also built and continues to enjoy the rewards of an older liberal democratic order. America is not adrift in uncharted seas. It is at the center of a world of its own making.

Note

1   Churchill insisted that the charter not mandate the dismantling of the British Empire and its system of trade preferences, and only last-minute sidestepping of this controversial issue made agreement possible.

7

Getting Hegemony Right

In May 1999 the Oxford Union debated the proposition, "Resolved, the United States is a rogue state." The resolution was ultimately defeated, but around the world there is growing unease about a global order dominated by American power – power unprecedented, unrestrained, and unpredictable. The unease is felt even by America's closest allies. "The United States of America today predominates on the economic level, the monetary level, on the technological level, and in the cultural area in the broadest sense of the word," French Foreign Minister Hubert Védrine observed in a speech in Paris in early 1999. "It is not comparable, in terms of power and influence, to anything known in modern history." European diplomats, following Védrine's coining of the term, have begun calling the United States a "hyperpower." During the Cold War, the Soviet Union and the United States kept each other in check. Today the restraints are less evident, and this has made American power increasingly controversial.

This is an unexpected turn of events. Just a little over a decade ago many pundits argued that the central problem of US foreign policy was the graceful management of the country's decline. Paul Kennedy's famous book, *The Rise and Fall of the Great Powers*, argued that the United States would go the way of all great powers – down. Japan was on the rise and Europe was awakening. World politics after the Cold War, it was widely assumed, was to be profoundly multipolar.

But the distribution of world power took a dramatic turn in America's favor. The sudden collapse of the Soviet Union, the decline in ideological rivalry, lagging economic fortunes in Japan and continental Europe, growing disparities in military and technological expenditure, and America's booming economy all intensified power disparities during the

1990s. Today it is not decline that the United States must manage but the fear, resentment, and instabilities created by a decade of rising American power.

A global backlash to US power is not inevitable, however, particularly if the United States remembers its own political history. Our leaders have the ideas, means, and political institutions that can allow for stable and cooperative order even in the midst of sharp and shifting asymmetries of power. The United States faced this problem after World War II and solved it by building what might be called a "stakeholder" hegemony. America can do it again today.

The Dangers of Success

The United States has a hegemony problem for a simple reason: it started the decade of the 1990s as the world's only superpower and then proceeded to have a better decade than any other power. Disparities in economic and military power between the United States and the other major states widened. Between 1990 and 1998, US economic growth (27 percent) was almost twice that of the European Union (15 percent) and three times that of Japan (9 percent).[1] The weakness of the euro since its launch is ultimately a result of these divergent European and US economic trends. While Europe and Japan have struggled with economic restructuring, America has ridden the wave of the "New Economy" and rising productivity. The United States also reduced defense spending at a slower rate after the Cold War than the other major powers, resulting in greater relative military capabilities by the end of the 1990s. In fact, it has come close in recent years to monopolizing military-related research and development, spending roughly 80 percent of the world's total.[2] These developments have resulted in an extremely lopsided distribution of world power. The US economy has slowed in recent months, but the disparities in wealth creation remain.

While such brute material disparities might normally be hidden below the surface, recent developments have rendered them salient and provocative. The US-led NATO air campaign over Kosovo in 1999 provided at times dramatic – and, to countries such as China and Russia, disturbing – evidence of America's military and technological advantage. The squabble between the United States and Germany over the leadership of the International Monetary Fund (IMF) also gave the impression that America had acquired a taste for dominance. Washington similarly bullied Japan during the East Asian financial crisis, opposing Tokyo's plan for an Asian Monetary Fund and insisting on American-approved remedies. Bipartisan support for a national missile defense, despite the opposition of the other major states and its potentially unsettling consequences for world security relationships, is another source of resentment and suspicion. In the meantime, the expansion and integration of world markets – unfolding under the banner of globalization – are seen by many as a Washington-directed phenomenon that spreads American values and disproportionately favors American interests. For these and many other reasons, it is widely believed around the world today that the global distribution of power is dangerously out of balance.

Realist thinkers argue that what is happening is not surprising. Balance of power theory makes a clear prediction: weaker states will resist and balance against the predominant state. According to realists, security – indeed survival – is the fundamental goal of states, and, because states cannot ultimately rely on the commitments or guarantees of other states to ensure their security, they will be very sensitive to their relative power position. When powerful states emerge, secondary states will seek protection in countervailing coalitions of weaker states. The alternative is to risk domination.[3] A leading scholar of balance of power theory, Kenneth Waltz, argues that with the end of the Cold War, relations between the United States and its allies will loosen and move toward a more traditional balance of power model. With the end of bipolarity, "the United States as the strongest power will often find other states edging away from it: Germany moving toward Eastern Europe and Russia, and Russia moving toward Germany and Japan."[4] According to this view, unipolarity is simply not stable. Eventually, the anarchic character of international politics will reassert itself: economic rivalry, security dilemmas, alliance decay, and balance of power politics among the major states.

The driving forces of this expected global reaction are the everyday frustrations and worries that are produced by sharp power disparities. Because of the size of the United States, little shifts in US policy can have huge consequences for other states. The Europeans will slowly expand their investments in autonomous military capabilities and increasingly articulate an independent strategic vision. Japan will expand its diplomatic engagement of East Asia, quietly launching independent security dialogues with other states in the region. At the same time, there is little in America's environment to discipline the exercise of Washington's power. It is hard for the world to ignore or work around the United States regardless of the issue – trade, finance, security, proliferation, or the environment.

But while the world worries about what America does next – or neglects to do – the United States needs to worry very little about what the rest of the world does. In such a benign and unchallenged environment, US foreign policy tends to be driven by domestic politics or the current policy tastes of its leaders. The sad fact is that in a world of unipolar power Americans need to know very little about what other governments or peoples think, but foreigners must worry increasingly about the vagaries of congressional campaigns and the idiosyncratic prejudices of congressional committee chairmen.

For those who see this world as inherently unstable, the existing world order will change not in large, dramatic leaps but in small steps. The great powers in Europe and Asia will begin making minute adjustments to protect themselves from the uncertainties of American power. Even in more balanced times, secondary states have worried about the ability of the United States simultaneously to restrain and commit itself. As the power imbalance has grown more extreme, America's willingness and ability to show restraint and make commitments is increasingly thrown into question. One can only imagine the discussions that go on, for example, in diplomatic cables between Paris and Berlin. Paris has never wanted to be a "junior partner in the American project," as one French official recently observed. Worried states are making small adjustments, creating alternatives to alliance with the United States. These small steps may not look important today, but eventually the ground will shift and the US-led postwar order will fragment and disappear.

The Acceptable Face of American Power

This bleak vision of backlash and strategic rivalry is not destiny. Indeed, the most striking fact of international life in the decade since the end of the Cold War is that stable and cooperative relations between the democratic great powers continue largely unabated. In some ways these relations have actually deepened, such as with the creation of the World Trade Organization and the expansion of intergovernmental working groups under the auspices of the G-7. One reason for this is simple enough: there is a broad convergence of interests among the advanced industrial countries, all of which share deeply held common commitments to economic openness, democracy, and multilateral management of global issues. The huge start-up costs of establishing an alternative to the US-centered system also probably deter the other major states.

A critical ingredient in stabilizing international relations in a world of radical power disparities is the character of America itself. The United States is indeed a global hegemon, but because of its democratic institutions and political traditions it is – or can be – a relatively benign one. Joseph Nye's arguments on "soft power" of course come to mind here, and there is much to his point. But, in fact, there are other, more significant aspects of the American way in foreign policy that protect the United States from the consequences of its own greatness.

When other major states consider whether to work with the United States or resist it, the fact that it is an open, stable democracy matters. The outside world can see American policy-making at work and can even find opportunities to enter the process and help shape how the overall order operates. Paris, London, Berlin, Moscow, Tokyo, and even Beijing – in each of these capitals officials can readily find reasons to conclude that an engagement policy toward the United States will be more effective than balancing against US power.

America in large part stumbled into this open, institutionalized order in the 1940s, as it sought to rebuild the postwar world and to counter Soviet communism. In the late 1940s, in a pre-echo of today's situation, the United States was the world's dominant state – constituting 45 percent of world GNP, leading in military power, technology, finance, and industry, and brimming with natural resources. But America nonetheless found itself building world order around stable and binding partnerships. Its calling card was its offer of Cold War security protection. But the intensity of political and economic cooperation between the United States and its partners went well beyond what was necessary to counter the Soviet threat. As the historian Geir Lundestad has observed, the expanding American political order in the half century after World War II was in important respects an "empire by invitation."[5] The remarkable global reach of American postwar hegemony has been at least in part driven by the efforts of European and Asian governments to harness US power, render that power more predictable, and use it to overcome their own regional insecurities. The result has been a vast system of America-centered economic and security partnerships.

Even though the United States looks like a wayward power to many around the world today, it nonetheless has an unusual ability to co-opt and reassure. Three elements matter most in making US power more stable, engaged, and restrained.

First, America's mature political institutions organized around the rule of law have made it a relatively predictable and cooperative hegemon. The pluralistic and regularized way in which US foreign and security policy is made reduces surprises and allows other states to build long-term, mutually beneficial relations. The governmental separation of powers creates a shared decision-making system that opens up the process and reduces the ability of any one leader to make abrupt or aggressive moves toward other states. An active press and competitive party system also provide a service to outside states by generating information about US policy and determining its seriousness of purpose. The messiness of a democracy can, indeed, frustrate American diplomats and confuse foreign observers. But over the long term, democratic institutions produce more consistent and credible policies – policies that do not reflect the capricious and idiosyncratic whims of an autocrat.

Think of the United States as a giant corporation that seeks foreign investors. It is more likely to attract investors if it can demonstrate that it operates according to accepted accounting and fiduciary principles. The rule of law and the institutions of policy-making in a democracy are the political equivalent of corporate transparency and accountability. Sharp shifts in policy must ultimately be vetted within the policy process and pass muster by an array of investigatory and decision-making bodies. Because it is a constitutional, rule-based democracy, outside states are more willing to work with the United States – or, to return to the corporate metaphor, to invest in ongoing partnerships.

This open and decentralized political process works in a second way to reduce foreign worries about American power. It creates what might be called "voice opportunities" – that is, opportunities for political access and, with it, the means for foreign governments and groups to influence the way Washington's power is exercised. In 1990 the political analyst Pat Choate wrote a bestseller entitled *Agents of Influence*, detailing the supposedly scandalous ways in which Japanese ministries and corporations were manipulating the American political process. High-priced lobbyists were advancing Tokyo's commercial interests within the hallowed halls of the American capital and undermining the pursuit of the US national interest. Today Washington is even more inundated by foreign diplomats and revolving-door lobbyists working to ensure that the interests of America's partners are not overlooked. Looked at from the perspective of the stable of functioning of America's hegemonic order, Choate was actually describing one of the brilliant aspects of the United States as a global power. By providing other states opportunities to play the game in Washington, they are drawn into active, ongoing partnerships that serve the long-term strategic interests of the United States.

A third and final element of the American order that reduces worry about power asymmetries is the web of multilateral institutions that mark the postwar world. After World War II, the United States launched history's most ambitious era of institution-building. The UN, IMF, World Bank, NATO, GATT and other institutions that emerged provided a more extensive rule-based structure for political and economic relations than anything seen before. The United States had been deeply ambivalent about making permanent security commitments to other states and about allowing its political and economic policies to be dictated by intergovernmental bodies. The Soviet menace was critical in overcoming these doubts.

Networks and political relationships were built that – paradoxically – made US power both more far-reaching and durable but also more predictable and malleable.

In effect, the United States spun a web of institutions that connected other states to an emerging American-dominated economic and security order. But in doing so, these institutions also bound the United States to other states and reduced – at least to some extent – Washington's ability to engage in the arbitrary and indiscriminate exercise of power. Call it an institutional bargain. The price for the United States was a reduction in Washington's policy autonomy, in that institutional rules and joint decision-making reduced US unilateralist capacities. But what Washington got in return was worth the price. America's partners also had their autonomy constrained, but in return were able to operate in a world where US power was more restrained and reliable.

Secretary of State Dean Rusk spelled out the terms of the bargain in testimony before the Senate Foreign Relations Committee in 1965:

> We are every day, in one sense, accepting limitations upon our complete freedom of action. . . . We have more than 4,300 treaties and international agreements, two-thirds of which have been entered into in the past 25 years. . . . Each one of which at least limits our freedom of action. We exercise our sovereignty going into these agreements.

But Rusk argued that these agreements also create a more stable environment within which the United States can pursue its interests. "Law is a process by which we increase our range of freedom" and "we are constantly enlarging our freedom by being able to predict what others are going to do."[6] The United States gets a more predictable environment and more willing partners.

There have been many moments when Asian and European allies have complained about the heavy-handedness of US foreign policy, but the open and institutionalized character of the American order has minimized the possibilities of hegemonic excess over the long term. The untoward implications of sharp power asymmetries are reduced, cooperation and reciprocity are regularized, and the overall hegemonic order is rendered more legitimate and stable. The bargain – on both sides – remains intact.

Renewing the Institutional Bargain

America's soaring power in the 1990s has put this open and rule-based postwar order to the test. Over the last 50 years, the advanced industrial states have been relatively confident that the institutional foundations of this order would guard against the worst abuses of US unilateralism and domination. The system had characteristics of a stakeholder hegemony that promoted stability and cooperation. Today, in various political circles around the world, it is harder for some people to make this judgment. Even the leader of a major US ally, German Chancellor Gerhard Schröder, has raised concerns. "That there is a danger of unilateralism, not by just anybody but by the United States, is undeniable."[7]

The implication of my argument is that the more America's brute power capabilities emerge from behind mutually acceptable rules and institutions, the more that power will provoke reaction and resistance. American leaders are indeed ambivalent about entangling the country in restraints and commitments. In the past, however, these leaders have consistently concluded that some restraint on US autonomy was a useful way to allay the worries of other states and bind them to America's postwar global political-economic order. As Robert Zoellick, former Under-Secretary of State and now US Trade Representative in the Bush administration, describes the operation of this postwar order:

> The more powerful participants in this system – especially the United States – did not forswear all their advantages, but neither did they exercise their strength without substantial restraint. Because the United States believed the Trilateral system was in its interest, it sacrificed some degree of national autonomy to promote it.[8]

What can America do to prevent the unraveling of this order? Three suggestions are offered here. First, US officials should keep the country's current good fortunes in historical perspective. This might induce a bit more modesty. America's long-time rival from outside the advanced democratic world – Russia – now has an economy about the size of Denmark's. America's one-time rival from within the advanced democratic world – Japan – has gone through ten years of economic stagnation, with no end in sight. China is still a developing country in terms of both economic and military capabilities, far from being able to challenge the United States in either arena. Western Europe is stable and expanding, but it is consumed with its own union, embarked on a politically difficult economic restructuring, and still is not capable of projecting global power. This unusual – perhaps unique – set of circumstances gives the United States a *de facto* license to act as the world's manager and CEO. But US officials should remember that the wheel of world power does turn. Russia will not be down forever, nor will Japan. Europe will eventually get its house in order. The way America treats the other major states when they are in decline will influence how these states treat America when – not if – they recover.

Second, the United States needs to renew the postwar institutional bargain by making it more explicit and more encompassing. This means that America must make it clear that it will play by multilateral rules in exchange for cooperation by other states on issues that matter most to us. The US government should bury once and for all legislation such as Super 301 and the Helms-Burton Act, which give the president authority to act unilaterally to protect narrow economic interests. Such exercises of US power create more problems than they solve. The United States should also expand its capacity to consult with other governments throughout the policy-making process. Washington is not just the capital of the country or even of "the West"; it is also – at least for a few more decades – the capital of a larger global order. These foreign stakeholders must be brought more fully into our policy process. Increasing opportunities to voice opinions can be achieved informally in the day-to-day willingness of US officials to consult with other governments. If not, Washington risks an ultimate shift toward some other form of global order.

President George W. Bush seemed to acknowledge the dangers of an overweening foreign policy – and chest thumping about America as the "indispensable nation" – during one of the presidential debates, when he called for more modesty as America operates around the world. The Bush team has also made "listening to our allies" a central theme of its foreign policy. Whether this is more than hollow campaign rhetoric will depend on how the new administration acts on such issues as US participation in peacekeeping operations, national missile defense, and a variety of proposed multilateral political and environmental accords.

Preserving the existing system through the redoubling of rule-based relationships will also require American elites to elevate the domestic debate on international commitments and institutions. The old canard that building international rules and authority threatens American sovereignty is still too tempting to many politicians on the Left and Right. The argument that many – if not most – of the existing multilateral institutions are inspired by US leadership and advance the country's goals needs to be made more convincing to the American people. Politicians are more likely to stress the short-term costs to the United States in terms of lost policy autonomy or sovereignty than the gains in building an enlightened order that serves long-term US interests.

Finally, the United States needs to find more ways to pursue its economic and security goals through joint or multilateral decision-making exercises. A good example of such intergovernmental processes that create stakeholder cooperation is the 1999 Perry commission on North Korea.

Responding to a congressional request for a reassessment of US policy toward North Korea, the Clinton administration charged former Secretary of Defense William Perry with the task of policy review. The deliberations eventually involved extensive talks with Japan and South Korea. In a *de facto* way, the commission became multilateral, and Japanese and South Korean officials were integrated into the process and ultimately helped shape its content. The Perry report helped clarify US policy toward North Korea, but the process by which it was generated also helped build consensus in the region on how to deal with that state. It also made American involvement in the region more consistent with the goals of partner states. The G-8 process – which in recent years has launched ongoing intergovernmental working groups to pursue common approaches to issues such as transnational organized crime and environmental policy – is also a place where coordinated policy-making can be expanded.

America's unipolar moment need not end in antagonistic disarray. But the United States needs to rediscover the solutions that it has brought to the problem of unequal power in the past. These solutions are celebrated in our national political tradition. The rule of law, constitutional principles, and inclusive institutions of political participation ensure that governance is not simply a product of wealth or power. The wealthy and the powerful must operate within principled institutional parameters. Because a rule-based order generates more stable and cooperative relations within the country, even the wealthy and powerful gain by avoiding social upheaval, which puts everyone's interests at risk. America can once again take this old domestic insight and use it to shape post-Cold War international relations. And it is time to do so now, when America's relative power may be at its peak.

Notes

1   Calculated from OECD statistics (July 1999 web edition). GDP measures are figured at 1990 prices and exchange rates.
2   See International Institute for Strategic Studies, *The Military Balance 1999/2000* (London: Oxford University Press, 1999). For additional indicators of an intensification of US power, see William C. Wohlforth, "The Stability of a Unipolar World," *International Security* (Summer 1999).
3   For views along these lines, see Peter W. Rodman, "The World's Resentment: Anti-Americanism as a Global Phenomenon," *The National Interest* (Summer 2000); and Samuel Huntington, "The Lonely Superpower," *Foreign Affairs* (March/April 1999).
4   Waltz, "The Emerging Structure of International Politics," *International Security* (Fall 1993): 75.

5 See Lundestad, "Empire by Invitation? The United States and Western Europe, 1945–1952," *The Journal of Peace Research* (September 1986).
6 Quoted in Edward C. Luck, *Mixed Messages: American Politics and International Organization, 1919–1999* (Washington, DC: Brookings Institution Press, 1999), p. 61.
7 Craig Whitney, *New York Times*, February 15, 1999.
8 Zoellick, "The United States", in Zoellick et al., *21st Century Strategies of the Trilateral Countries: In Concert or Conflict?*, Report No. 53 (New York: Trilateral Commission, 1999), p. 5.

8

American Grand Strategy in the Age of Terror

The surprise attacks on the World Trade Center and the Pentagon have been called this generation's Pearl Harbor, exposing America's vulnerabilities to the outside world and triggering a fundamental reorientation of foreign policy. President George W. Bush's speech to Congress on September 20 has likewise been seen by some as the most important statement of American grand strategy since President Harry Truman's Greece and Turkey speech of March 12, 1947, when the United States declared its determination to fight communism worldwide. Indeed, to some, September 11, 2001 marks the end of the post-Cold War era. The 1990s was a decade of peace and prosperity during which the "new economy," budget surpluses, and momentary geopolitical stability bred a sort of naive liberal optimism about the future. But in reality, according to this view, these years were merely an historical interlude between eras of struggle. After a decade of drift, the United States has finally rediscovered its grand strategic purpose.[1]

This evocative image of historical transition in American foreign policy and world order is misleading. The events of September 11 and the Bush administration's declaration of war on terrorism will have an enduring impact on world politics, but primarily in reinforcing the existing Western-centered international order and providing new sinews of cohesion among the great powers, including Russia and China. The most profound diplomatic achievement of the 1990s was the preservation of relatively stable and cooperative relations among the major states. Cold War bipolarity turned into American unipolarity without great geopolitical upheaval. The Bush administration's coalition strategy of fighting terrorism relies on and – if Washington plays its cards well – promises to strengthen this structure of cooperative relations. Europe, Japan, and the United States form the core of this order. If Russia becomes more tightly connected to the West, there will be a "critical mass" among the great powers committed to international order organized around alliance partnership and cooperative security. If China follows its strategic interests that favor continued integration into the international system, and the United States remains committed to an inclusive global strategy of anti-terrorism, it is possible that engagement and accommodation – rather than balance of power and security rivalry – will continue to define great power relations well into the future.

The most immediate consequence of the recent terrorist events could be within the Bush administration itself, pushing it back toward a more centrist foreign policy. Divergent philosophies of international order and American leadership coexist uneasily within the administration. A pragmatic orientation – that stresses alliances, multilateral cooperation, and a commitment to building order around practical and mutually beneficial rules and institutions – competes with a more unilateral orientation that stresses military preponderance, selective engagement, and national autonomy. In its first six months in office, the Bush administration signaled a move toward a more hardline unilateralist position. It rejected a series of international treaties and agreements, championed missile defense, and stated its desire to abrogate the ABM Treaty. However, the administration's new ambition to lead a global coalition against terrorism makes unilateralism untenable. Much as leadership of the free-world coalition during the Cold War forced the United States reluctantly to make policy compromises and commitments, so too will its leadership of an anti-terrorist coalition.

The rise of a unipolar American order after the Cold War has not triggered a global backlash, but it has unsettled relationships worldwide. Europeans worry about the steadiness of American leadership. Other governments and peoples resent the extent and intrusiveness of American power, markets, and culture. Some intellectuals in the West even suggest that an arrogant America brought the terrorism of September 11 on itself.[2] Aside from diffuse resentments, the practical reality for many states is that they need the United States more than it needs them – or so it would seem. In the early months of the Bush administration, the political consequences of a unipolar superpower seemed all too obvious. It could walk away from treaties and agreements with other countries – on global warming, arms control, trade, business regulation, and so forth – and suffer fewer consequences than its partners. But to conduct a campaign against terrorism successfully, the United States now needs the rest of the world. This is a potential boon to cooperation across the board.

The core of today's international order – what might be called the "American system" – is built on two grand bargains that the United States made with other countries around the world. One is a "realist" bargain that grew out of the Cold War. The United States provides its European and Asian partners with security protection and access to American markets, technology, and supplies within an open world economy. In return, these countries agree to be stable partners that provide diplomatic, economic, and logistical support for the United States as it leads the wider American-centered postwar order. The other is a "liberal" bargain that addresses the uncertainties of American power. Asian and European states agree to accept American leadership and operate within an agreed-upon political-economic system. In return, the United States opens itself up and binds itself to its partners, in effect building an institutionalized coalition of partners, and reinforces the stability of these long-term relations by making itself more "user friendly" – that is, by playing by the rules and creating ongoing political processes with these other states that facilitate consultation and joint decision-making. The United States makes its power safe for the world and in return the world agrees to live within the American system. These bargains date from the 1940s but continue to undergird the post-Cold War order.

To pursue a global campaign against terrorism successfully, Washington will need to renew these two critical bargains. How Washington fights the war on terrorism matters. Cooperative strategies that reinforce norms of international conduct do constrain the ways in which the US uses military force, but they also legitimate that use of force and make other states more willing to join the coalition. If the United States acts with an eye on the logic and historic bargains of the existing international order, the terrible events of September 11 will provide an opportunity to strengthen the pillars of democratic community and great power peace.

Post-Cold War Orders: Real and Imagined

Many observers expected that the end of the Cold War would usher in dramatic and destabilizing shifts in world politics. But despite the collapse of the Soviet Union – and despite great swings in the international distribution of power – the United States and its partners navigated their way into a new era while maintaining stable and cooperative relations. Indeed, the most important characteristic of the current international order is the remarkable absence of serious strategic rivalry and competitive balancing among the great powers. At the core of this order are the major industrial democracies of Europe, North America, and East Asia – a community of states with stable governments, liberal societies, and advanced market economies, linked by security alliances, economic interdependence, and a variety of multilateral governance institutions.[3] The United States – whose military, technological, and economic superiority increased during the 1990s – sits at the order's epicenter.

Stable peace among the great powers was not a widely anticipated outcome. One group of "realist" analysts forecast the return of great-power rivalry.[4] Without the cohesion provided by a common external threat, the argument went, the major powers would revert to competitive strategies driven by the underlying structure of anarchy. In this view, Germany and Japan would rearm and loosen their subordinate security ties to the United States, NATO and the US–Japan alliance would unravel, and a competitive multipolar scramble for power would emerge. The post-Cold War world would look more like the late nineteenth-century system of shifting alliances and great power conflict. Security cooperation and the willingness of European and Asian partners to operate within an American-centered global order were considered artifacts of the Cold War.

Another scenario of breakdown in the American security system has focused on shifting geopolitical ambitions in Europe and the United States. The United States may be "indispensable" to the stable operation of global order, but American voters are not really aware of this or much impressed by its imperatives. Charles Kupchan argues that a shrinking American willingness to be the global protector of last resort will be the primary engine of a change to that order.[5] Today's hegemonic order will crack from a growing mismatch between domestic support and external commitments: "The foundation is shaky because America has a dwindling interest in paying the construction and upkeep. . . . Rather than pursue a hollow hegemony that misleads and creates unmet expectations, it is better for the United States to give advance notice that its days as a guarantor of last resort may be numbered."[6] The big oak tree of American hegemony has grown steadily over the decades. Others still want it and benefit from it and the fact of its existence makes alternative ordering systems less viable – but it still depends on a subterranean water supply – United States public support – that could be drying up. The rise of a united Europe that seeks an independent security role and its own leadership presence around the world adds to the coming conflict.

A second group of analysts has focused on shifts in the economic structure of the existing order. This group anticipated that the world would return to the problems of the 1930s: open multilateralism would give way to rival geoeconomic regions. Europe and East Asia would each pull away from the United States and pursue their own visions of regional economic order. Markets would become more political, trade conflict would rise, and the three major regions would compete for supremacy.[7] The severity of these regional clashes would be intensified – in the view of some – because of deep differences in the character of each region's capitalism. Continental Europe, Anglo-America, and East Asia each has its own values and institutions that gives each a distinctive approach to state and market. Chalmers Johnson, for example, has argued that with the end of artificial Cold War constraints, Japan will eventually reassert its economic independence from the United States, triggering greater conflict across the Pacific.[8]

The themes of both these post-Cold War visions are fragmentation and conflict. The "problems of anarchy" will reassert themselves: economic closure, hypernationalism, arms races, and regional competition and strategic rivalry.

Yet these grim predictions have not come to pass. Despite losing the Soviet Union as a common threat, Japan and the United States during the 1990s reaffirmed their alliance partnerships, contained political conflict, expanded trade and investment across the Atlantic and Pacific, and avoided a return to balance-of-power politics. Germany and other European states are reducing their defense expenditures rather than increasing their independent military capacity. Japan is rethinking its defense posture in Asia but not questioning its fundamental alliance link with the United States. Russia and China remain outside the core community of industrial democracies, but even as they voice opposition to America's hegemonic global presence they are also seeking greater integration into the Western-oriented world system. This stable peace among the great powers is noted by Robert Jervis: "Although the causes can be debated, the fact is striking: we are experiencing the longest period of peace among the great powers in history. . . . This is a breathtaking change in world politics, which previously consisted of the state of war among the great powers."[9] Part of this stability was achieved in the decades after World War II, a response to Cold War bipolarity and nuclear weapons. But since the end of superpower struggle, it is clear that this stable order among the great powers is rooted in the more general relationship between the United States and the outside world.

Political Foundations of the American System

Forecasts of post-Cold War breakdown and disarray missed an important fact: in the shadow of the Cold War, a distinctive and durable political order was being assembled among the major industrial countries. This order might be called the American system – evoking the multifaceted character of this American-centered order organized around layers of security alliances, open markets, multilateral institutions, and forums for consultation and governance. It is an order built on common interests and values and anchored in capitalism and democracy. But it is also an engineered political order built on American power, institutional relationships, and political bargains.

The American system is a product of two postwar order-building exercises. One – commonly seen as the defining feature of the era – was containment. Truman, Dean Acheson, George Kennan, and other American foreign policy-makers were responding to the specter of Soviet power, organizing a global anti-communist alliance and fashioning an American grand strategy. America's strategy was to "prevent the Soviet Union from using the power and position it won . . . to reshape the postwar international order."[10] This is the grand strategy, and international order based on it, that was swept away in 1991.

But there was another order created after World War II. American officials worked with Britain and other countries to build new relationships among the Western industrial democracies. The political order among these countries, aimed at solving the problems of the 1930s, was articulated in such statements as the Atlantic Charter of 1941, the Bretton Woods agreements of 1944, and the Marshall Plan speech in 1947. Unlike containment, there was not a singular statement of strategy and purpose. It was a collection of ideas about open markets, social stability, political integration, international institutional cooperation, and collective security. Even the Atlantic Pact of 1949 was as much aimed at reconstruction and integrating Europe and binding the democratic world together as it was an alliance created to balance Soviet power.[11]

The American system is based on a vision of open economic relations, intergovernmental cooperation, and liberal democratic society. But the most consequential aspect of the order is its security structure. Although the United States remained deeply ambivalent about extending security guarantees or forward-deploying troops in Europe and Asia, it ultimately bound itself to the other advanced democracies through alliance partnerships.[12] This strategy of security binding has provided a structure of commitments, restraints, and mechanisms of reassurance.

The American-centered alliances have always been doing more "work" than is usually appreciated.[13] The traditional understanding of alliances is that they are created to balance against external power and threats. But America's postwar alliances with Europe and Japan were created to achieve a lot more. Stabilizing and managing relations between alliance partners was as much a function of these alliances as countering hostile states. This was true even during the Cold War, but it is even more fundamentally the case today. The alliances serve to bind Japan, the United States, and Western Europe together and thereby reduce conflict and the potential for strategic rivalry between these traditional great powers. The alliances help these states establish credible commitment to a cooperative structure of relations and provide institutional mechanisms that allow each state to gain access to the policy-making processes in the others. Moreover, by binding Germany to Western Europe and Japan to the United States, the alliances help prevent security dilemmas and strategic rivalry that might otherwise break out in Europe and East Asia.[14] The alliances allow the United States to both project power around the world and limit and channel how that power is exercised. These functions of the alliances fit together, constituting a long-term institutional bargain between the United States and its European and Asian partners.

The durability of the American system rests on preponderant American power and a distinctive form of open and institutionalized hegemony. American power has been essential to the building and maintenance of the existing order. After World War II, the United States commanded about 50 percent of the world's wealth. While the other major powers were destroyed or diminished by war, the United States economy reached new levels of growth and technological advancement. Again today, the United States has only about 4 percent of the world's population but produces approximately 27 percent of global output. Its nearest rivals – China and Japan – produce about half this amount with four times the population between them.[15] As in the 1940s, America's military and technological supremacy is unchallenged and unprecedented.[16]

One explanation for the durability of the American system involves an appeal to a version of the "democratic peace" thesis: that open democratic polities are less able or willing to use power in an arbitrary and indiscriminate manner against other democracies.[17] The calculations of smaller and weaker states as they confront a democratic hegemon are thereby altered. Fundamentally, power asymmetries are less threatening or destabilizing when they exist between democracies. This might be so for several reasons. Open polities make the exercise of power more visible and easy to anticipate. Accountable governments make the exercise of power more predictable and institutionalized. Democracies are more externally accessible than non-democracies. Leaders who rise through the ranks within democratic countries are more inclined to participate in "give and take" with other democratic leaders than their counterparts in autocratic and authoritarian states. Processes of interaction between democracies make the crude and manipulative exercise of power less likely or consequential. Institutions and norms of consultation and reciprocal influence are manifest in relations across the democratic world. These facets of democracy are stressed by John Gaddis: "Negotiation, compromise, and consensus-building came naturally to statesmen steeped in the uses of such practices at home: in this sense, the American political tradition served the country better than its realist critics – Kennan among them – believed it did."[18] This system of alliances and multilateral institutions is the core of today's world order. American power both undergirds this system and is transformed by it. By enmeshing itself in a postwar web of alliances and multilateral commitments, the United States is able to project its influence outward and create a relatively secure environment in which to pursue its interests. But that order also shapes and restrains American power and makes the United States a more genial partner for other states. Likewise, the array of institutions and cooperative security ties that link Europe, the United States, Japan, and the rest of the democratic community create a complex and stable order that by sheer size overwhelms any alternative. Russia, China, or any other combination of states or movements are too small to mount a fundamental challenge to the American system. This order provides the ready foundation for a concerted campaign against terrorism.

America's Competing Grand Strategies

The Bush administration has still not completely come to terms with – or accepted the logic of – the American system. The events of September 11 expose the deep divides within the Bush administration over the exercise of American power and visions of international order. Two distinct strategies are competing for primacy. One is the liberal multilateralism that generally characterized the approach of the previous Bush and Clinton administrations as well as American policy toward the West during the post-World War II era. This is the strategy that gave rise to and reinforces the American system. But some Bush administration officials embrace a more unilateral – even imperial – grand strategy, based on a starkly realist vision of American interests and global power realities. In this view, American preponderance allows it selectively to engage Europe and Asia, dominating world politics with military forces that are both unchallenged and less bound to United Nations or alliance controls. Cooperative security, arms control, and multilateral cooperation play a reduced role in this global strategy. But the events of September 11 have rendered this strategy deeply problematic. The logic of the Bush administration's war on terrorism – with its emphasis on leading an international coalition of states – necessarily reorients the administration's foreign policy in ways that will push it back in the direction of postwar liberal multilateralism.

Grand strategies are really bundles of security, economic and political strategies based on assumptions about how best to advance national security and build international order. Administrations inevitably pursue a mix of policies and strategies.[19] In general, however, the strategy of liberal multilateralism has been the dominant strand of American policy in the decade after the Cold War, with the elder Bush and Clinton administrations drawing on ideas and commitments from the post-World War II era that gave shape to the American system. This liberal grand strategy is based on the view that American security and national interests can be best advanced by promoting international order organized around democracy, open markets, multilateral institutions, and binding security ties.

James Baker, Secretary of State in the previous Bush administration, captured aspects of this strategy in his reflection on American policy in the immediate aftermath of the Cold War, likening the first Bush administration's thinking to American strategy after 1945: "Men like Truman and Acheson were above all, though we sometimes forget, institution builders. They created NATO and the other security organizations that eventually won the Cold War. They fostered the economic institutions . . . that brought unparalleled prosperity. . . . At a time of similar opportunity and risk, I believed we should take a leaf from their book."[20] This strategy was reflected in the first Bush administration's support for the North American Free Trade Area (NAFTA), Asia-Pacific Economic Cooperation (APEC), the World Trade Organization (WTO), and its initial steps to expand NATO's association with countries in the former Soviet Union. The Clinton administration pursued an even more ambitious and explicitly articulated version of liberal multilateralism under various rubrics such as "enlargement" and "engagement."[21]

The new Bush administration speaks with a more mixed voice on grand strategy.[22] To be sure, it has reaffirmed basic aspects of the multilateral economic and security order and America's leadership position within it. It has moved forward aggressively with freer trade and investment in the Western hemisphere and called for a new round of global multilateral trade negotiations. But lurking in some quarters of the government is a deep skepticism about operating within a rule-based international order and a preference for unilateralism and selective engagement. "It is not isolationist but unilateralist, unashamed of using military power," one journalist notes.[23] It is a unilateral grand strategy that resists involvements in regional and multilateral entanglements that are deemed marginal to America's own security needs. It envisions American power acting in the world but not being entangled by it.

The most visible sign of this tendency was the dramatic sequence of Bush administration rejections of pending international agreements, including the Kyoto Protocol, the International Criminal Court, the Biological Weapons Convention, and UN action on the trade in small arms and light weapons. In pushing national missile defense, the administration has also signaled its willingness to withdraw from the 1972 Anti-Ballistic Missile Treaty, which many regard as the cornerstone of modern arms-control agreements. There is room for serious debate about the merits of various aspects of these agreements. But together the chorus of rejections underscore the misgivings the Bush administration has about multilateral and rule-based cooperation in general.[24]

The current administration is also retooling defense strategy in a way that will inevitably loosen alliance partnerships. The high-tech revolution in military capabilities will increasingly allow the United States to project force from the United States rather than from platforms in Europe, Asia, and the Middle East. These include more long-distance bombers, precision missiles, and space-based weapons. Missile defense – depending on which options are pursued – can also loosen alliance ties by making the United States more secure without a forward-based presence. Missile defense has been defended by some as a technology that will strengthen America's defense commitment to its European and Asian allies. If the United States feels secure from counter-attack from North Korea, they say, it is more likely to come to the defense of Japan and Korea. But in the longer term, a comprehensive national missile defense capacity will have the opposite effect: with its own homeland protected, American political leaders will be less certain why the United States needs to be spending money protecting people in faraway places.

The vision that lies behind this grand strategy and military posture is deeply rooted in old ideas about the country's place in the world – ideas that over the last 50 years have been pushed to the sidelines.[25] It is a vision of a country that is big enough, powerful enough, and remote enough to go it alone, free from the dangerous and corrupting conflicts festering in all the other regions of the world. It is a vision that is deeply suspicious of international rules and institutions. "It is the difference between those who would rely on lawyers to defend America and those who rely on engineers and scientists," observed Newt Gingrich, in explaining why his "Contract with America" included a commitment to national missile defense.[26] The dream that propels many missile-defense proponents is not a limited missile shield that might stop an errant missile launched by a rogue state, but a national shield that will abolish the postwar system of nuclear deterrence – based as it is on the ugly logic of mutual assured destruction.

The tension between the liberal multilateral and unilateral grand strategies has been heightened in the aftermath of September 11, but it has also been altered by these events. Richard Perle, the Bush administration's head of the Defense Policy Board at the Pentagon, suggested that there were real limits on a coalition-based approach to fighting terrorism: "It's wonderful to have the support of our friends and allies, but our foremost consideration has to be to protect this country and not take a vote among others as to how we should do it." When Perle's remark was brought to the attention of Secretary of State Colin Powell, he responded:

> I have not scheduled a vote for any members of this coalition to participate in. . . . But the President has made it very clear that the kinds of things that will probably be most successful in the campaign against terrorism are intelligence-sharing, controlling people going across borders, financial transactions and how to get at their financial systems. You can't do this, America alone. You need coalitions.[27]

This embrace of multilateralism does not mean that the United States submits itself fully to a rule-based order on an equilateral basis. In the American system, the United States accepts restraints on its power, but this is not the same as the absolute and across-the-board acceptance of formally binding rules. The restraint is manifest in more subtle ways that entail conducting foreign policy in a way that is sensitive to norms and processes of multilateral cooperation. Some administration officials – embracing unilateralist ideas – have bridled at the constraints that an alliance and coalition-based approach implies, particularly the limitations that it imposes on the countries and targets that the United States can go after. But the logic of the situation has strengthened the hand of those seeking to pursue American interests through multilateral and alliance-based tools.

It is unclear whether the Bush administration's discovery of the virtues of a multilateral coalition in fighting terrorism will spill over to its grand strategy. But there will be pressures and incentives for it to move back to a more general multilateral orientation. At least, it will be difficult for the US to ask for new forms of cooperation – intelligence, logistical support, political solidarity – from other states and resist their strongly-held views on missile defense, global warming, and other major issues. American unilateralism – exhibited in the first six months of the Bush term – was built on ideology and a practical reality. The ideology was a unilateral or imperial grand strategy embraced by a vocal and articulate group of officials. The practical reality was that the United States could in fact say no to agreements and not pay a huge price. Today, that ideology has not disappeared but it is less credible. The new practical reality is that the United States does want something from its partners, so it will need to give things in return.

To fight terrorism on a global scale, the Bush administration will need to rediscover the two bargains that the United States has made with the world. The realist bargain exchanges America's security support and access to markets and technology for the diplomatic and logistical support needed by the United States to pursue its geopolitical objectives. To fight terrorism effectively, the United States needs partners: the military and logistical support of allies, intelligence sharing, and the practical cooperation of front-line states. The transnational character of modern terrorism makes a national strategy impotent. Fighting terrorism entails tracing bank accounts and sharing criminal information and other basic tasks of transnational law enforcement. As Fareed Zakaria has indicated, "the crucial dimensions of the struggle are covert operations, intelligence gathering and police work. All of this requires the active cooperation of many other governments. US Marines cannot go into Hamburg and arrest suspects. We cannot shut down banks in the United Arab Emirates. We cannot get intelligence from Russia except if the Russians share it with us."[28] The simple logic of problem-solving moves the United States into the realm of multilateral, rule-based foreign policy. Aerial bombing may root out terrorists and destroy their camps, but the long-term demands of a campaign against terrorism is to work within and strengthen rules, laws, and institutions.

The liberal bargain also needs to be renewed. The United States obtains the cooperation of other states by offering to restrain and commit itself in return. To the surprise of many observers, the Bush administration did not rush the use of force after September 11, but waited while Secretary of State Powell built an informal coalition of support and defined the war aims in sufficiently precise and limited terms to keep other states on board. While reserving the right to act unilaterally, the United States signaled patience and restraint. There are practical incentives for the United States to do so. If the world perceives the war on terrorism to be between an arrogant and narrowly self-interested America and an aggrieved Islamic people, the war will be difficult to win. A war between the civilized, democratic world and murderous outlaws, on the other hand, can be won. Coalitions do not just aggregate power, they also legitimate it, particularly when they are organized around shared principles and values.

The Future of Great Power Cooperation

"One knows where a war begins but one never knows where it ends" – so remarked a diplomat looking back on the bloodiest war in history, the collapse of European empires, and the chaotic spectacle of Versailles, all of which seemed to follow from a single shot fired in Sarajevo in 1914. States rarely finish wars for the same reasons they start them. To build support for the waging of war, leaders need to define the struggle in terms that will make the sacrifice worthwhile. Leaders tend to promise that if their countrymen are willing to bear the burdens of war, a better world awaits on the other side. In the Atlantic Charter of 1941, Churchill and Roosevelt articulated ideas for war-weary Britain and war-wary America of a prosperous and stable peace built on a united community of nations. If history is a guide, the American-led war on terrorism will lead Western leaders to cast their actions in terms of broad principles and values which will in turn influence the response to future conflicts.

The war on terrorism is different from the great wars of the past, and likening it to the Cold War obscures as much as it reveals. In one sense, today's terrorism is more disturbing than the violence of past wars. If it is rooted in a clash between Western modernity and failed and threatened Islamic fundamentalism, the war will not end soon.[29] Wars between states are easier to understand, and if it is territory that is in dispute, they are easier to settle. In another sense, the struggle today is not a war at all, but is more like fighting organized crime. The solution is not deploying troops but traditional law enforcement. If this is true, the impact of this war will be primarily within societies, reshaping the balance between civil liberties and the reach of the state. Governments will have greater incentives to coordinate their domestic security and law-enforcement operations. They will also need to tackle the problems of failed states that harbor terrorists, promoting responsible regimes and the rule of law. This is an important agenda, but it does not evoke the memory of 1815, 1919, or 1945.

Nevertheless, the aftermath of September 11 will have important impacts beyond the immediate struggle with terrorism – impacts within the Western democratic world and between that world and the outside powers. The Bush administration's response to the attacks is illuminating the logic of the American order. In seeking partners in its struggle, the United States is rediscovering that the strategic partnerships it has built over the decades still exist and are useful. After NATO voted its support of the American campaign, Secretary of State Powell remarked that 50 years of steady investment in the alliance had paid off.[30] When the United States ties itself to a wider grouping of states it is more effective, but this requires some compromise of national autonomy. The US must both restrain and commit its power. The logic of this grand strategy is captured by Robert Jervis:

> Binding itself to act multilaterally by forgoing the capability to use large-scale force on its own would then provide a safeguard against the excessive use of American power. This might benefit all concerned: the United States would not be able to act on its own worst impulses; others would share the

costs of interventions and would also be less fearful of the United States and so, perhaps, more prone to cooperate with it.[31]

The struggle between unilateral and multilateral grand strategies today is a debate over the costs and benefits of binding American power to wider alliance and global groupings. The United States may give up some discretion, but it gains partners. The coalition-based struggle against terrorism is providing an object lesson in how best to strike the balance.

The American system is encouraging this collaborative approach to terrorism. European and other world leaders trooped into Washington in the weeks following the September 11 attacks. Each offered its support but also weighed in on how best to wage the coming campaign. The actions of Prime Minister Tony Blair exemplify this strategy of engaging America. The British leader has tied himself to the American anti-terrorist plan but in doing so, he has made it an Anglo-American – and even alliance-based – campaign. By binding itself to the superpower, Britain gains a stake in the struggle but also a voice in the policy. America's allies are surely hoping that the administration's new-found embrace of multilateralism is not a single-issue affair. At least for now, post-September 11 allied diplomacy shows the dynamic character of the American system: the United States has ready friends and America's allies have ready access to American decision-making. Allied interactions tend to moderate policy, soften the sharp edges of allied disagreements, and move the countries toward a more concerted strategy.

The American campaign against terrorism is also changing the wider terms of great power cooperation. Russian President Vladimir Putin is the best example of a leader seeking to exploit this new opportunity to bargain. By throwing his support to the American cause, he is opening the way for support and accommodation by the United States on a range of issues crucial to the Russian agenda: economic aid, Chechnya, NATO expansion, and missile defense. Prior to September 11, the United States had been seeking to recast its strategic relationship with Russia. While the Bush strategy has been to offer that strategic relationship in exchange for accommodation on missile defense, the ultimate result might be some more expansive form of cooperative security between Russia and the West. Indeed, Russian cooperation on terrorism may in the long run strengthen the argument that Russia should be brought fully into the Western security framework, including perhaps NATO membership.[32] China is more quiet but it too may find ways to exchange its support of the American anti-terrorist campaign for a stable policy of engagement by the United States. This was the first call to arms by an American president where the enemy was not another great power, or a totalitarian ideology linked to a great power. This new transnational threat offers incentives to deepen strategic cooperation among all the great powers.

All this could go sour. The United States could decide that its desire to oppose terrorist regimes such as Iraq was more important than maintaining the coalition. In this case it might use force in a way that split the allies into fragmented groups each seeking a separate settlement. The United States could also return to its unilateral ways on other issues, allowing the deep disagreements and latent antagonisms between America and Europe – currently not visible because of the temporary united front against terrorism – to break out into the open. The deals that the United States and its allies make with repressive regimes in the Middle East and South Asia could also come back to haunt the Western democracies by undercutting the credibility of the West's commitment to democracy and human rights and creating locales for breeding the next generation of terrorists.

Yet overall, the events of September 11 do not seem to signal the unraveling of the old international order. The Bush administration is launching its war on terrorism from a foundation of stable and cooperative relations built over many decades. It may well be that historians remember the global response to September 11 more than those dramatic events themselves. Certainly the terrorist events present the United States, Europe, and other states with an opportunity to renew and expand the political bargains on which the current international order rests.

Notes

1 See Steven Mufson, "Foreign Policy's Pivotal Moment," *The Washington Post*, September 27, 2001; Joel Garreau, "Hinges of Opportunity," *The Washington Post*, October 14, 2001.
2 See for example, Steven Erlanger, "In Europe, Some Say the Attacks Stemmed from American Failings," *The New York Times*, September 22, 2001; and Elaine Sciolino, "Who Hates the US? Who Loves It?" *The New York Times*, September 23, 2001. For imperial views of American power, see Chalmers Johnson, *Blowback: The Costs and Consequences of American Empire* (New York: Henry Holt and Co., 2000); and Michael Hardt and Antonio Negri, *Empire* (Cambridge, Mass.: Harvard University Press, 2000).
3 For descriptions of this democratic core, see Daniel Deudney and G. John Ikenberry, "The Nature and Sources of Liberal International Order," *Review of International Studies* 25 (Spring 1999); Bruce Cumings, "Trilateralism and the New World Order," *World Policy Journal* 8: 3 (Spring 1991): 195–222; James M. Goldgeier and Michael MacFaul, "A Tale of Two Worlds: Core and Periphery in the Post-Cold War Era," *International Organization* 46 (Spring 1992): 467–91; and Richard L. Kugler, "Controlling Chaos: New

Axial Strategic Principles." in Kugler and Ellen L. Frost, eds., *The Global Century: Globalization and National Security* (Washington, DC: National Defense University Press, 2000), vol. 1, pp. 75–107.

4 See Kenneth Waltz, "The Emerging Structure of International Politics," *International Security* 18: 2 (Fall 1993); Waltz, "Structural Realism after the Cold War," *International Security* 25: 1 (Summer 2000); John J. Mearsheimer, "Back to the Future: Instability of Europe After the Cold War," *International Security* 15 (Summer 1990): 5–57; Mearsheimer, "Why We Will Soon Miss the Cold War," *The Atlantic* 266 (August 1990): 35–50; Christopher Layne, "The Unipolar Illusion: Why New Great Powers Will Arise," *International Security* 17: 4 (Spring 1993): 5–51; and Christopher Layne, "What's Built Up Must Come Down," *The Washington Post*, November 14, 1999. For a new statement of this view, see John J. Mearsheimer, *The Tragedy of Great Power Politics* (New York: W. W. Norton, 2001).

5 Charles A. Kupchan, "After Pax Americana: Benign Power, Regional Integration, and the Sources of Stable Multipolarity," *International Security* 23: 3 (Fall 1998): 40–79.

6 See Charles Kupchan, "Fractured US Resolve," *The Washington Post*, Outlook Section, June 13, 1999, pp. B1, B4.

7 For one version of coming regional economic conflict, see Lester Thurow, *Head to Head: The Coming Economic Battle among Japan, Europe, and America* (New York: William Morrow and Company, 1992).

8 Chalmers Johnson, "History Restarted: Japanese–American Relations at the End of the Century," in Johnson, *Japan: Who Governs? The Rise of the Developmental State* (New York: Norton, 1995).

9 Robert Jervis, "America and the Twentieth Century: Continuity and Change," in Michael J. Hogan, ed., *The Ambiguous Legacy: US Foreign Relations in the "American Century"* (New York: Cambridge University Press, 1999), p. 100.

10 John Lewis Gaddis, *Strategies of Containment: A Critical Appraisal of Postwar American National Security Policy* (New York: Oxford University Press, 1982), p. 4.

11 See Mary N. Hampton, "NATO at the Creation: US Foreign Policy, West Germany, and the Wilsonian Impulse," *Security Studies* 4: 3 (Spring 1995): 610–56; and Hampton, *The Wilsonian Impulse: US Foreign Policy, the Alliance, and German Unification* (Westport, Conn.: Praeger, 1996).

12 On the complex, ambivalent, and evolving American thinking on its postwar security commitment to Europe, see Marc Trachtenberg, *A Constructed Peace: The Making of the European Settlement, 1945–1963* (Princeton: Princeton University Press, 1999); and Melvin Leffler, *A Preponderance of Power: National Security, The Truman Administration, and the Cold War* (Stanford: Stanford University Press, 1992).

13 This argument is developed in G. John Ikenberry, *After Victory: Institutions, Strategic Restraint, and the Rebuilding of Order after Major War* (Princeton: Princeton University Press, 2001).

14 For discussion of security dilemmas, see John Herz, "Idealist Internationalism and the Security Dilemma," *World Politics* 2 (1949/50);

and Robert Jervis, "Cooperation under the Security Dilemma," *World Politics* 30 (1978): 167–214.

15 World Bank figures cited in Gerard Baker, "Liberty's Triumph," *The Financial Times*, December 23, 1999.

16 On global power disparities and America's pre-eminent position, see William Wohlforth, "The Stability of a Unipolar World," *International Security* 24: 1 (Summer 1999): 5–41.

17 See Bruce Russett and John O'Neal, *Triangulating Peace: Democracy, Interdependence, and International Organizations* (New York: Norton, 2001).

18 John Lewis Gaddis, *We Now Know: Rethinking Cold War History* (New York: Oxford University Press, 1997), p. 50.

19 A large and growing literature has emerged on American grand strategy. For surveys, see Barry R. Posen and Andrew L. Ross, "Competing Visions for US Grand Strategy," *International Security* 21: 3 (Winter 1996–7); and G. John Ikenberry, ed., *American Unrivalled: The Future of the Balance of Power* (Ithaca: Cornell University Press, 2002).

20 James A. Baker, *The Politics of Diplomacy: Revolution, War and Peace 1989–92* (New York: G. P. Putnam's Sons, 1995), pp. 605–6.

21 See White House, *A National Security Strategy of Engagement and Enlargement* (Washington, DC: White House, July 1994).

22 The US State Department's Director of Policy Planning, Richard Haass, has coined the term "à la carte multilateralism" to describe the administration's approach, but important differences in thinking exist across the administration. See Thom Shanker, "White House Says the US is Not a Loner, Just Choosy," *The New York Times*, July 31, 2001.

23 Stephen Fidler, "Between Two Camps," *Financial Times*, February 14, 2001.

24 See Gerard Baker, "Bush Heralds Era of US Self-Interest," *International Herald Tribune*, April 24, 2001.

25 See Thomas E. Ricks, "US Urged to Embrace an 'Imperial' Role," *International Herald Tribune*, August 22, 2001.

26 Stephen Fidler, "Conservatives Determined to Carry Torch for US Missile Defence," *Financial Times*, July 11, 2001.

27 Secretary of State Powell, National Public Radio Interview, October 27, 2001.

28 Fareed Zakaria, "Back to the Real World," *The Washington Post*, October 2, 2001.

29 See Martin Wolf, "The Economic Failure of Islam," *Financial Times*, September 26, 2001.

30 Secretary Colin Powell, public statement, October 10, 2001.

31 Robert Jervis, "International Primacy: Is the Game Worth the Candle?" *International Security* 17 (1993): 66.

32 See Quentin Peel, "Washington's Balancing Act," *Financial Times*, October 1, 2001; and Timothy Garton Ash, "A New War Reshapes Old Alliances," *The New York Times*, October 12, 2001.

9

America's Imperial Ambition

The Lures of Pre-emption

In the shadows of the Bush administration's war on terrorism, sweeping new ideas are circulating about US grand strategy and the restructuring of today's unipolar world. They call for American unilateral and pre-emptive, even preventive, use of force, facilitated if possible by coalitions of the willing – but ultimately unconstrained by the rules and norms of the international community. At the extreme, these notions form a neo-imperial vision in which the United States arrogates to itself the global role of setting standards, determining threats, using force, and meting out justice. It is a vision in which sovereignty becomes more absolute for America even as it becomes more conditional for countries that challenge Washington's standards of internal and external behavior. It is a vision made necessary – at least in the eyes of its advocates – by the new and apocalyptic character of contemporary terrorist threats and by America's unprecedented global dominance. These radical strategic ideas and impulses could transform today's world order in a way that the end of the Cold War, strangely enough, did not.

The exigencies of fighting terrorism in Afghanistan and the debate over intervening in Iraq obscure the profundity of this geopolitical challenge. Blueprints have not been produced, and Yalta-style summits have not been convened, but actions are afoot to dramatically alter the political order that the United States has built with its partners since the 1940s. The twin new realities of our age – catastrophic terrorism and American unipolar power – do necessitate a rethinking of the organizing principles of international order. America and the other major states do need a new consensus on terrorist threats, weapons of mass destruction (WMD), the use of force, and the global rules of the game. This imperative requires a better appreciation of the ideas coming out of the administration. But in turn, the administration should understand the virtues of the old order that it wishes to displace.

America's nascent neo-imperial grand strategy threatens to rend the fabric of the international community and political partnerships precisely at a time when that community and those partnerships are urgently needed. It is an approach fraught with peril and likely to fail. It is not only politically unsustainable but diplomatically harmful. And if history is a guide, it will trigger antagonism and resistance that will leave America in a more hostile and divided world.

Proven Legacies

The mainstream of American foreign policy has been defined since the 1940s by two grand strategies that have built the modern international order. One is realist in orientation, organized around containment, deterrence, and the maintenance of the global balance of power. Facing a dangerous and expansive Soviet Union after 1945, the United States stepped forward to fill the vacuum left by a waning British Empire and a collapsing European order to provided a counterweight to Stalin and his Red Army.

The touchstone of this strategy was containment, which sought to deny the Soviet Union the ability to expand its sphere of influence. Order was maintained by managing the bipolar balance between the American and Soviet camps. Stability was achieved through nuclear deterrence. For the first time, nuclear weapons and the doctrine of mutual assured destruction made war between the great powers irrational. But containment and global power-balancing ended with the collapse of the Soviet Union in 1991. Nuclear deterrence is no longer the defining logic of the existing order, although it remains a recessed feature that continues to impart stability in relations among China, Russia, and the West.

This strategy has yielded a bounty of institutions and partnerships for America. The most important have been the NATO and US–Japan alliances, American-led security partnerships that have survived the end of the Cold War by providing a bulwark for stability through commitment and reassurance. The United States maintains a forward presence in Europe and East Asia; its alliance partners gain security protection as well as a measure of regularity in their relationship with the world's leading military power. But Cold War balancing has yielded more than a utilitarian alliance structure; it has generated a political order that has value in itself.

This grand strategy presupposes a loose framework of consultations and agreements to resolve differences: the great powers extend to each other the respect of equals, and they accommodate each other until vital interests come into play. The domestic affairs of these states remain precisely that – domestic. The great powers compete with each other, and although war is not unthinkable, sober statecraft and the balance of power offer the best hope for stability and peace.

George W. Bush ran for president emphasizing some of these themes, describing his approach to foreign policy as "new realism": the focus of American efforts should shift away from Clinton-era preoccupations with nation building, international social work, and the promiscuous use of force, and toward cultivating great power relations and rebuilding the nation's military. Bush's efforts to integrate Russia into the Western security order have been the most important manifestation of this realist grand strategy at work. The moderation in Washington's confrontational rhetoric toward China also reflects this emphasis. If the major European and Asian states play by the rules, the great power order will remain stable. (In a way, it is precisely because Europe is not a great power – or at least seems to eschew the logic of great power politics – that it is now generating so much discord with the United States.)

The other grand strategy, forged during World War II as the United States planned the reconstruction of the world economy, is liberal in orientation. It seeks to build order around institutionalized political relations among integrated market democracies, supported by an opening of economies. This agenda was not simply an inspiration of American businessmen and economists, however. There have always been geopolitical goals as well. Whereas America's realist grand strategy was aimed at countering Soviet power, its liberal grand strategy was aimed at avoiding a return to the 1930s, an era of regional blocs, trade conflict, and strategic rivalry. Open trade, democracy, and multilateral institutional relations went together. Underlying this strategy was the view that a rule-based international order, especially one in which the United States uses its political weight to derive congenial rules, will most fully protect American interests, conserve its power, and extend its influence.

This grand strategy has been pursued through an array of postwar initiatives that look disarmingly like "low politics": the Bretton Woods institutions, the World Trade Organization (WTO), and the Organization for Economic Cooperation and Development are just a few examples. Together, they form a complex layer cake of integrative initiatives that bind the democratic industrialized world together. During the 1990s, the United States continued to pursue this liberal grand strategy. Both the first Bush and the Clinton administrations attempted to articulate a vision of world order that was not dependent on an external threat or an explicit policy of balance of power. Bush the elder talked about the importance of the transatlantic community and articulated ideas about a more fully integrated Asia-Pacific region. In both cases, the strategy offered a positive vision of alliance and partnership built around common values, tradition, mutual self-interest, and the preservation of stability. The Clinton administration likewise attempted to describe the post Cold War order in terms of the expansion of democracy and open markets. In this vision, democracy provided the foundation for global and regional community, and trade and capital flows were forces for political reform and integration.

The current Bush administration is not eager to brandish this Clinton-looking grand strategy, but it still invokes that strategy's ideas in various ways. Support for Chinese entry into the WTO is based on the liberal anticipation that free markets and integration into the Western economic order will create pressures for Chinese political reform and discourage a belligerent foreign policy. Administration support for last year's multilateral trade-negotiating round in Doha, Qatar, also was premised on the economic and political benefits of freer trade. After September 11, US Trade Representative Robert Zoellick even linked trade expansion authority to the fight against terrorism: trade, growth, integration, and political stability go together.

Richard Haass, policy planning director at the State Department, argued recently that "the principal aim of American foreign policy is to integrate other countries and organizations into arrangements that will sustain a world consistent with US interests and values" – again, an echo of the liberal grand strategy. The administration's recent protectionist trade actions in steel and agriculture have triggered such a loud outcry around the world precisely because governments are worried that the United States might be retreating from this postwar liberal strategy.

America's Historic Bargains

These two grand strategies are rooted in divergent, even antagonistic, intellectual tradition. But over the last 50 years they have worked remarkably well together. The realist grand strategy created a political rationale for establishing major security commitments around the world. The liberal strategy created a positive agenda for American leadership. The United States could exercise its power and achieve its national interests, but it did so in a way that helped deepen the fabric of international community. American power did not destabilize world order; it helped create it. The development of rule-based agreements and political-security partnerships was good both for the United States and for much of the world. By the end of the 1990s, the result was an international political order of unprecedented size and success: a global coalition of democratic states tied together through markets, institutions, and security partnerships.

This international order was built on two historic bargains. One was the US commitment to provide its European and Asian partners with security protection and access to American markets, technology, and supplies within an open world economy. In return, these countries agreed to be reliable partners providing diplomatic, economic, and logistical support for the United States as it led the wider Western postwar order. The other is the liberal bargain that addressed the uncertainties of American power. East Asian and European states agreed to accept American leadership and operate within an agreed-upon political-economic system. The United States, in response, opened itself up and bound itself to its partners. In effect, the United States built an institutionalized coalition of partners and reinforced the stability of these mutually beneficial relations by making itself more "user-friendly" – that is, by playing by the rules and creating ongoing political processes that facilitated consultation and joint decision-making. The United States made its power safe for the world, and in return the world agreed to live within the US system. These bargains date from the 1940s, but they continue to shore up the post-Cold War order. The result has been the most stable and prosperous international system in world history. But new ideas within the Bush administration – crystallized by September 11 and US dominance – are unsettling this order and the political bargains behind it.

A New Grand Strategy

For the first time since the dawn of the Cold War, a new grand strategy is taking shape in Washington. It is advanced most directly as a response to terrorism, but it also constitutes a broader view about how the United States should wield power and organize world order. According to this new paradigm, America is to be less bound to its partners and to global rules and institutions while it steps forward to play a more unilateral and anticipatory role in attacking terrorist threats and confronting rogue states seeking WMD. The United States will use its unrivaled military power to manage the global order.

This new grand strategy has seven elements. It begins with a fundamental commitment to maintaining a unipolar world in which the United States has no peer competitor. No coalition of great powers without the United States will be allowed to achieve hegemony. Bush made this point the centerpiece of American security policy in his West Point commencement address in June: "America has, and intends to keep, military strengths beyond challenges – thereby making the destabilizing arms races of other eras pointless, and limiting rivalries to trade and other pursuits of peace." The United States will not seek security through the more modest realist strategy of operating within a global system of power balancing, nor will it pursue a liberal strategy in which institutions, democracy, and integrated markets reduce the importance of power politics altogether. America will be so much more powerful than other major states that strategic rivalries and security competition among the great powers will disappear, leaving everyone – not just the United States – better off.

This goal made an unsettling early appearance at the end of the first Bush administration in a leaked Pentagon memorandum written by then Assistant Secretary of Defense Paul Wolfowitz. With the collapse of the Soviet Union, he wrote, the United States must act to prevent the rise of peer competitors in Europe and Asia. But the 1990s made this strategic aim moot. The United States grew faster than the other major states during the decade, it reduced military spending more slowly, and it dominated investment in the technological advancement of its forces. Today, however, the new goal is to make these advantages permanent – a *fait accompli* that will prompt other states to not even try to catch up. Some thinkers have described the strategy as "breakout," in which the United States moves so quickly to develop technological advantages (in robotics, lasers, satellites, precision munitions, etc.) that no state or coalition could ever challenge it as global leader, protector, and enforcer.

The second element is a dramatic new analysis of global threats and how they must be attacked. The grim new reality is that small groups of terrorists – perhaps aided by outlaw states – may soon acquire highly destructive nuclear, chemical, and biological weapons that can inflict catastrophic destruction. These terrorist groups cannot be appeased or deterred, the administration believes, so they must be eliminated. Secretary of Defense Donald Rumsfeld has articulated this frightening view with elegance: regarding the threats that confront the United States, he said, "There are things we know that we know. There are known unknowns. That is to say, there are things that we know we don't know. But there are also unknown unknowns. There are things we don't know we don't know. . . . Each year, we discover a few more of those unknown unknowns." In other words, there could exist groups of terrorists that no one knows about. They may have nuclear, chemical, or biological weapons that the United States did not know they could get, and they might be willing and able to attack without warning. In the age of terror, there is less room for error. Small networks of angry people can inflict unimaginable harm on the rest of the world. They are not nation-states, and they do not play by the accepted rules of the game.

The third element of the new strategy maintains that the Cold War concept of deterrence is outdated. Deterrence, sovereignty, and the balance of power work together. When deterrence is no longer viable, the larger realist edifice starts to crumble. The threat today is not other great powers that must be managed through second-strike nuclear capacity, but the transnational terrorist networks that have no home address. They cannot be deterred because they are either willing to die for their cause or able to escape retaliation. The old defensive strategy of building missiles and other weapons that can survive a first strike and be used in a retaliatory strike to punish the attacker will no longer ensure security. The only option, then, is offense.

The use of force, this camp argues, will therefore need to be pre-emptive and perhaps even preventive – taking on potential threats before they can present a major problem. But this premise plays havoc with the old international rules of self-defense and United Nations norms about the proper use of force. Rumsfeld has articulated the justification for pre-emptive action by stating that the "absence of evidence is not evidence of absence of weapons of mass destruction." But such an approach renders international norms of self-defense – enshrined by Article 51 of the UN Charter – almost meaningless. The administration should remember that when Israeli jets bombed the Iraqi nuclear reactor at Osirak in 1981 in what Israel described as an act of self-defense, the world condemned it as an act of aggression. Even British Prime Minister Margaret Thatcher and the American ambassador to the UN Jeane Kirkpatrick criticized the action, and the United States joined in passing a UN resolution condemning it.

The Bush administration's security doctrine takes this country down the same slippery slope. Even without a clear threat, the United States now claims a right to use pre-emptive or preventive military force. At West Point, Bush put it succinctly when he stated that "the military must be ready to strike at a moment's notice in any dark corner of the world. All nations that decide for aggression and terror will pay a price." The administration defends this new doctrine as a necessary adjustment to a more uncertain and shifting threat environment. This policy of no regrets errs on the side of action – but it can also easily become national security by hunch or inference, leaving the world without clear-cut norms for justifying force.

As a result, the fourth element of this emerging grand strategy involves a recasting of the terms of sovereignty. Because these terrorist groups cannot be deterred, the United States must be prepared to intervene anywhere, anytime to pre-emptively destroy the threat. Terrorists do not respect borders, so neither can the United States. Moreover, countries that harbor terrorists, either by consent or because they are unable to enforce their laws within their territory, effectively forfeit their rights of sovereignty. Haass recently hinted at this notion in *The New Yorker*:

> What you are seeing in this administration is the emergence of a new principle or body of ideas . . . about what you might call the limits of sovereignty. Sovereignty entails obligations. One is not to massacre your own people. Another is not to support terrorism in any way. If a government fails to meet these obligations, then it forfeits some of the normal advantages of sovereignty, including the right to be left alone inside your own territory. Other governments, including the United States, gain the right to intervene. In the case of terrorism, this can even lead to a right of preventive . . . self-defense. You essentially can act in anticipation if you have grounds to think it's a question of when, and not if, you're going to be attacked.

Here the war on terrorism and the problem of the proliferation of WMD get entangled. The worry is that a few despotic states – Iraq in particular, but also Iran and North Korea – will develop capabilities to produce weapons of mass destruction and put these weapons in the hands of terrorists. The regimes themselves may be deterred from using such capabilities, but they might pass along these weapons to terrorist networks that are not deterred. Thus another emerging principle within the Bush administration: the possession of WMD by unaccountable, unfriendly, despotic governments is itself a threat that must be countered. In the old era, despotic regimes were to be lamented but ultimately tolerated. With the rise of terrorism and weapons of mass destruction, they are now unacceptable threats. Thus states that are not technically in violation of any existing international laws could nevertheless be targets of American force – if Washington determines that they have a prospective capacity to do harm.

The recasting of sovereignty is paradoxical. On the one hand, the new grand strategy reaffirms the importance of the territorial nation-state. After all, if all governments were accountable and capable of enforcing the rule of law within their sovereign territory, terrorists would find it very difficult to operate. The emerging Bush doctrine enshrines this idea: governments will be held responsible for what goes on inside their borders. On the other hand, sovereignty has been made newly conditional: governments that fail to act like respectable, law-abiding states will lose their sovereignty.

In one sense, such conditional sovereignty is not new. Great powers have willfully transgressed the norms of state sovereignty as far back as such norms have existed, particularly within their traditional spheres of influence, whenever the national interest dictated. The United States itself has done this within the Western hemisphere since the nineteenth century. What is new and provocative in this notion today, however, is the Bush administration's inclination to apply it on a global basis, leaving to itself the authority to determine when sovereign rights have been forfeited, and doing so on an anticipatory basis.

The fifth element of this new grand strategy is a general depreciation of international rules, treaties, and security partnerships. This point relates to the new threats themselves: if the stakes are rising and the margins of error are shrinking in the war on terrorism, multilateral norms and agreements that sanction and limit the use of force are just annoying distractions. The critical task is to eliminate the threat. But the emerging unilateral strategy is also informed by a deeper suspicion about the value of international agreements themselves. Part of this view arises from a deeply felt and authentically held American belief that the United States should not get entangled in the corrupting and constraining world of multilateral rules and institutions. For some Americans, the belief that American sovereignty is politically sacred leads to a preference for isolationism. But the more influential view – particularly after September 11 – is not that the United States should withdraw from the world but that it should operate in the world on its own terms. The Bush administration's repudiation of a remarkable array of treaties and institutions – from the Kyoto Protocol on global warming to the International Criminal Court to the Biological Weapons Convention – reflects this new bias. Likewise, the United States signed a formal agreement with Russia on the reduction of deployed nuclear warheads only after Moscow's insistence; the Bush administration wanted only a "gentlemen's agreement." In other words, the United States has decided it is big enough, powerful enough, and remote enough to go it alone.

Sixth, the new grand strategy argues that the United States will need to play a direct and unconstrained role in responding to threats. This conviction is partially based on a judgment that no other country or coalition – even the European Union – has the force-projection capabilities to respond to terrorist and rogue states around the world. A decade of US defense spending and modernization has left allies of the United States far behind. In combat operations, alliance partners are increasingly finding it difficult to mesh with US forces. This view is also based on the judgment that joint operations and the use of force through coalitions tend to hinder effective operations. To some observers, this lesson became clear in the allied bombing campaign over Kosovo. The sentiment was also expressed during the US and allied military actions in Afghanistan. Rumsfeld explained this point earlier this year, when he said, "The mission must determine the coalition; the coalition must not determine the mission. If it does, the mission will be dumbed down to the lowest common denominator, and we can't afford that."

No one in the Bush administration argues that NATO or the US–Japan alliance should be dismantled. Rather, these alliances are now seen as less useful to the United States as it confronts today's threats. Some officials argue that it is not that the United States chooses to depreciate alliance partnerships, but that the Europeans are unwilling to keep up. Whether that is true, the upgrading of the American military, along with its sheer size relative to the forces of the rest of the world, leaves the United States in a class by itself. In these circumstances, it is increasingly difficult to maintain the illusion of true alliance partnership. America's allies become merely strategic assets that are useful depending on the circumstance. The United States still finds attractive the logistical reach that its global alliance system provides, but the pacts with countries in Asia and Europe become more contingent and less premised on a vision of a common security community.

Finally, the new grand strategy attaches little value to international stability. There is an unsentimental view in the unilateralist camp that the traditions of the past must be shed. Whether it is withdrawal from the Anti-Ballistic Missile Treaty or the resistance to signing other formal arms-control treaties, policy-makers are convinced that the United States needs to move beyond outmoded Cold War thinking. Administration officials have noted with some satisfaction that America's withdrawal from the ABM Treaty did not lead to a global arms race but actually paved the way for a historic arms-reduction agreement between the United States and Russia. This move is seen as a validation that moving beyond the old paradigm of great power relations will not bring the international house down. The world can withstand radically new security approaches, and it will accommodate American unilateralism as well. But stability is not an end in itself. The administration's new hawkish policy toward North Korea, for example, might be destabilizing to the region, but such instability might be the necessary price for dislodging a dangerous and evil regime in Pyongyang.

In this brave new world, neo-imperial thinkers contend that the older realist and liberal grand strategies are not very helpful. American security will not be ensured, as realist grand strategy assumes, by the preservation of deterrence and stable relations among the major powers. In a world of asymmetrical threats, the global balance of power is not the linchpin of war and peace. Likewise, liberal strategies of building order around open trade and democratic institutions might have some long-term impact on terrorism, but they do not address the immediacy of the threats. Apocalyptic violence is at our doorstep, so efforts at strengthening the rules and institutions of the international community are of little practical value. If we accept the worst-case imagining of "we don't know what we don't know," everything else is secondary: international rules, traditions of partnership, and standards of legitimacy. It is a war. And as Clausewitz famously remarked, "War is such a dangerous business that the mistakes which come from kindness are the very worst."

Imperial Dangers

Pitfalls accompany this neo-imperial grand strategy, however. Unchecked US power, shorn of legitimacy and disentangled from the postwar norms and institutions of the international order, will usher in a more hostile international system, making it far harder to achieve American interests. The secret of the United States' long brilliant run as the world's leading state was its ability and willingness to exercise power within alliance and multinational frameworks, which made its power and agenda more acceptable to allies and other key states around the world. This achievement has now been put at risk by the administration's new thinking.

The most immediate problem is that the neo-imperialist approach is unsustainable. Going it alone might well succeed in removing Saddam Hussein from power, but it is far less certain that a strategy of counter-proliferation, based on American willingness to use unilateral force to confront dangerous dictators, can work over the long term. An American policy that leaves the United States alone to decide which states are threats and how best to deny them weapons of mass destruction will lead to a diminishment of multilateral mechanisms – most important of which is the nonproliferation regime.

The Bush administration has elevated the threat of WMD to the top of its security agenda without investing its power or prestige in fostering, monitoring, and enforcing nonproliferation commitments. The tragedy of September 11 has given the Bush administration the authority and willingness to confront the Iraqs of the world. But that will not be enough when even more complicated cases come along – when it is not the use of force that is needed but concerted multilateral action to provide sanctions and inspections. Nor is it certain that a pre-emptive or preventive military intervention will go well; it might trigger a domestic political backlash to American-led and military-focused interventionism. America's well-meaning imperial strategy could undermine the principled multilateral agreements, institutional infrastructure, and cooperative spirit needed for the long-term success of nonproliferation goals.

The specific doctrine of pre-emptive action poses a related problem: once the United States feels it can take such a course, nothing will stop other countries from doing the same. Does the United States want this doctrine in the hands of Pakistan, or even China or Russia? After all, it would not require the intervening state to first provide evidence for its actions. The United States argues that to wait until all the evidence is in, or until authoritative international bodies support action, is to wait too long. Yet that approach is the only basis that the United States can use if it needs to appeal for restraint in the actions of others. Moreover, and quite paradoxically, overwhelming American conventional military might, combined with a policy of pre-emptive strikes, could lead hostile states to accelerate programs to acquire their only possible deterrent to the United States: WMD. This is another version of the security dilemma, but one made worse by a neo-imperial grand strategy.

Another problem follows. The use of force to eliminate WMD capabilities or overturn dangerous regimes is never simple, whether it is pursued unilaterally or by a concert of major states. After the military intervention is over, the target country has to be put back together. Peacekeeping and state building are inevitably required, as are long-term strategies that bring the UN, the World Bank, and the major powers together to orchestrate aid and other forms of assistance. This is not heroic work, but it is utterly necessary. Peacekeeping troops may be required for many years, even after a new regime is built. Regional conflicts inflamed by outside military intervention must also be calmed. This is the "long tail" of burdens and commitments that comes with every major military action.

When these costs and obligations are added to America's imperial military role, it becomes even more doubtful that the neo-imperial strategy can be sustained at home over the long haul – the classic problem of imperial overstretch. The United States could keep its military predominance for decades if it is supported by a growing and increasingly productive economy. But the indirect burdens of cleaning up the political mess in terrorist-prone failed states levy a hidden cost. Peacekeeping and state building will require coalitions of states and multilateral agencies that can be brought into the process only if the initial decisions about military intervention are hammered out in consultation with other major states. America's older realist and liberal grand strategies suddenly become relevant again.

A third problem with an imperial grand strategy is that it cannot generate the cooperation needed to solve practical problems at the heart of the US foreign policy agenda. In the fight on terrorism, the United States needs cooperation from European and Asian countries in intelligence, law enforcement, and logistics. Outside the security sphere, realizing US objectives depends even more on a continuous stream of amicable working relations with major states around the world. It needs partners for trade liberalization, global financial stabilization, environmental protection, deterring transnational organized crime, managing the rise of China, and a host of other thorny challenges. But it is impossible to expect would-be partners to acquiesce to America's self-appointed global security protectorate and then pursue business as usual in all other domains.

The key policy tool for states confronting a unipolar and unilateral America is to withhold cooperation in day-to-day relations with the United States. One obvious means is trade policy; the European response to the recent American decision to impose tariffs on imported steel is explicable in these terms. This particular struggle concerns specific trade issues, but it is also a struggle over how Washington exercises power. The United States may be a unipolar military power, but economic and political power is more evenly distributed across the globe. The major states may not have much leverage in directly restraining American military policy, but they can make the United States pay a price in other areas.

Finally, the neo-imperial grand strategy poses a wider problem for the maintenance of American unipolar power. It steps into the oldest trap of powerful imperial states: self-encirclement. When the most powerful state in the world throws its weight around, unconstrained by rules or norms of legitimacy, it risks a backlash. Other countries will bridle at an international order in which the United States plays only by its own rules. The proponents of the new grand strategy have assumed that the United States can single-handedly deploy military power abroad and not suffer untoward consequences; relations will be coarser with friends and allies, they believe, but such are the costs of leadership. But history shows that powerful states tend to trigger self-encirclement by their own overestimation of their power. Charles V, Louis XIV, Napoleon, and the leaders of post-Bismarck Germany sought to expand their imperial domains and impose a coercive order on others. Their imperial orders were all brought down when other countries decided they were not prepared to live in a world dominated by an overweening coercive state. America's imperial goals and *modus operandi* are much more limited and benign than were those of age-old emperors. But a hard-line imperial grand strategy runs the risk that history will repeat itself.

Bring in the Old

Wars change world politics, and so too will America's war on terrorism. How great states fight wars, how they define the stakes, how they make the peace in its aftermath – all give lasting shape to the international system that emerges after the guns fall silent. In mobilizing their societies for battle, wartime leaders have tended to describe the military struggle as more than simply the defeat of an enemy. Woodrow Wilson sent US troops to Europe not only to stop the kaiser's army but to destroy militarism and usher in a worldwide democratic revolution. Franklin Roosevelt saw the war with Germany and Japan as a struggle to secure the "four great freedoms." The Atlantic Charter was a statement of war aims that called not just for the defeat of fascism but for a new dedication to social welfare and human rights within an open and stable world system. To advance these visions, Wilson and Roosevelt proposed new international rules and mechanisms of cooperation. Their message was clear: If you bear the burdens of war, we, your leaders, will use this dreadful conflict to usher in a more peaceful and decent order among states. Fighting the war had as much to do with building global relations as it did with vanquishing an enemy.

Bush has not fully articulated a vision of postwar international order, aside from defining the struggle as one between freedom and evil. The world has seen Washington take determined steps to fight terrorism, but it does not yet have a sense of Bush's larger, positive agenda for a strengthened and more decent international order.

This failure explains why the sympathy and goodwill generated around the world for the United States after September 11 quickly disappeared. Newspapers that once proclaimed, "We are all Americans," now express distrust toward America. The prevailing view is that the United States seems prepared to use its power to go after terrorists and evil regimes, but not to use it to help build a more stable and peaceful world order. The United States appears to be degrading the rules and institutions of international community, not enhancing them. To the rest of world, neo-imperial thinking has more to do with exercising power than with exercising leadership.

In contrast, America's older strategic orientations – balance-of-power realism and liberal multilateralism – suggest a mature world power that seeks stability and pursues its interests in ways that do not fundamentally threaten the positions of other states. They are strategies of co-option and reassurance. The new imperial grand strategy presents the United States very differently: a revisionist state seeking to parlay its momentary power advantages into a world order in which it runs the show. Unlike the hegemonic states of the past, the United States does not seek territory or outright political domination in Europe or Asia; "America has no empire to extend or utopia to establish," Bush noted in his West Point address. But the sheer power advantages that the United States possesses and the

228 Unipolarity and Multilateralism

doctrines of pre-emption and counter-terrorism that it is articulating do unsettle governments and people around the world. The costs could be high. The last thing the United States wants is for foreign diplomats and government leaders to ask, "How can we work around, undermine, contain, and retaliate against US power?"

Rather than invent a new grand strategy, the United States should reinvigorate its older strategies, those based on the view that America's security partnerships are not simply instrumental tools but critical components of an American-led world political order that should be preserved. US power is both leveraged and made more legitimate and user-friendly by these partnerships. The neo-imperial thinkers are haunted by the specter of catastrophic terrorism and seek a radical reordering of America's role in the world. America's commanding unipolar power and the advent of frightening new terrorist threats feed this imperial temptation. But it is a grand strategic vision that, taken to the extreme, will leave the world more dangerous and divided – and the United States less secure.

10

The End of the
Neo-Conservative Moment

The neo-conservative moment is over. In the past two years, a set of hard-line, fundamentalist ideas have taken Washington by storm and provided the intellectual rationale for a radical post-September 11 reorientation of American foreign policy. Driven by fear of terrorism, contempt for perceived European pacifism and a willingness to take big risks, and emboldened by the rise of American unipolar power, these "new fundamentalist" thinkers argue for an era of American global rule organized around the bold unilateral exercise of American military power, gradual disentanglement from the constraints of multilateralism, and an aggressive push to bring freedom and democracy to countries where evil lurks. The conquest of Iraq was the neo-conservatives' defining goal and their crowning achievement.

But the new fundamentalism has turned into a costly misadventure. As a grand strategic approach to global leadership, it has failed. It is hard to think of another instance in American diplomatic history where a strategic wrong turn has done so much damage to the country's international position – its prestige, credibility, security partnerships, and goodwill of other countries – in such a short time, with so little to show for it. A single-minded American campaign against terrorism and rogue states in which countries are either "with us or against us" and bullied into support is not leadership but a geostrategic wrecking ball that will destroy America's own half-century-old international architecture. Long after the new fundamentalist thinking fades away, American diplomats will be repairing the damaged relations and political disarray it wrought.

To be sure, a legion of neo-conservative policy-makers and pundits will continue to champion their radical ideas. But the strategic vision behind the hard-right turn in American foreign policy has been exposed for what it is – intellectually and politically untenable. In retrospect, the intellectual high-water mark of the new fundamentalism was probably the October 2002 National Security Strategy report. Its political high tide was probably the moment President George W. Bush landed in a flight-suit on the USS *Abraham Lincoln* to pronounce the "end" of major hostilities in Iraq.

Future American presidents and policy-makers will want to learn from today's debacle. The rise of global terrorism and American unipolar power do not require an unbound America to enforce world order unilaterally. Quite the contrary: the tested American strategy of alliance partnership and multilateral rule-making will be crucial in an era of new threats and shifting power relations. At the heart of this old order is a strategic bargain that has served America well for decades: the United States ties itself to other democratic states and agrees to develop its policies in concert with them, in the process giving up some modest procedural and political freedom of action. In return, the United States acquires dependable allies who share the burden and operate within rules and institutions that serve American interests over the long term.

The New Fundamentalism

The neo-conservative vision of world order is based on unrivaled American military might and a cultivated belief in American exceptionalism. While the intellectuals and journalists who make up this school of thought disagree on many matters and stress different themes, they tend to share four convictions. First, the United States should increasingly stand aloof from the rest of the world and use its unipolar power – most importantly, its military power – to arbitrate right and wrong and enforce the peace. In a Hobbesian world of anarchy, the United States must step forward as the order-creating Leviathan. The United States will refuse to play by the same rules as other states: this is the price that the world must pay for the unipolar provision of security. America's older, postwar approach to order – organized around alliances, multilateral cooperation, and strategic bargains with other key states – falls away.

This new geopolitical aloofness is reflected in Defense Secretary Donald Rumsfeld's aphorism that "the mission determines the coalition" rather than the other way around.[1] The United States will determine what is a threat and how to respond; relevant and willing partners will be invited to join in. But gone is the notion that the alliance determines the mission. New fundamentalists are not against security partnerships per se – but "coalitions of the willing" will be formed only if other countries sign on to America's unilaterally defined goal. This approach is also reflected in the October 2002 National Security Strategy's new doctrine of pre-emption under which the United States claims a new right to use force "to act against emerging threats before they are fully formed."[2] Gone are the old justifications of war based on self-defense and imminent threat enshrined in Article 51 of the United Nations charter. "When it comes to our security," President Bush affirmed, "we really don't need anybody's permission."[3]

Second, the new fundamentalists argue that military power – and the willingness to use it robustly in pursuit of the national interest – must be returned to the center of American foreign policy. Early neo-conservative thinking in the 1970s made this a central tenet of its critique of American foreign policy in the post-Vietnam era. That policy, in the minds of neo-conservatives, had become too liberal, too soft and unwilling to confront Soviet expansionism. Power must be put back in the service of American principles and the national interest. During the Clinton years, the new fundamentalists argue, the United States was not taken seriously as a global military power – commander-in-chief Clinton sent a few cruise missiles to Baghdad on several occasions, but never threatened real force – and when enemies stop fearing the United States, they are emboldened to strike.

Third, new fundamentalists are frustrated with the entangling rules and institutions of liberal internationalism. They advocate pulling back from treaties and international agreements that jeopardize American sovereignty and constrain the exercise of power. The neo-conservative pundit Charles Krauthammer calls it the "new unilateralism":

> After eight years during which foreign policy success was largely measured by the number of treaties the president could sign and the number of summits he could attend, we now have an administration willing to assert American freedom of action and the primacy of American national interests. Rather than contain power within a vast web of constraining international agreements, the new unilateralism seeks to strengthen American power and unashamedly deploy it on behalf of self-defined global ends.[4]

Some advocates of this view simply appeal to the new realities of terrorism: in an new era where small groups of determined individuals can unleash massive violence against the civilized world without warning, the old system of rules and multilateral cooperation must give way to action – whatever it takes, in short, to "get them before they get us." Other new fundamentalists offer more political–philosophical attacks on multilateralism and rule-based order. In one of the most far-fetched versions,

Under-Secretary of State John Bolton, prior to joining the administration, argued that a great struggle was unfolding between what he calls "Americanists" and "Globalists."[5] Globalists are depicted as elite activist groups who seek to strengthen "global governance" through a widening net of agreements on environment, human rights, labor health, and political–military affairs, and whose not-so-hidden agenda is to enmesh the United States in international laws and institutions that rob the country of its sovereignty. Americanists, according to Bolton, have finally awoken and are now seizing back the country's control over its own destiny. This is a cartoonish view of a complex reality that evinces not just a healthy skepticism of multilateralism, but raises American resistance to international rules and agreements to the status of patriotic duty.

Fourth, the new fundamentalists also incorporate Wilsonian ideas into their vision in urging the spread of democracy. This is not merely idealism, according to neo-conservatives; it is good national security policy. If democracy and the rule of law are established in troubled countries around the world, they cease being threats. This argument was given a conservative imprimatur in Ronald Reagan's celebrated 1982 speech to the UK Parliament in which he called for the promotion of democracy as a fundamental global security imperative. In the hands of new fundamentalists, this aspiration has become, in Pierre Hassner's apt phrase, "Wilsonian in boots."[6] The promotion of democracy is not left to the indirect, long-term forces of economic development and political engagement; when necessary, it is purveyed through military force. Some think-tank fundamentalists, such as Tom Donnelly and Max Boot, go even further and argue for formal quasi-imperial control over strategically valuable failed states, backed up by new American bases and an imperial civil service.[7]

Why Neo-Conservative Ideas Fail

Together, these ideas propose a radical transformation in America's traditional global role and the current organization of unipolar world politics. But it is a profoundly flawed vision of order built on false assumptions, failed policies, misread history, and misguided notions of power. There are nine reasons why the new fundamentalism cannot serve as a successful guide to effective foreign policy.

Grand strategic failure

The war in Iraq was suppose to be a showcase of the new fundamentalist world-view. To these strategists, regime change was always about more than simply eliminating the "gathering threat" of weapons of mass destruction. The decisive use of American power to oust Saddam Hussein would accomplish three larger objectives: it would send a signal to other "axis of evil" states that they could face a similar fate were they to acquire nuclear capacities; it would pave the way for the emergence of a stable, democratic Iraqi regime, setting in motion a democratic transformation across the Middle East; and it would alter the geopolitical realities in the region – reassuring Israel and undercutting support for Palestinian terrorism – thereby giving impetus to the Middle East peace process. Amid the deteriorating conditions of postwar Iraq, none of these fundamentalist goals looks remotely realizable. Rather than induce Iran and North Korea to cease their nuclear programmes, these countries seem more determined than ever to acquire a deterrent capability. The establishment of a stable order in Iraq – let alone democracy – is elusive. In the wake of the war, Arab nationalism, Muslim fundamentalism, and resistance to an American presence are more evident than a region-wide search for democracy. An Israeli–Palestinian settlement is nowhere in sight. Even the public – if only partial – explanation for the war has been undercut; months after the war is over, no weapons of mass destruction have been found. As Talleyrand, diplomat for Napoleon and later for the restored monarchy, once said in reference to a foreign-policy misadventure he himself had committed, "that was worse than a crime; it was a mistake."

Unsustainable at home

"Wilsonianism in boots" is expensive. American democracy will not sustain the new fundamentalist agenda; rather, this cycle of crisis, escalating costs, and ever more rancorous debate will force the United States back to its traditional multilateral-alliance based orientation. In going back to the United Nations for a resolution that creates a multilateral force in Iraq, the Bush administration has begun to raise the unilateralist white flag. It has good reason to do so. On September 7, 2003, President Bush went before the American people to ask for $87 billion for the reconstruction of Iraq. This is on top of $54 billion already budgeted. Vice-President Dick Cheney has suggested that more requests are likely to follow. Very soon the cost of the Iraqi occupation will reach a quarter-trillion dollars. Yet even now, public opinion polls indicate that the American people think the price for stabilizing Iraq is too high; indeed, confidence in the president actually dropped in the polls after his September 7 speech to the nation.[8]

There is no doubt that the United States has sufficient economic and military resources to succeed in stabilizing and rebuilding Iraq – if the country wanted to pay the price. If it dared, the Bush administration could raise taxes, expand the armed forces, and increase funding to Iraq. It could throw massive resources at Iraq and, perhaps, triumph in the end. This is precisely what the neo-conservative champions of the Iraq War, such as William Kristol, are advocating.[9] But this ambitious strategy founders on the rocks of American democracy. The American people don't want to pay the price to pursue an open-ended and expensive occupation and rebuilding effort in Iraq – let alone do so around the world.

As the costs swell, Congress will be obligated to grant the president's budget requests so as to avoid an even worse disaster in Iraq. But voices will also increasingly insist that if the American taxpayer is going to fund the reconstruction of Iraq, the Bush administration must go back to the international community for help. American unilateralism got the United States into this predicament: American taxpayers are getting stuck with the bill, while the European Union – slighted in the Bush administration's rush to war – has offered only $250 million for Iraqi reconstruction in 2004. Today, all roads lead to the United Nations and away from the neo-conservative vision of a unilateral America remaking the Middle East. The challenge over the medium run will not be to resist UN and allied involvement, but rather, how to induce them to get involved in the perilous Iraqi occupation.

Mis-measure of American power

American power advantages – massive, useable, and enduring – are the linchpin of the new fundamentalist go-it-alone strategy of maintaining global order through American domination. To get other states to bend to American goals, the United States must be able to successfully threaten, induce, coerce, and punish other states. The United States must also be powerful enough to go it alone when other states refuse to cooperate. With the rise of American unipolarity, fundamentalists were confident the United States could now lead the global order on its own terms. Washington could do so not by strengthening the international community or signaling a willingness to support and operate within multilateral rules and institutions, but by wielding a big stick.

But this strategy is premised on a radically inflated view of American power. The United States is pre-eminent, not omnipotent. Its military power is without peer or precedent. But in economic and political realms, the world is not really unipolar at all. The failure of the Bush administration to get Turkey and Russia to cooperate in the run-up to the Iraq War is revealing. Despite intense efforts, American leverage over Russia and Turkey was extraordinarily limited. In the end, both countries have more important trade and economic relationships with the European Union than with the United States. They are also both fledgling democracies – and democracies are notoriously unresponsive to bullying or pressure tactics by a more powerful state.

American military power is overwhelming – and it does, in fact, give the United States extraordinary global influence. But in an age where terrorism is the overriding security threat, offering or withholding American security cooperation does not mean as much as it did during the Cold War. Back then – when the threats were clear and aimed at Europe and Asia as much as North America – the United States was truly indispensable to its allies. Current threats are less geographically fixed and the United States feels more at risk than its major Asian or European allies. Yet the United States needs those allies for assistance in intelligence, law enforcement, and a thousand small cooperative gestures every week in the war on terrorism. Contrary to new fundamentalist thinking, the United States does not hold all the cards. Indeed, in many ways other countries – notably those in the EU – may have a stronger hand when it comes to terrorism.

Legitimacy matters

New fundamentalists are mystified why the United States would want to legitimate its military actions by seeking the approval of the UN Security Council or other collective bodies. Prior to the invasion of Iraq, neo-con pundit Charles Krauthammer disparaged the notion that the support of the other major powers conferred any greater "rectitude" on the approaching American war: "I think that need for outside legitimacy bespeaks a very strong lack of confidence in the legitimacy of Americans acting in congress, assembled, if you like, under their own counsel."[10] This is an extraordinarily short-sighted – and potentially quite dangerous – view. It is odd to think that a great nation trying to secure its interests and build a framework for its power through the search for great power consensus or the normative blessings of other countries is a sign of lack of confidence. The opposite is more surely the case. Indeed, our disdain for compromise and cooperation is historically a trait associated with revanchist, not established, powers. It's the self-confidence of your position that allows you to look for opportunities to concert it with others, to leverage it through cooperation. This logic of leveraging power is what must have taken President Bush to the United Nations on September 12, 2002, and transformed the debate over Iraq – at least for a while.

Legitimacy is not something that only academics puzzle over. It is an intrinsic aspect of power. It is also something that the United States has cared about during the eras of its most historic international accomplishments. One of the great differences between the United States and the Soviet Union after World War II was that the Soviet Union was, in effect, a coercive unilateralist. It pursued its own narrow interests of gaining territory and direct political control over Eastern Europe. The United States pursued what might be called a milieu strategy, where it combined its power with the other democratic countries, helping to create democracy and build institutions. American power was rendered legitimate, gaining great advantage over the Soviet Union during the Cold War. To be sure, the United States has pursued crude imperial policies before – most notably in Latin America and in the Middle East – but they remained largely exceptions rather than the guiding logic of its foreign policy.

To care about legitimacy is not to cede American power to the United Nations or – to raise a particularly sore issue for neo-conservatives – to give France an absolute veto right over the American use of force. American presidents have never done this in the past. But they *have* found ways to define American goals and exercise of power in ways that attracted the support of others. American leaders did it because they realized that to legitimate American power was to turn coercion and domination into authority and consent. In Rousseau's famous formulation: "The strongest is never strong enough to be always master, unless he transforms strength into right and obedience into duty."

This insight is not part of new fundamentalist thinking. This is ironic. The fundamentalist power wielders in post-September 11 unipolar America fancy themselves as savvy practitioners of realpolitik. But they too easily confuse force with power and power with authority. They endanger America by stripping us of our legitimacy as the pre-eminent global power and the authority that flows from such a status.

Power as fear backfires

New fundamentalists enshrine Machiavelli's advice – that it "is much safer to be feared than loved, when, of the two, either must be dispensed with." For today's hardliners, it follows that America's problem in the Middle East and elsewhere is that America's enemies do not sufficiently fear Washington. The Afghan and Iraqi wars were championed in part by new fundamentalists as a way to restore fear of American power. Max Boot argues, for example, that the invasion of Afghanistan "provided a vital boost for US security, not only by routing the terrorist network, but also by dispelling the myth of US weakness." Likewise, in March 2003, he claimed that "the invasion of Iraq will be another vital step toward restoring a healthy fear of US power."[11]

The effort to make people fear American power reinforces all the other new fundamentalist impulses – to take big risks, ignore international rules and norms, disparage concerns for legitimacy, and side-step the restraints of alliance partnership. The "fear strategy" is also premised on the optimistic fundamentalist view about the utter dominance of American power – you have to be powerful and threatening all the times and places and ways, otherwise you invite retaliation.

But fear is a dangerous and self-defeating strategy of global leadership. There is no persuasive evidence that the "demonstration effect" of the Iraq War is working with North Korea or Iran or other troublesome states. (Some will claim that the recent British success in gaining Libyan agreement to end its WMD programs was made possible by the fear of an Iraq-style invasion, but the long secret history of the negotiations suggest more complex causes, including the patient workings of sanctions and low-key diplomacy.) The more likely outcome is that these regimes will continue to seek and keep nuclear weapons so as to establish some deterrence against an American invasion. This is not an irrational response, given the Bush administration's rhetoric and actions. After all, the United States has announced to the world that it has a right to use force when it wants to act against states that are not yet imminent threats. It has announced in its 2002 Nuclear Posture statement that it intends – in violation of the Nuclear Non-proliferation Treaty – to develop "bunker buster" nuclear weapons and will not forswear the right to use them against non-nuclear states.[12] In short, the fundamentalists' fear strategy is backfiring. At the end of their tenure in office, the world will be more armed and dangerous and some of those arms will be nuclear.

The irony is that in the aftermath of the neo-conservative "shock and awe" exercise of American power, the United States appears weaker and less in command than it did before this high-risk strategy was launched. The exercise of power can create power – but can also diminish it.

Multilateralism is a tool of American power

It is an article of faith among fundamentalists that multilateralism and rule-based international order are dangerous constraints on American power. After all, as Robert Kagan has famously put it, "multilateralism is a weapon of the weak."[13] When the United States was weak, it too sought refuge in rules and institutions that protected it from the brute power of other countries. Now that the United States is strong, it is natural and sensible for it to resist such entanglements. As Max Boot puts it: "Power breeds unilateralism. It is as simple as that."[14] For these thinkers, it follows that America should exercise its power more directly – less mediated or constrained by international rules, institutions, or alliances. Because America is powerful, it should move toward a power-based rather than a rule-based international order.

But this is a profound misreading of history and American diplomacy. International rules and institutions are not the enemy of American power and interests. At each of the great postwar historical junctions of the twentieth century – 1919, 1945, and 1991 – the United States understood that its interests would be advanced by the construction of a global framework of rules and institutions that lock in a favorable international environment and legitimate American power. Power is most profound and durable when it is manifest in the rules and principles of order itself. American values – which fundamentalists apparently want to champion – have been spread on a global level precisely because the United States has sponsored institutions – such as the United Nations, NATO, and the Bretton Woods machinery – that directly and indirectly embody these values. As European Union diplomat Javier Solana – a great admirer of the United States – has argued:

> A rules-based approach is not a ploy to constrain the US. America wrote much of the great body of international law that has served us so well in the post-war period. Upholding and strengthening the rule of law is the best means for America to preserve her position as the benign world power and to continue to project her values.[15]

Multilateral rules and institutions also leverage American power. It is the oldest bargain underpinning American leadership over the last half-century: that the United States would commit itself to East Asia and Europe – provide security, open its markets, and make its foreign policies in consultation with friends and allies – and in return these other countries would work with – rather than against – American leadership. The United States has been the most powerful state in the world for most of the last century. What has made other countries willing to cooperate with and engage Washington across the decades has been America's willingness – to be sure, often ambivalent – to bind itself to others. The cost in lost freedom of action is more than made up in the gains of added support.

NATO is one component of this institutional bargain that underlies the older American order. Retired general and presidential aspirant Wesley Clark argues that by waging war on Kosovo through NATO, the United States lost some autonomy but gained legitimacy and support: "NATO wasn't an obstacle to victory in Kosovo; it was the reason for our victory." The time-consuming process of getting allied agreement was not always easy. "But in the end," Clark argues, "this was the decisive process for success, because whatever we lost in theoretical military effectiveness we gained many-fold in actual strategic impact by having every NATO nation on board."[16]

Misreading of the end of the Cold War

New fundamentalists are inspired by a particular view of how the Cold War was won – and it is their lessons from this great victory that guide their strategy today. It was not engagement, détente, "paper" agreements, and mutual interest that brought the Soviet Union down, but the Reagan administration's hard-line policy of confrontation, military build-up and ideological warfare. Reagan raised the stakes in the struggle with the Soviet Union by boosting military spending and putting ideological pressure on the "evil empire." This historical narrative provides the ultimate defense for hardline fundamentalist policies.

The problem is that it is flawed history. Reagan was not quite the hard-liner many fundamentalists remember. Reagan campaigned in 1980 against Carter administration weakness, but promptly ended the grain embargo against the Soviet Union – something he had promised Iowa farmers. Reagan also signaled to Soviet President Mikhail Gorbachev a willingness to make radical reductions in nuclear arsenals, much to the surprise and horror of hardliners arrayed around the American president.[17] In the meantime, hardliners – such as those from the Committee on the Present Danger – grossly overestimated Soviet economic and military capabilities. When Gorbachev made his heroic decision to seek radical reform of the Soviet system, he did so confronting a non-communist West that was dynamic and powerful, but also restrained and unlikely to exploit Moscow in its time of crisis. Indeed, when the collapse of the Soviet Union finally came during the administration of Reagan's vice-president, George H. W. Bush, the United States took pains not to strike too "triumphalist" a posture.

Gorbachev saw not just the bluster of Reagan administration hardliners but also the European peace movement. The mobilization of Western public opinion created a political climate in which the rhetoric of the early Reagan administration was a political liability. By the presidential election of 1984, the Reagan administration embraced arms-control goals it had previously spurned. This new line culminated in a speech by Reagan at the UN in September 1984. To the Soviet leaders whom he had previously called "the focus of evil in the modern world," the American president made a new appeal: "For the sake of a peaceful world . . . let us approach each other with ten-fold trust and thousand-fold affection." In the background, Gorbachev's advisors had gathered ideas for Moscow's "new thinking" from years of Western engagement of the Soviet Union that allowed track-two dialogue, transnational exchange, and the flow of ideas.[18]

The real lesson of the end of the Cold War is that the West won because it was united. The United States led the way in building a multilateral economic and security order that generated historically unprecedented prosperity and alliance protection. The United States tied itself down and opened itself up to its Western partners, thereby creating a great engine of political cooperation and geopolitical power. The fundamentalists have it exactly wrong. The Reagan era experience shows that a single, consistent, and unambiguous hardline policy was structurally impossible to sustain within the Western order – and this is why the Cold War ended as successfully as it did.

No stable grand vision of order

New fundamentalists offer an impoverished image of American-dominated world order. Their ideas are essentially a crude "owner's manual" for the unilateral waging of a war against evil regimes and terrorists. But beyond that, they are silent on the full range of global challenges and opportunities that America faces. Nor do their ideas provide a compelling vision for other states – no sense of why they should join this unipolar order or how they fit into it.

There are two problems here. One is that the organizing idea of new fundamentalist grand strategy is focused on the immediate menace of terrorism. The doctrine of security is reduced to a simple, even primitive, maxim: "kill them before they kill us."[19] It is a global strategy based on threats and fear. It offers no inspiring and unifying vision that can provide the basis for sustained cooperation with other countries. Fundamentalists hint that they admire FDR and Truman – but they have failed to draw the most important lesson from these past American leaders. These presidents articulated inspiring visions of world order based on the opportunities that existed to promote rights and safeguards within a strengthened international community. The 1941 Atlantic Charter – agreed upon by Roosevelt and Churchill – was a statement of Anglo-American war aims that offered a vision of a more stable, secure, and prosperous postwar international order. In effect, FDR was telling Americans and world public opinion that if you bear the burdens of waging this awful war, your leaders will endeavor to reconstruct a better world. When Truman unexpectedly became president in April 1945, his first public announcement was to reaffirm America's commitment to the San Francisco conference that was to lay the foundation for a postwar United Nations. The United States drew other peoples and countries into its order by signaling its intention to strengthen rather than rend apart the international community.

Second, the new fundamentalist idea of order has no room for the other traditional great powers. Where does France – or Europe as a whole – fit in today's unipolar American-dominated order? They have no role – they are either irrelevant or expected to acquiesce to American leadership. It is no wonder that Western European governments bridle at unilateral pronouncements from Washington. At the most extreme, the fundamentalist vision is a sort of "hub and spoke" American empire. The United States makes unilateral decisions and expects subordinate states to follow or pay the consequences. Willing junior partners will be rewarded with military bases and trade agreements. Some states will prosper and others will be sidelined in this hierarchical system. But it is an order that will divide the world and leave the United States increasingly alone.

Breaking the bonds of trust

One of the most damaging legacies of the Vietnam War was the decline in trust that the American people had in their government to conduct foreign policy. That trust was gradually restored in the years that followed, and President Bush was able to take advantage of that trust in his first decisions following September 11, but the subsequent controversies over the war in Iraq – overestimating the threat and underestimating the costs – may haunt this and future administrations. The exaggerations of the Iraqi threat and its conflation with the September 11 attacks provide momentary surges of public support, but a longer-term diminishment. Americans may be less willing to trust their leaders in future crises. The president may not be taken at his word – a disturbing development in an era where shadowy threats can strike before they are evident.[20]

Misleading the American people may not be inherent to the fundamentalist project, but it is now part of the historical record. Hardliners were unwilling to go public with their private reasons for going to war in Iraq: transforming the Middle East and re-establishing fear of American power. Instead, the Bush administration justified the war by citing the failure of the Iraqi regime to comply with past United Nations disarmament resolutions. Fundamentalists fancy themselves tough-minded thinkers. But they didn't have the courage of their convictions to level with the American people on what this geopolitical adventure in Iraq was really about and what it would cost. Instead, they seem to have determined that American support for the war and postwar reconstruction can only be sustained if Iraq is linked to terrorism and the September 11 attacks. The temptation to conflate the war in Iraq and the war on terrorism was too great to resist.

But the Bush administration – and the United States – is paying the price in lost credibility. It will be very hard for an American president to come forward and say to the people: "trust me, the intelligence information I have suggests a gathering threat – and we must act."

Lasting Damage

What is the most lasting image of two years of neo-conservative American foreign policy? Is it the impressive display of military power on the road to Baghdad in April 2003 or is it the inability of the United States to gain the support of Canada, Mexico, and Chile in the United Nations Security Council on the eve of war? New public opinion polls show that the world admires America's principles and open society, but also that it is increasingly troubled by its leadership of global politics. Many in Europe and elsewhere suspect that the Bush administration willfully misled the world about the threat posed by Iraq; others see its efforts to gain UN support for the US invasion as a transparent and high-handed exercise in simple bullying. The new fundamentalists have squandered America's most important foreign policy asset – its moral authority.

The new fundamentalists believe that American power is good for the world: America is naturally benign and a provider of global public goods. Charles Krauthammer argues that the "American claim to benignity is not mere self-congratulation. We have a track record."[21] Precisely. But that track record from the post-1945 era provides a refutation of fundamentalist thinking rather than support. Our success after World War II was based on bargains with allies that neo-conservatives now want to repudiate, on a willingness to cooperate and compromise that they now deride as weakness and, above all, on a broadly shared trust in the United States that fundamentalists seem bent on replacing with brute power. Their history is defective, their policies ineffective. Only two years after its ascendancy in the wake of the September 11 attacks, the new fundamentalist approach is already showing signs of immense foreign and domestic strain. It is time to jettison it now, before more – and perhaps irreversible – damage is done to an international order painstakingly created by visionary American statesmen over the course of half a century.

Notes

Many thanks to Thomas Wright for his valuable research assistance, and to Joe Barnes for his comments and suggestions.

1   Donald Rumsfeld, remarks on *Face the Nation*, CBS, September 23, 2001.
2   Office of the President, *National Security Strategy of the United States*, September 2002.
3   Quoted in Dan Baltz, "President Puts Onus Back on Iraqi Leader," *The Washington Post*, March 7, 2003, p. A1.
4   Charles Krauthammer, "The New Unilateralism," *The Washington Post*, June 8, 2001, p. A29.
5   John Bolton, "Should We Take Global Governance Seriously?" *Chicago Journal of International Law* 1: 2 (2000): 205–22.
6   Pierre Hassner, "The United States: The Empire of Force or the Force of Empire?" *Chaillot Papers* 54 (September 2002): 43.
7   See Max Boot, "American Imperialism? No Need to Run Away from Label," *USA Today*, May 6, 2003, p 15A; Boot, "Washington Needs a Colonial Office," *Financial Times*, July 3, 2003, p. 19; and Tom Donnelly, "There's No Place Like Iraq . . . for US Military Bases," *Weekly Standard* (Washington DC), May 5, 2003.
8   See Mike Allen, "What the $87 Billion Speech Cost Bush," *The Washington Post*, September 20, 2003, p. A02.
9   William Kristol and Robert Kagan, "The United States Must be Serious About Its 'generational commitment'," *The Weekly Standard*, September 1 and 8, 2003 (double issue).
10 Charles Krauthammer, quote from panel debate, Eisenhower National Security conference, September 2002.
11 Max Boot, "Iraq War Can Make Up for Earlier US Missteps," *USA Today*, March 25, 2003.
12 For Libya's change of heart, see Stephen Fidler, Roula Khalaf, and Mark Husband, "Return to the Fold: How Gadaffi was Persuaded to Give Up His Nuclear Goals," *Financial Times*, January 27, 2004, p. 13. For American departures from the Non-proliferation Treaty and other arms-control failings, see Nicole Deller, Arjun Makhijani, and John Burroughs, *Rule of Power or Rule of Law: An Assessment of US Policies and Actions Regarding Security Related Treaties* (New York: Apex Press, 2003).
13 Robert Kagan, *Of Paradise and Power* (New York: Knopf, 2003).
14 Max Boot, "The Doctrine of the 'Big Enchilada'," *Washington Post*, October 14, 2002, p. A29.
15 Javier Solana, "Mars and Venus Reconciled: A New Era for Transatlantic Relations," *Albert H. Gordon Lecture*, Kennedy School of Government, Harvard University, April 7, 2003.
16 Wesley Clark, "An Army of One: In the War on Terrorism, Alliances are Not an Obstacle to Victory," *The Washington Monthly*, September 2002.
17 See Daniel Deudney and G. John Ikenberry, "Who Won the Cold War?" *Foreign Policy 87* (Summer 1992): 123–38; and Deudeny and Ikenberry, "The International Sources of Soviet Change," *International Security* 16: 3 (Winter 1991–2): 74–118.

18   See G. John Ikenberry, *After Victory: Institutions, Strategic Restraint and the Rebuilding of Order After Major War* (Princeton: Princeton University Press, 2001), ch. 7.

19   See Ivo Daalder and James Lindsay, *America Unbound: The Bush Revolution in American Foreign Policy* (Washington DC: The Brookings Institution, 2003).

20   This point is stressed by Zbigniew Brzezinski in a speech delivered on October 28, 2003, to a conference entitled "New American Strategies for Security and Peace," co-sponsored by the Center for American Progress, *The American Prospect* and The Century Foundation.

21   Charles Krauthammer, "The Unipolar Moment Revisited," *The National Interest* (Winter 2002–3).

11

Is American Multilateralism in Decline?

American foreign policy appears to have taken a sharp unilateral turn. A half century of US leadership in constructing an international order around multilateral institutions, rule-based agreements, and alliance partnerships seems to be giving way to a new assertive – even defiant – unilateralism. Over the last several years, the Bush administration has signaled a deep skepticism of multilateralism in a remarkable sequence of rejections of pending international agreements and treaties, including the Kyoto Protocol on Climate Change, the Rome Statute of the International Criminal Court (ICC), the Germ Weapons Convention, and the Programme of Action on Illicit Trade in Small and Light Arms. It also unilaterally withdrew from the 1970s Anti-Ballistic Missile Treaty, which many experts regard as the cornerstone of modern arms-control agreements. More recently, spurred by its war on terrorism, the Bush administration has advanced new, provocative ideas about the American unilateral and pre-emptive use of force – and under this go-it-alone-if-necessary banner, it defied allies and world public opinion by launching a preventive war against Iraq. "When it comes to our security," President Bush proclaimed, "we really don't need anybody's permission."[1]

Unilateralism, of course, is not a new feature of American foreign policy. In every historical era, the United States has shown a willingness to reject treaties, violate rules, ignore allies, and use military force on its own.[2] But many observers see today's US unilateralism as something much more sweeping – not an occasional ad hoc policy decision, but a new strategic orientation. Capturing this view, one pundit calls it the "new unilateralism":

After eight years during which foreign policy success was largely measured by the number of treaties the president could sign and the number of summits he could attend, we now have an administration willing to assert American freedom of action and the primacy of American national interests. Rather than contain power within a vast web of constraining international agreements, the new unilateralism seeks to strengthen American power and unashamedly deploy it on behalf of self-defined global ends.[3]

Indeed, Richard Holbrooke, former US ambassador to the United Nations, has charged that the Bush administration threatens to make "a radical break with 55 years of a bipartisan tradition that sought international agreements and regimes of benefit to us."[4]

America's "new unilateralism" has unsettled world politics. The stakes are high because in the decade since the end of the Cold War, the United States has emerged as an unrivaled and unprecedented global superpower. At no other time in modern history has a single state loomed so large over the rest of the world. But as American power has grown, the rest of the world is confronted with a disturbing double bind. On the one hand, the United States is becoming more crucial to other countries in the realization of their economic and security goals; it is increasingly in a position to help or hurt other countries. But on the other hand, the growth of American power makes the United States less dependent on weaker states, and so it is easier for the United States to resist or ignore these states.

Does this Bush-style unilateralism truly represent a major turn away from the long postwar tradition of multilateralism in American foreign policy? It depends on whether today's American unilateralism is a product of deep structural shifts in the country's global position or if it reflects more contingent and passing circumstances. Does American unipolarity "select" for unilateralism? Do powerful states – when they get the chance – inevitably seek to disentangle themselves from international rules and institutions? Or are more complex considerations at work? The answers to these questions are relevant to determining whether the rise of American pre-eminence in the years since the end of the Cold War is ultimately consistent with or destined to undermine the post-1945 multilateral international order.

This essay makes three arguments. First, the new unilateralism is not an inevitable reaction to rising American power. The international system may give the United States more opportunities to act unilaterally, but the incentives to do so are actually complex and mixed. And arguably, these incentives make a multilateral approach more – not less – desirable for Washington in many areas of foreign policy.

Second, despite key officials' deep and ideologically driven skepticism about multilateralism, the Bush administration's opposition to multilateralism represents in practical terms an attack on specific types of multilateral agreements more than it does a fundamental assault on the "foundational" multilateralism of the postwar system. One area is arms control, nonproliferation, and the use of force, where many in the administration do resist the traditional multilateral, treaty-based approach. Likewise, some of the other new multilateral treaties that are being negotiated today represent slightly different trade-offs for the United States. In the past, the United States has embraced multilateralism because it provided ways to protect American freedom of action: escape clauses, weighted voting, and veto rights. The "new unilateralism" is in part a product of the "new multilateralism," which offers fewer opportunities for the United States to exercise political control over others and fewer ways to escape the binding obligations of the agreements.

Weaker states have responded to the rise of American unipolarity by seeking to embed the United States further in binding institutional relationships (in effect, to "tie Gulliver down"), while American officials attempt to get the benefits of a multilateral order without accepting greater encroachments on its policy autonomy. We are witnessing not an end to multilateralism but a struggle over its scope and character. A "politics of institutions" is being played out between the United States and the rest of the world within the United Nations, the North Atlantic Treaty Organization (NATO), the World Trade Organization (WTO), and other postwar multilateral fora.

Third, the circumstances that led the United States to engage in multilateral cooperation in the past are still present and, in some ways, have actually increased. In particular, there are three major sources of multilateralism: functional demands for cooperation (e.g., institutional contracts between states that reduce barriers to mutually beneficial exchange); hegemonic power management, both to institutionalize power advantages and, by reducing the arbitrary and indiscriminate exercise of power, to make the hegemonic order more stable and legitimate; and the American legal-institutional political tradition of seeing this domestic rule-of-law orientation manifest in the country's approach to international order.

I begin by looking at the logic and dimensions of multilateralism. Next, I present and critique the structural, power-based explanation for the new unilateralism. I then look at three theoretical traditions that offer explanations for continued multilateralism. To be sure, unipolarity creates opportunities for unilateralist foreign policy officials to push their agenda, particularly in the areas of arms control and the use of force, where multilateral rules and norms have been weak even under the most favorable circumstances. The incentives and pressures for multilateralism are altered but not extinguished with the rise of American unipolarity.

System	Sovereign state system: constitution of legal actors; principles of mutual recognition, formal equality, diplomatic practice
Ordering	Basic organizing principles and features of the international order
	Indivisibility of economic and security areas
Contract	Individual agreements/treaties among groups of states

Figure 11.1   Types of multilateral relations

What is Multilateralism?

Multilateralism involves the coordination of relations among three or more states according to a set of rules or principles. It can be distinguished from other types of interstate relations in three ways. First, because it entails the coordination of relations among a group of states, it can be contrasted with bilateral, "hub and spoke," and imperial arrangements. Second, the terms of a given relationship are defined by agreed-upon rules and principles – and sometimes by organizations – so multilateralism can be contrasted with interactions based on ad hoc bargaining or straightforward power politics. Third, multilateralism entails some reduction in policy autonomy, since the choices and actions of the participating states are – at least to some degree – constrained by the agreed-upon rules and principles.[5]

Multilateralism can operate at three levels of international order: system multilateralism, ordering or foundational multilateralism, and contract multilateralism (see figure 11.1). At the most basic level, it is manifest in the Westphalian state system, where norms of sovereignty, formal equality, and legal-diplomatic practice prevail.[6] This is multilateralism as it relates to the deep organization of the units and their mutual recognition and interaction; this notion is implicit in both realist and neoliberal theories of international order. At a more intermediate level, multilateralism can refer to the political-economic organization of regional or international order. John Ruggie notes that "an 'open' and 'liberal' international economic order is multilateral in form."[7] The overall organization of relations among the advanced industrial countries has this basic multilateral characteristic. As Robert Keohane observes, "Since the end of World War II, multilateralism has become increasingly important in world politics, as manifest in the proliferation of multinational conferences on a bewildering variety of themes and an increase in the number of multilateral intergovernmental organizations from fewer than 100 in 1945 to about 200 in 1960 and over 600 in 1980."[8] At the surface level, multilateralism also refers to specific

System	Complex interdependence, unipolarity, the rise of nonstate violent collective action
Institutional	Autonomous influence of pre-existing multilateral institutions
Domestic	American identity, limiting domestic fiscal and manpower costs, election cycles
Agentic	Ideologies of foreign policy elites, nongovernmental organizations, how specific treaties get structured

Figure 11.2   Sources of multilateralism

intergovernmental treaties and agreements. These can be thought of as distinct "contracts" among states.

Multilateralism can also be understood in terms of the binding character of the rules and principles that guide interstate relations. In its loosest form, multilateralism can simply entail general consultations and informal adjustments among states.[9] This form of multilateralism can be traced back to the diplomatic practices of the Concert of Europe, where the great powers observed a set of unwritten rules and norms about the balance of power on the continent. For instance, no major power would act alone in matters of diplomacy and territorial adjustments, and no great power could be isolated or humiliated.[10] This loose, nonbinding type of multilateralism can be found today in the Asia Pacific Economic Cooperation (APEC), which was established in the early 1990s to promote regional economic cooperation. The WTO and other multilateral economic institutions entail more formal, treaty-based agreements that specify certain commitments and obligations. But the binding character of these multilateral agreements is still qualified: escape clauses, weighted voting, opt-out agreements, and veto rights are all part of the major post-1945 multilateral agreements. The most binding multilateral agreements are ones where states actually cede sovereignty in specific areas to supranational authorities. The European Union is the most important manifestation of this sovereignty-transferring, legally binding multilateralism.[11]

Multilateralism (as well as unilateralism) can also be understood in terms of its sources (see figure 11.2). It can emerge from the international system's structural features, including the distribution of power (i.e., the rise or decline of American dominance), the growth of complex interdependence, and the emergence of non-state violent collective action. Incentives for multilateralism can also come from the independent influence of pre-existing multilateral institutions. For example, the postwar multilateral order might in various ways put pressure on the United States to maintain or even expand its commitments. Incentives for multilateralism may also come from inside a state, manifest in national political identity and tradition or more specific factors such as fiscal and manpower costs and election cycles. Finally, multilateralism can be traced to agentic sources, such as the ideologies of government elites, the ideas pressed upon government by nongovernmental organizations, and the maneuvering of elites over treaty conditions and ratification.

When deciding whether to sign a multilateral agreement, a state faces a trade-off. In choosing to abide by the rules and norms of the agreement, the state must accept a reduction in its policy autonomy. That is, it must agree to some constraints on its freedom of action – or independence of policy-making – in a particular area. But in exchange, it expects other states to do the same. The multilateral bargain will be attractive to a state if it concludes that the benefits that flow to it through the coordination of policies are greater than the costs of lost policy autonomy. In an ideal world, a state might want to operate in an international environment in which all other states are heavily rule-bound while leaving itself entirely unencumbered by rules and institutional restraints.[12] But because all states are inclined in this way, the question becomes one of how much autonomy each must relinquish in order to get rule-based behavior out of the others.

A state's willingness to agree to a multilateral bargain will hinge on several factors that shape the ultimate cost–benefit calculation. One is whether the policy constraints imposed on other states (*states b, c*, and *d*) really matter to the first state (*state a*). If the "unconstrained" behavior of other states is judged to have no undesirable impact on *a*, then *a* will be unwilling to give up any policy autonomy of its own. It also matters if the participating states can credibly restrict their policy autonomy. If *a* is not convinced that *b, c*, and *d* can actually be constrained by multilateral rules and norms, it will not be willing to sacrifice its own policy autonomy.[13] Likewise, if the agreement is to work, *a* will need to convince the other states that it too will be constrained. These factors are all continuous rather than dichotomous variables, so the states must make judgments about the degree of credibility and relative value of constrained policies.[14]

When multilateral bargains are made by states with highly unequal power, the considerations can be more complex. The more that a powerful state is capable of dominating or abandoning weaker states, the more the weaker states will care about constraints on the leading state's policy autonomy. In other words, they will be more eager to see some limits placed on the arbitrary and indiscriminate exercise of power by the leading state. Similarly, the more that the powerful state can restrain itself in a credible fashion, the more that weaker states will be interested in multi-lateral rules and norms that accomplish this end. When both these conditions hold – when the leading state can use its power to dominate and abandon, and when it can restrain and commit itself – the weaker states will be particularly eager for a deal. They will, of course, also care about the positive benefits that accrue from cooperation. Of course, the less important the policy behavior of weaker states – and the less certain the leading state is that weaker states can in fact constrain their policies – the less the leading state will offer to limit its own policy autonomy.

Varieties of Multilateralism

In this light, it is easy to see why the United States sought to build a post-1945 order around multilateral economic and security agreements such as the Bretton Woods agreements on monetary and trade relations and the NATO security pact. The United States ended World War II in an unprecedented power position, so the weaker European states attached a premium to taming and harnessing this newly powerful state. Britain, France, and other major states were willing to accept multilateral agreements to the extent that they also constrained and regularized US economic and security actions. American agreement to operate within a multilateral economic order and make an alliance-based security commitment to Europe was worth the price: it ensured that Germany and the rest of Western Europe would be integrated into a wider, American-centered international order. At the same time, the actual restraints on US policy were minimal. Convertible currencies and open trade were in the United States' basic national economic interest. The United States did make a binding security guarantee to Western Europe, and this made American power more acceptable to Europeans, who were then more eager to cooperate with the United States in other areas.[15] But the United States did not forswear the right to unilaterally use force elsewhere. It supported multilateral economic and security relations with Europe, and it agreed to operate economically and militarily within multilateral institutions organized around agreed-upon rules and principles. In return, it ensured that Western Europe would be firmly anchored in an Atlantic and global political order that advanced America's long-term national interest.

The United States was less determined or successful in establishing a multilateral order in East Asia. Proposals were made for an East Asian version of NATO, but security relations quickly took the shape of bilateral military pacts. Conditions did not favor Atlantic-style multilateralism. Europe had a set of roughly equal-sized states that could be brought together in a multilateral pact tied to the United States, while Japan largely stood alone.[16] But another factor mattered as well: the United States was dominant in East Asia yet wanted less out of the region, so the United States found it less necessary to give up policy autonomy in exchange for institutional cooperation there. In Europe, the United States had an elaborate agenda of uniting European states, creating an institutional bulwark against communism, and supporting centrist democratic governments. These ambitious goals could not be realized simply by exercising brute power. To get what it wanted, the United States had to bargain with the Europeans, and this meant agreeing to institutionally restrain and commit its power. In East Asia, the building of order around bilateral pacts with Japan, Korea, and other states was a more desirable strategy because multilateralism would have entailed more restraints on policy autonomy. As Peter Katzenstein argues:

> It was neither in the interest of the United States to create institutions that would have constrained independent decision making in Washington nor in the interest of subordinate states to enter into institutions in which they would have minimal control while forgoing opportunities for free-riding and dependence reduction. Extreme hegemony thus led to a system of bilateral relations between states rather than a multilateral system that emerged in the North Atlantic area around the North Atlantic Treaty Organization (NATO) and the European Community.[17]

Despite these regional variations, the international order that took shape after 1945 was decidedly multilateral. A core objective of American postwar strategists was to ensure that the world did not break apart into 1930s-style closed regions.[18] An open system of trade and investment – enshrined in the General Agreement on Tariffs and Trade (GATT) and the Bretton Woods agreement – provided one multilateral foundation to the postwar order. The alliance ties between the United States and Europe provided another. NATO was not just a narrow security pact but was seen by its founders as an extension of the collective self-defense provision of the UN Charter. The security of Europe and America are bound together; the parties thus have substantial consultative and decision-making obligations to each other. This indivisibility of economic and security relations is what has given the Western-centered international order a deep multilateral character. The United States makes commitments to other participating states – that is, it provides security protection and access to its markets, technology, and society in the context of an open international system. In exchange, other states agree to be stable political partners with the United States and offer it economic, diplomatic, and logistical support.

This is multilateralism as Ruggie has described it – as an organizational form.[19] The parts of this Western order are connected by economic and

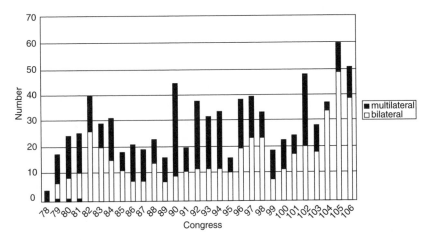

Source: Schocken and Caron 2001.

Figure 11.3   Treaties completed by Congress, 1945–2000

security relationships that are informed by basic rules, norms, and institutions. The rules and institutions are understood by participating states to matter, reflecting loosely agreed-upon rights, obligations, and expectations about how "business" will be done within the order. It is an open system in which members exhibit "diffuse reciprocity."[20] Power does not disappear from this multilateral order, but it operates in a bargaining system in which rules and institutions – and power – play an interactive role. At this foundational or ordering level, multilateralism still remains a core feature of the contemporary Western international system, despite the inroads of the "new unilateralism."

On top of this foundational multilateral order, a growing number and variety of multilateral agreements have been offered up and signed by states. At a global level, between 1970 and 1997, the number of international treaties more than tripled; and from 1985 through 1999 alone, the number of international institutions increased by two-thirds.[21] What this means is that an expanding number of multilateral "contracts" is being proposed and agreed to by states around the world. The United States has become party to more and more of these contracts. This is reflected in the fact that the number of multilateral treaties in force for the United States steadily grew during the twentieth century. There were roughly 150 multilateral treaties in force in 1950, 400 in 1980, and close to 600 in 2000. In the most recent five-year period, 1996 through 2000, the United States ratified roughly the same number of treaties as in earlier postwar periods.[22] Other data, summarized in figure 11.3, indicate an increase in bilateral treaties passed by the Congress and a slight decrease in the number of multilateral treaties from 1945 through 2000.[23] Measured in these rough aggregate terms, the United States has not significantly backed away from what is a more and more dense web of international treaties and agreements.[24]

Two conclusions follow from these observations. First, in the most general of terms, there has not been a dramatic decline in the propensity of the United States to enter into multilateral treaties. In fact, the United States continues to take on multilateral commitments at a steady rate. But the sheer volume of "contracts" that are being offered around the world for agreement has steadily expanded – and while the American "yield" on proposed multilateral treaties may not be substantially lower than in earlier decades, the absolute number of rejected contracts is necessarily larger. The United States has more opportunities to look unilateral today than in the past, even though it is not more likely when confronted with a specific "contract" to be any less multilateral than in earlier years. Second, even if the United States does act unilaterally in opposing specific multilateral treaties that come along, it is important to distinguish these rejected "contracts" from the older foundational agreements that give the basic order its multilateral form. These is no evidence of "rollback" at this deeper level of order. But it is necessary to look more closely at the specific explanations for American multilateralism and the recent unilateral turn.

Unipolar Power and Multilateralism

The simplest explanation for the new unilateralism is that the United States has grown in power during the 1990s, thereby reducing its incentives to operate within a multilateral order. As one pundit has put it: "Any nation with so much power always will be tempted to go it alone. Power breeds unilateralism. It is as simple as that."[25] This is a structural-realist explanation that says, in effect, that because of the shifting distribution of power in favor of the United States, the international system is increasingly "selecting" for unilateralism in its foreign policy.[26] The United States has become so powerful that it does not need to sacrifice its autonomy or freedom of action within multilateral agreements. Unipolar power gives the United States the ability to act alone and do so without serious costs.

Today's international order, then, is at the early stage of a significant transformation triggered by what will be a continuous and determined effort by a unipolar America to disentangle itself from the multilateral restraints of an earlier era. It matters little who is president and what political party runs the government. The United States will exercise its power more directly – less mediated or constrained by international rules, institutions, or alliances. The result will be an international order that is more hegemonic than multilateral, more power-based than rule-based. The rest of the world will complain, but will not be able or willing to impose sufficient costs on the United States to alter its growing unilateral orientation.

This explanation for the decline of American multilateralism rests on several considerations. First, the United States has turned into a unipolar global power without historical precedent. The 1990s surprised the world. Many observers expected the end of the Cold War to usher in a multipolar order with increasingly equal centers of power in Asia, Europe, and America. Instead, the United States began the decade as the world's only superpower and proceeded to grow more powerful at the expense of the other major states. Between 1990 and 1998, the United States' gross national product grew 27 percent, Europe's 16 percent, and Japan's 7 percent. Today, the American economy is equal to the economies of Japan, the United Kingdom, and Germany combined. The United States' military capacity is even more in a league of its own. It spends as much on defense as the next 14 countries taken together. It has bases in 40 countries. Eighty percent of world military research and development takes place in the United States.[27] What the 1990s wrought is a unipolar America that is more powerful that any other great state in history.[28]

Second, these massive power advantages give the United States opportunities to resist entanglements in multilateral rules and institutions. Multilateralism can be a tool or expedient in some circumstances, but states will avoid or shed entanglements in rules and institutions when they can.[29] This realist vision of multilateralism is captured by Robert Kagan, who argues that multilateralism is a "weapon of the weak." He adds: "When the United States was weak, it practiced the strategies of indirection, the strategies of weakness; now that the United States is powerful, it behaves as powerful nations do."[30]

Put another way, power disparities make it easier for the United States to walk away from potential international agreements. Across the spectrum of economic, security, environmental, and other policy issues, the sheer size and power advantages of the United States make it easier to resist multilateral restraints. That is, the costs of non-agreement are lower for the United States than for other states – which gives it bargaining advantages but also a greater ability to forgo agreement without suffering consequences.[31]

According to this view, the American willingness to act multilaterally during the postwar era was an artifact of the bipolar struggle. The United States needed allies, and the construction of this "free world" coalition entailed some American willingness to agree to multilateral commitments and restraints. Yet even during the Cold War decades, realists note, multilateral economic and security commitments did not entail great compromises on American policy autonomy. Voting shares, veto power, and escape clauses have been integral to American multilateralism during this earlier era. Today, even these contingent multilateral commitments and restraints are unnecessary.

Third, the shifting power differentials have also created new divergent interests between the United States and the rest of the world, a fact that further reduces possibilities for multilateral cooperation. For example, the sheer size of the American economy – and a decade of growth unmatched by Europe, Japan, or the other advanced countries – means that US obligations under the Kyoto Protocol would be vastly greater than those of other states.[32] The United States has global interests and security threats that no other state has. Its troops are the ones most likely to be dispatched to distant battlefields, which means that it is more exposed than other states to the legal liabilities of the ICC. The United States must worry about threats to its interests in all major regions of the world. Such unipolar power is a unique target for terrorism. It is not surprising that Europeans and Asians make different assessments of terrorist threats and rogue states seeking weapons of mass destruction than American officials do. Since multilateralism entails working within agreed-upon rules and institutions about the use of force, this growing divergence will make multilateral agreements less easy to achieve – and less desirable in the view of the United States.

This structural-power perspective on multilateralism generates useful insights. One such insight is that the United States – as well as other states – has walked away from international rules and agreements when they did not appear to advance American interests. This helps to explain a lot about American foreign policy over many decades. For example, when the US intervention in Nicaragua was brought before the International Court of Justice on the grounds of a violation of Nicaragua's sovereignty, the court ruled in Nicaragua's favor. The US response was immediately to move to rescind the court's jurisdiction over the United States. In this sense, Kenneth Waltz is surely correct when he argues that "strong states use institutions, as they interpret laws, in ways that suit them."[33]

But the more general claim about unipolarity and the decline of multilateralism is misleading. To begin with, at earlier moments of power preeminence, the United States did not shy away from multilateralism. As Fareed Zakaria notes:

> America was the most powerful country in the world when it proposed the creation of an international organization, the League of Nations, to manage international relations after the First World War. It was the dominant power

at the end of the Second World War, when it founded the United Nations, created the Bretton Woods system of international economic cooperation, and launched most of the world's key international organizations.[34]

During the 1990s, the United States again used its unrivaled position after the end of the Cold War to advance new multilateral agreements, including the WTO, NAFTA (the North American Free Trade Agreement), and APEC. There is no necessary or simple connection between a state's power position and its inclinations toward multilateralism, a tool that weak and strong alike can use.[35]

What is most distinctive about American policy is its mixed record on multilateralism. The United States is not rolling back its commitments to foundational multilateralism, but it is picking and choosing among the variety of multilateral agreements being negotiated today. Power considerations – and American unipolar power – surely are part of the explanation for both the calculations that go into American decisions and the actions of other states. The United States had actively championed the WTO but is resisting a range of arms control treaties. One has to look beyond gross power distributions and identify more specific costs and incentives that inform state policy.

The chief problem with the structural-power explanation for America's new unilateralism is that it hinges on an incomplete accounting of the potential costs of unilateralism. The assumption is that the United States has become so powerful that other countries are unable to impose costs if it acts alone. On economic, environmental, and security issues, the rhetorical question that the United States can always ask when confronted with opposition to American unilateralism is this: they may not like it, but what are they going to do about it? According to this view, the United States is increasingly in the position that it was in East Asia during the early Cold War: it is so hegemonic that it has few incentives to tie itself to multilateral rules and institutions, and it can win on issues that it cares about by going it alone or bargaining individually with weaker states. This view – as we shall see below – is a very superficial reading of the situation.

Unipolarity and unilateralist ideologies

One source of the new unilateralism does follow – at least indirectly – from unipolar power. The United States is so powerful that the ideologies and policy views of a few key decision-makers in Washington can have a huge impact on the global order, even if these views are not necessarily representative of the wider foreign policy community or of public opinion. In effect, the United States is so powerful that the structural pressures associated with anarchy – which lead to security competition and relative gains calculations – decline radically. The passing views of highly placed administration elites matter more than in other states or international structural circumstances.[36]

Indeed, the Bush administration does have a large group of officials who have articulated deep intellectual reservations about international treaties and multilateral organizations.[37] Many of America's recent departures from multilateralism are agreements dealing with arms control and proliferation. In this area, American policy elites are deeply divided on how to advance the nation's security – a division that dates back to right-wing opposition to American arms control diplomacy with the Soviet Union during the Nixon–Kissinger era.[38] The skeptical view of arms control made its appearance during the Reagan administration in the embrace by hardliners of the Star Wars missile defense program. It reappeared in the 1990s, when conservative Republicans again championed national missile defense. When asked why missile defense was part of the Republican "Contract with America" campaign in 1994, Representative Newt Gingrich remarked: "It is the difference between those who would rely on lawyers to defend America and those who rely on engineers and scientists."[39]

The circumstances of the post-Cold War era also complicate arms control and nonproliferation agreements. The arms control of the Soviet era had a more immediate and reciprocal character. The United States agreed to restraints on its nuclear arsenal; but in return, it got relatively tangible concessions from the Soviets, and the agreements themselves were widely seen to have a stabilizing impact on the global order – something both sides desired.[40] The arms control agenda today is more diverse and problematic. New types of agreements are being debated in a more uncertain and shifting international security environment. With the Comprehensive Test Ban Treaty and the Land Mines Treaty, for example, the United States accepts restraints on its military capabilities without the same degree of confidence that they will generate desired reciprocal action.[41] The realms of arms control – along with the calculations of costs and benefits, at least among some American elites – have changed. This helps explain why American unilateralism today is so heavily manifest in this policy area.[42]

Some observers contend that the Bush administration has embraced a more ambitious unilateralist agenda aimed at rolling back and disentangling the United States from post-1945 foundational multilateral rules and institutions. Grand strategic ideas of this sort are circulating inside and outside the administration. One version of this thinking is simply old-style nationalism that sees international institutions and agreements as a basic threat to American sovereignty.[43] Another version – increasingly influential in Washington – is advanced by the so-called neoconservative movement, which seeks to use American power to single-handedly reshape entire countries, particularly in the Middle East, so as to make them more congenial with American interests.[44] This is a neo-imperial vision of American order that requires the United States to unshackle itself from the norms and institutions of multilateral action (and from partners that reject the neo-imperial project).

It is possible that this neo-imperial agenda could undermine the wider and deeper multilateral order. Given sufficient time and opportunity, a small group of determined foreign policy officials could succeed in subverting multilateral agreements and alliance partnerships – even if such steps were opposed by the wider foreign policy community and the American public. This could be done intentionally or it could happen indirectly if, by violating core multilateral rules and norms, the credibility of American commitment to the wider array of agreements and norms becomes suspect and the entire multilateral edifice crumbles. The possibility of unilateral action against self-interest does exist. Great powers have often in the past launched themselves in aggressive directions (often unilateral) that appear in retrospect to have not been in their interest. Examples include Wilhelmine Germany (1890–1918), Nazi Germany, Fascist Italy, the Soviet Union during most of its history, France and Britain in the Crimean War, ancient Athens' expedition to Syracuse, and the United States in Vietnam.[45]

It is extremely doubtful, however, that a neo-imperial foreign policy can be sustained at home or abroad. There is no evidence that the American people are eager for or willing to support such a transformed global role. It is not clear that the country will even be willing to bear the costs of rebuilding Iraq, let alone undertake a global neo-imperial campaign to overturn and rebuild other countries in the region. Moreover, if the neo-conservative agenda is really focused on promoting democracy in the Arab and Muslim world, the unilateral use of force will be of limited and diminishing importance, while the multilateral engagement of the region will be critical. In the end, a determined, ideologically motivated policy elite can push the United States in dramatic new directions, but electoral cycles and democratic politics make it difficult for costly and self-destructive policy orientations to be sustained over the long term.[46]

Multilateral rule-breaking and rule-making

Even if the United States takes advantage of its unipolar power to act unilaterally in various policy areas, the action can lead to multilateralism – no matter what the United States intended. Britain used its position as the leading naval power of the nineteenth century to suppress piracy on the high seas, which eventually led to agreements and concerted action among the major states to protect ocean shipping.[47] President Nixon unilaterally "closed the gold window" of the Bretton Woods monetary regime in the early 1970s, which upset Japan and European countries but eventually led to the creation of the International Monetary Fund (IMF) and the G-8 summit process. President Reagan pursued unilateral trade policies in some instances during the 1980s, but this led to the establishment of the GATT dispute settlement mechanism. Rule-breaking can lead to rule-making.[48]

Unilateralism leading to new multilateral rules is a dynamic that is particularly likely to emerge when new issues and circumstances alter the interest calculations of leading states. In the 1990s, the United States and other states showed a willingness to go beyond long-standing UN norms about sovereignty in the use of force in humanitarian crises. This experience appears to be leading to new multilateral understandings about when the UN Charter sanctions international action in defense of human rights.[49] Further, the United States has recently advanced new ideas about the preemptive – and even preventative – use of force to combat terrorism. This unilateral assertion of American rights has triggered a world debate on UN principles regarding the use of force, and the result could well be a new agreement that adapts existing rules and norms to cope with the new circumstances of global terrorism.[50] So it is useful to look more closely at the factors that give rise to multilateralism.

Sources of Multilateralism

The United States is not structurally destined to disentangle itself from the multilateral order and go it alone. Indeed, there continue to be deep underlying incentives for the United States to support multilateralism – incentives that in many ways are increasing. The sources of US multilateralism stem from the functional demands of interdependence, the long-term calculations of power management, and American political tradition and identity.

Interdependence and functional multilateralism

American support for multilateralism is likely to be sustained, even in the face of resistance and ideological challenges to multilateralism within the Bush administration, in part because of a simple logic: as global economic interdependence grows, so does the need for multilateral coordination of policies. The more economically interconnected states become, the more dependent they are on the actions of other states for the realization of objectives. "As interdependence rises," Keohane argues, "the opportunity costs of not co-ordinating policy increase, compared with the costs of sacrificing autonomy as a consequence of making binding agreements."[51] Rising economic interdependence is one of the great hallmarks of the contemporary international system. Over the postwar era, states have actively and consistently sought to open markets and reap the economic, social, and technological gains that derive from integration into the world economy. If this remains true in the years ahead, it is easy to predict that the demands for multilateral agreements – even, and perhaps especially, by the United States – will increase.

One theoretical tradition, neoliberal institutionalism, provides an explanation for the rise of multilateral institutions under these circumstances. Institutions perform a variety of functions, such as reducing uncertainty and the costs of transactions between states.[52] Mutually beneficial exchanges are missed in the absence of multilateral rules and procedures, which help states overcome collective action, asymmetrical information, and the fear that other states will cheat or act opportunistically. In effect, multilateral rules and institutions provide a contractual environment within which states can more easily pursue joint gains. Likewise, as the density of interactions between states increases, so will the demand for rules and institutions that facilitate these interactions. In this sense, multilateralism is self-reinforcing. A well-functioning contractual environment facilitates the promulgation of additional multilateral rules and institutions. As Keohane points out, the combination of growing interdependence and successful existing institutions should lead to the expansion in the tasks and scope of multilateralism in the relevant policy area.[53]

This argument helps explain why a powerful state might support multilateral agreements, particularly in trade and other economic policy areas. To return to the cost-benefit logic of multilateralism discussed earlier, the leading state has a major interest in inducing smaller states to open their economies and participate in an integrated world economy. As the world's leading economy, it has an interest in establishing not just an open system but also a predictable one – that is to say, it will want rules, principles, and institutions that create a highly stable and accessible order. As the density and sophistication of these interactions grow, the leading state will have greater incentives for a stable, rule-based economic order. What the dominant state wants from other states grows along with its economic size and degree of interdependence. But to get weaker states to commit themselves to an open and increasingly elaborate rule-based regime, it must establish its own reliability. It must be willing to commit itself credibly to the same rules and institutions.[54] It will be necessary for the dominant state to reduce its policy autonomy – and do so in a way that other states find credible.

The American postwar commitment to a multilateral system of economic rules and institutions can be understood in this way. As the world's dominant state, the United States championed GATT and the Bretton Woods institutions as ways of locking other countries into an open world economy that would ensure massive economic gains for itself. But to get these states to organize their postwar domestic orders around an open world economy – and accept the political risks and vulnerabilities associated with openness – the United States had to signal that it too would play by the rules and not exploit or abandon these weaker countries. The postwar multilateral institutions facilitated this necessary step. As the world economy and trading system have expanded over the decades, this logic has continued. It is reflected in the WTO, which replaced the GATT in 1995 and embodies an expansive array of legal-institutional rules and mechanisms.[55] The United States demands an expanding and ever-more complex international economic environment, but to get the support of other states, the United States must itself become more embedded in this system of rules and institutions.

This perspective is particularly useful in identifying specific policy realms – such as trade – where multilateralism is an attractive tool to advance American interests. Accordingly, it is not surprising that the Bush administration has succeeded in gaining "fast track" authority from Congress and led the launch of a new multilateral trade round. This view does acknowledge that American support for multilateralism will be uneven across policy realms. But it is not clear how American support for trade multilateralism may or may not spill over to other policy realms, such as the environment or the use of force.

Hegemonic power and strategic restraint

American support for multilateralism also stems from a grand strategic interest in preserving power and creating a stable and legitimate international order. This logic is particularly evident at major historical turning points – such as 1919, 1945, and after the Cold War – when the United States has faced choices about how to use power and organized interstate relations. The support for multilateralism is a way to signal restraint and commitment to other states, thereby encouraging the acquiescence and cooperation of weaker states.[56] The United States has pursued this strategy to varying degrees across the twentieth century – and this reflects the remarkably durable and legitimate character of the existing international order. From this perspective, multilateralism – and the search for rule-based agreements – should increase rather than decrease with the rise of American unipolarity. Moreover, the existing multilateral order, which itself reflects an older multilateral bargain between the United States and the outside world, should rein in the Bush administration, and the administration should respond to general power management incentives and limit its tilt toward unilateralism.[57]

This theoretical perspective begins by looking at the choices that dominant states face when they are in a position to shape the fundamental character of the international order. A state that wins a war, or through some other turn of events finds itself in a dominant global position, faces a choice: it can use its power to bargain and coerce other states in struggles over the distribution of gains, or, knowing that its power position will someday decline and that there are costs to enforcing its way within the order, it can move toward a more rule-based, institutionalized order in exchange for the acquiescence and compliant participation of weaker states. In seeking a more rule-based order, the leading state is agreeing to engage in strategy restraint – it is acknowledging that there will be limits on the way in which it can exercise its power. Such an order, in effect, has "constitutional" characteristics. Limits are set on what a state within the order can do with its power advantages. Just as in constitutional polities, the implications of "winning" in politics are reduced. Weaker states realize that the implications of their inferior position are limited and perhaps temporary; operation within the order, despite their disadvantages, does not risk everything, nor will it give the dominant state a permanent advantage. Both the powerful and weak states agree to operate within the same order, regardless of radical asymmetries in the distribution of power.[58]

Multilateralism becomes a mechanism by which a dominant state and weaker ones can reach a bargain over the character of international order. The dominant state reduces its "enforcement costs" and succeeds in establishing an order where weaker states will participate willingly rather than resist or balance against the leading power.[59] It accepts some restrictions on how it can use its power. The rules and institutions that are created serve as an "investment" in the longer-run preservation of its power advantages. Weaker states agree to the order's rules and institutions. In return, they are assured that the worst excesses of the leading state – manifest as arbitrary and indiscriminate abuses of state power – will be avoided, and they gain institutional opportunities to work and help influence the leading state.[60]

Arguably, this institutional bargain has been at the heart of the postwar Western order. After World War II, the United States launched history's most ambitious era of institution building. The UN, the IMF, the World Bank, GATT, NATO, and other institutions that emerged provided the most rule-based structure for political and economic relations in world history. The United States was deeply ambivalent about making permanent security commitments to other states or allowing its political and economic policies to be dictated by intergovernmental bodies. The Soviet threat during the Cold War was critical in overcoming these doubts. Networks and political relationships were built that made American power farther-reaching and durable but also more predictable and restrained. As a former State Department official (now a Special Trade Representative) described this postwar bargain: "The more powerful participants in the system – especially the United States – did not forswear all their advantages, but neither did they exercise their strength without substantial restraint. Because the United States believed the Trilateral system was in its interests, it sacrificed some degree of national autonomy to promote it."[61]

In its most extreme versions, today's new unilateralism appears to be a violation of this postwar bargain. Certainly this is the view of some Europeans and others around the world. But if the Bush administration's unilateral moves are seen as more limited – and not emerging as a basic challenge to the foundations of multilateralism – this observation might be incorrect. The problem with the argument about order built on an institutional bargain and strategic restraint is that it reflects judgments by decision-makers about how much institutional restraint and commitment by the dominant state is necessary to secure how much participatory acquiescence and compliance by weaker states. The Bush administration might calculate that the order is sufficiently stable that the United States can resist an entire range of new multilateral agreements and still not trigger costly responses from its partners. It might also *miscalculate* in this regard and do great damage to the existing order. Yet if the thesis about the constitutional character of the postwar Western order is correct, a basic turn away from multilateralism should not occur. The institutionalized order, which facilitates intergovernmental bargaining and "voice opportunities" for America's weaker partners, should have some impact on American policy. The multilateral processes and "pulling and hauling" within the order should, at least to some extent, lead the United States to adjust its policies so as not to endanger the basic postwar bargain. And the Bush administration should act as if it recognizes the virtues of strategic restraint.

The struggle between the United States and its security partners over how to deal with Iraq put American strategic restraint and multilateral security cooperation to the test. Governments around the world were extremely uncomfortable with the prospect of American unilateral use of force. Reflecting this view, a French diplomat recently noted: "France is not interested in arguing with the United States. This is a matter of prin-

ciple. This is about the rules of the game in the world today. About putting
the Security Council in the center of international life. And not permitting
a nation, whatever nation it may be, to do what it wants, when it wants,
where it wants."[62] During the run-up to the Iraq war, the Bush administration insisted on its right to act without the multilateral approval of the
United Nations – but its decision to take the issue of Iraq back to the United
Nations in September 2002 is an indication that the administration sensed
the costs of unilateralism.[63] By seeking a UN Security Council resolution
that demands tough new weapons inspections and warning that serious
consequences will flow from an Iraqi failure to comply, the United States
acted to place its anti-Saddam policy in a multilateral framework.[64]

In the end, the Bush administration went to war with Iraq almost alone,
ignoring an uproar of international opposition, and without an explicit
Security Council resolution authorizing the use of force. Governments that
opposed the war had attempted to use the Security Council as a tool to
restrain the American unilateral and pre-emptive use of force, while the
Bush administration had attempted to use it to provide political cover for
its military operations aimed at regime change in Baghdad. The episode
reveals a search by the United States for a modicum of legitimacy for its
provocative act, but also a willingness to incur political costs and go it
alone if necessary. Still, the administration sought to wrap itself in the
authority of the United Nations. In making the case for war, President Bush
and UN Ambassador John Negreponte did not refer to the administration's
controversial National Security Strategy, which claimed an American unilateral right to use force at any time and place in anticipation of future
threats.[65] Rather, they defended the intervention in terms of the continuing
authority of UN resolutions and the failure of the Iraqi regime to comply
with disarmament agreements. The Bush administration pulled back from
the extreme unilateral brink: instead of asserting a new doctrine of preventive force, it couched its actions in terms of UN authority.

The diplomatic struggle at the United Nations over the American use
of force in Iraq reflects a more general debate among major states over
whether there will be agreed-upon rules and principles to guide and limit
the exercise of US power. The Bush administration seeks to protect its
freedom to act alone while giving just enough ground to preserve the
legitimacy of America's global position and garner support for the practical
problems of fighting terrorism. The administration is again making trade-
offs between autonomy and gaining the multilateral cooperation of other
states in confronting Iraq.

The pressure for multilateralism in the American use of force is weaker
and more diffuse than in other policy areas, such as trade and other economic realms. The incentives have less to do with the realization of specific

material interests and more to do with the search for legitimacy – which brings with it the possibility of greater cooperation by other countries and a reduction of the general political "drag" on the American exercise of power. But the Iraq war episode shows how these considerations can give way when a president and his advisors are utterly determined in their policy agenda.

Finally, this same basic struggle has been played out in the controversy over the ICC. European governments are moving forward to establish a world court with universal jurisdiction and strong independent judicial authority in the area of war crimes. This necessarily entails an encroachment on American sovereignty in cases where crimes by its own citizens are alleged. The US position during the Clinton years, when the treaty was being negotiated, was that the UN Security Council should be able to veto cases that were brought before the ICC. The United States sought to adopt the traditional postwar approach for multilateral agreements – that is, to give the major powers special opt-out and veto rights that make the binding obligations more contingent and subject to state review.[66] The proponents of contingent multilateralism calculated that escape clauses made the signing of such agreements more likely and that rules and norms promulgated by the agreements would nonetheless have a long-term impact even on powerful states. The ICC represents a newer style of multilateralism in which the scope of the agreement is universal and the binding character is law-based and anchored in international judicial authority.[67] The Europeans offered compromises in the ICC treaty: the court's statutes, framed to meet American concerns about political prosecutions, provide explicit guarantees that jurisdiction lies first with national governments.[68] This suggests that the gap between the "old" and "new" multilateralism is not inherently unbridgeable.

Political identity and multilateralism

Another source of American multilateralism emerges from the polity itself. The United States has a distinctive self-understanding of its political order, and this has implications for how it thinks about international political order. To be sure, there are multiple political traditions in the United States that reflect divergent and often competing ideas about how the United States should relate to the rest of the world.[69] These traditions variously counsel isolationism and activism, realism and idealism, aloofness and engagement in the conduct of American foreign affairs. But behind these political-intellectual traditions are deeper aspects of the American political identity that inform the way the United States seeks to build order in the larger global system. The enlightenment origin of the American founding has given the United States a political identity of self-perceived universal significance and scope.[70] The republican democratic tradition that enshrines the rule of law reflects an enduring American view that polities – domestic or international – are best organized around rules and principles of order. America's tradition of civic nationalism also reinforces this notion that the rule of law is the source of legitimacy and political inclusion. This tradition provides a background support for a multilateral foreign policy.[71]

The basic distinction between civic and ethnic nationalism is useful in locating this feature of the American political tradition. Civic identity is group identity composed of commitments to the nation's political creed. Race, religion, gender, language, and ethnicity are not relevant in defining a citizen's rights and inclusion within the polity. Shared beliefs in the country's principles and values embedded in the rule of law is the organizing basis for political order, and citizens are understood to be equal and rights-bearing individuals. Ethnic nationalism, in contrast, maintains that individual rights and participation within the polity are inherited – based on ethnic or racial or religious ties.[72]

Civic national identity has several implications for the multilateral orientation of American foreign policy. First, civic identity has tended to encourage the outward projection of US domestic principles of inclusive and rule-based international political organization. The American national identity is not based on ethnic or religious particularism but on a more general set of agreed-upon and normatively appealing principles. Ethnic and religious identities and disputes are pushed downward into civil society and removed from the political arena. When the United States gets involved in political conflicts around the world, it tends to look for the establishment of agreed-upon political principles and rules to guide the rebuilding of order. And when the United States promotes rule-based solutions to problems, it is strengthening the normative and principled basis for the exercise of its own power – and thereby making disparities in power more acceptable.

Because civic nationalism is shared with other Western states, it tends to be a source of cohesion and cooperation. Throughout the industrial democratic world, the dominant form of political identity is based on abstract and juridical rights and responsibilities that coexist with private ethnic and religious associations. Just as warring states and nationalism tend to reinforce each other, so do Western civic identity and cooperative political relations. Political order – domestic and international – is strengthened when there exists a substantial sense of community and shared identity. It matters that the leaders of today's advanced industrial states are not seeking to legitimate their power by making racial or imperialist appeals. Civic nationalism, rooted in shared commitment to democracy and the rule of law, provides a widely embraced identity across most of the American hegemonic order. At the same time, potentially divisive identity conflicts – rooted in antagonistic ethnic, religious, or class divisions – are dampened by being relegated to secondary status within civil society.[73] The notion that the United States participates in a wider Western community of shared values and like-minded states reinforces American multilateralist impulses.[74]

Third, the multicultural character of the American political identity also reinforces internationalist – and ultimately multilateral – foreign policy. Ruggie notes that culture wars continue in the United States between a pluralistic and multicultural identity, and between nativist and parochial alternatives, but that the core identity is still "cosmopolitan liberal" – an identity that tends to support instrumental multilateralism: "[T]he evocative significance of multilateral world order principles – a bias against exclusive bilateralist alliances, the rejection of discriminatory economic blocs, and facilitating means to bridge gaps of ethos, race, and religion – should resonate still for the American public, insofar as they continue to reflect its own sense of national identity."[75] US society is increasingly heterogeneous in race, ethnicity, and religion. This tends to reinforce an activist and inclusive foreign policy orientation and a bias in favor of rule-based and multilateral approaches to the conduct of American foreign policy.[76]

To be sure, American leaders can campaign against multilateral treaties and institutions and win votes. But this has been true across the last century, manifest most dramatically in the rejection of the League of Nations treaty in 1919, but also reflected in other defeats, such as the International Trade Organization after World War II. When President George W. Bush went to the United Nations to rally support for his hardline approach to Iraq, he did not articulate a central role for the world body in promoting international security and peace. He told the General Assembly: "We will work with the UN Security Council for the necessary resolutions." But he also made it clear that "[t]he purposes of the United States should not be doubted. The Security Council resolutions will be enforced . . . or action will be unavoidable."[77] In contrast, just 12 years earlier, when the elder President Bush appeared before the General Assembly to press his case for resisting Iraq's invasion of Kuwait, he offered a "vision of a new partnership of nations . . . a partnership based on consultations, cooperation and collective action, especially through international and regional organizations, a partnership united by principle and the rule of law and supported by an equitable sharing of both cost and commitment."[78] It would appear that American presidents can articulate quite divergent visions of American foreign policy, each resonating in its own way with ideas and beliefs within the American polity. If this is true, American presidents do have political and intellectual space to shape policy – and they are not captives of a unilateralist-minded public.

Recent public opinion findings confirm this view and actually suggest that the American public is quite willing and eager to conduct foreign policy within multilateral frameworks. In a comprehensive poll of American and European attitudes on international affairs, the German Marshall Fund and the Chicago Council on Foreign Relations found that a clear majority of Americans actually favored joining the European Union in ratifying the Kyoto accord on global warming and the treaty creating the ICC. American public attitudes reveal a general multilateral bent. When given three alternatives about the role of the United States in solving international problems, most Americans (71 percent) said that the United States should act to solve problems together with other countries, and only 17 percent said that "as the sole remaining superpower the United States should continue to be the pre-eminent world leader in solving international problems." There is also high – and increased – support for strengthening the United Nations, participating in UN peacekeeping operations, and using diplomatic methods to combat terrorism. When asked if the United States should or should not take action alone if it does not have the support of allies in responding to international crises, 61 percent said that the United States should not act alone. Only a third of the American public indicated that the United States should act alone.[79]

Conclusion

The rise of unipolarity is not an adequate explanation for recent unilateralism in American foreign policy. Nor is the United States doomed to shed its multilateral orientation. The dominant power position of the United States creates opportunities to go it alone, but the pressures and incentives that shape decisions about multilateral cooperation are quite varied and crosscutting. The sources of multilateralism – which can be traced to system, institutional, and domestic structural locations – still exist and continue to shape and restrain the Bush administration, unilateral inclinations notwithstanding.

Multilateralism can be manifest at the system, ordering, and contract levels of international order. The critical question is not whether the Bush administration is more inclined than previous administrations to reject specific multilateral treaties and agreements (in some instances, it is), but whether the accumulation of these refusals undermines the deeper organizational logic of multilateralism in the Western and global system. At the ordering or foundational level, multilateralism is manifest in what might be termed "indivisible" economic and security relations. The basic organization of the order is multilateral in that it is open and tied together through diffuse reciprocity and cooperative security. But there is little or no evidence that ordering multilateralism is eroding or under attack.[80]

The sources of unilateralism are more specific and contingent. The United States has always been ambivalent about multilateral commitments. Political judgments about the costs of reduced policy autonomy and the benefits of rule-based order are at the heart of this ambivalence. The dominant area of American unilateralism is arms control and the use of force. The Bush administration has brought into office a policy elite that represents the skeptical side of a long-standing debate within the foreign policy community about the merits and limits of arms control. The shift from Cold War arms control to the more uncertain and unwieldy world of weapons of mass destruction (WMD) and nonproliferation reinforces these biases. But even in the area of WMD proliferation, the United States has incentives to develop multilateral mechanisms to pursue sanctions, inspections, and the use of force.

Beyond these conclusions, three questions remain in the debate over the future of multilateralism. First, what precisely are the costs of unilateralism? The unilateralists in the Bush administration act under the assumption that they are minimal. If aggrieved states are not able to take action against the United States – such action ultimately would entail the threat of some sort of counterhegemonic coalition – then the costs of unilateralism will never truly threaten the American global position. This is particularly true in the area of world politics that has been historically the most immune to binding multilateral rules and institutions – namely, arms control and the use of force. But in areas such as trade, other countries can impose tangible costs on the United States. This helps explain why the United States has been more multilaterally forthcoming in trade than in other areas. The economic gains that flow from the coordination of economic relations also reinforce multilateralism. Additionally, a less tangible cost of unilateralism is when such foreign policy actions threaten the overall legitimacy of the American global position. When the United States exercises its power in ways generally seen around the world as legitimate, its "costs of enforcement" go down. But when legitimacy declines, the United States must engage in more difficult and protracted power struggles with other states. Other states cannot fundamentally challenge the United States, but they can make its life more difficult. Threats to the international legitimacy of the United States can register within the American policy as a violation of its own political identity. The United States wants to act abroad in a way that is consistent with its self-image as a law-abiding, responsible country. How, when, and to what extent the costs of unilateralism matter is an ongoing puzzle.

Second, to what extent does the existing multilateral order reinforce current choices about multilateralism? I have pointed out that the United States created a web of multilateral rules and institutions over the last half century that has taken the shape of a mature political order – and the United States is now embedded in this order. A vast latticework of intergovernmental processes and institutional relationships exists across the advanced industrial democracies. This multilateral complex ultimately serves to reduce the uncertainties and worries that weaker states would otherwise have about operating in a system dominated by a singularly powerful America. But questions linger: How powerful are the effects of this multilateral complex on American foreign policy? Does the "pulling and hauling" that is set in motion by this multilateral order actually discipline American power and its unilateral temptations?

Third, how significant is the challenge of the "new multilateralism" to the older-style postwar multilateralism that the United States championed? I argue in this paper that Washington's resistance to new multilateral agreements has something to do with the new *type* of multilateralism. The older multilateralism came with escape clauses, veto rights, and weighted voting mechanisms that allowed the United States and other major states to protect their interests and gave room for maneuvering. The new multilateralism is more legally binding in character. The ICC is perhaps the best example. But how much "new multilateralism" is really out there? Is this a clash that is primarily centered on the ICC but not on the wider range of policy areas, or is it a more basic and serious emerging divide? How wide is the gap? Some experts argue that the exceptions and protections built into the Rome Treaty of the ICC did move in the direction of the old multilateral safeguards. Moreover, although the WTO manifests "new multilateralism" characteristics, the United States has been one of its major champions. So it is not clear how wide the divide is between old and new multilateralism or even if the conflict over these types of multilateralism pits the United States against the rest of the world. We need to know more about the sources of the new multilateralism. Is it a result of functional adjustments to more complex socioeconomic relations – as the WTO would seem to suggest – or a result of new issues, such as human rights and norms of justice, that make escape clauses and exceptions more difficult to countenance?

What is certain is that deep forces and incentives keep the United States on a multilateral path – rooted in considerations of economic interest, power management, and political tradition. To ignore these pressures and incentives would entail a revolution in American foreign policy that even the most hardline unilateralist in Washington today does not imagine. The worst unilateral impulses coming out of the Bush administration are so harshly criticized around the world because so many countries have accepted the multilateral vision of international order that the United States has articulated over most of the twentieth century.

Notes

1 Quoted in Balz 2003: A1. This unilateral turn did not begin with the Bush administration. Although the Clinton administration articulated a foreign policy strategy of "assertive multilateralism," its record was more mixed. In June 1997, the Clinton administration declined to join most of the world's countries in signing the Ottawa Convention on the Banning of Land Mines. In 1999 the Senate rejected the Comprehensive Test Ban Treaty, ignoring warnings from experts that such a move would weaken global nonproliferation norms, and it signaled its opposition to the Kyoto Protocol and the ICC. The Clinton administration did not await UN Security Council approval for its 1998 bombing of Iraq, nor did it seek such approval in the American-led North Atlantic Treaty Organization bombing campaign against Serbia in the spring of 1999. For an excellent summary of recent multilateral agreements rejected by the United States, see Patrick 2002.
2 Schlesinger 2000.
3 Krauthammer 2001: A29.
4 Purdum 2002: 1.
5 This definition of multilateralism draws on Keohane 1990 and Ruggie 1993. See also Van Oudenaren 2003.
6 Bull 1977. The norm of sovereign equality is what Philpott 2001 calls the "side by side" principle. See also Reus-Smit 1997.
7 Ruggie 1993: 12.
8 Keohane 1990: 731.
9 This distinction points to what might be called informal manifestations of multilateralism. The United States has at least four routes to take action: (1) it can go it alone, without consulting others; (2) it can consult others, but then go it alone; (3) it can consult and take action with others, not on the basis of agreed-upon rules and principles that define the terms of its relationship with those others, but rather on the basis of the current situation's needs; or (4) it can take action with others, on the basis of agreed-upon rules and principles. The first route is clearly unilateral. The second and third can be coded as multilateral, even though action is not taken in accord with formal multilateral rules and institutions. In areas such as the use of force, where formal and binding multilateral rules and principles are least evident, the difference between unilateral and multilateral action will likely fall between the first route and the second and third. For a discussion of formal and informal institutions, see Koromenos et al. 2001.
10 Schroeder 1994; Elrod 1976.

11 Goldstein et al. 2001.

12 This is the story told by Crozier 1964 about politics within large-scale organizations. Each individual within a complex organizational hierarchy is continually engaged in a dual struggle: to tie his colleagues to precise rule-based
behavior, thereby creating a more stable and certain environment in which
to operate, and to retain as much autonomy and discretion as possible for
himself.

13 Fearon 1997.

14 I sketch this logic in Ikenberry 2003.

15 On the way in which NATO multilateralism restrained American exercise of
power, see Weber 1993.

16 For discussions of America's divergent postwar institutional strategies in
Europe and East Asia, see Grieco 1997 and Hemmer and Katzenstein
2002.

17 Katzenstein 1997: 37.

18 This is emphasized by Leffler 1992 and Pollard 1985.

19 Ruggie 1993.

20 Keohane 1986.

21 National Intelligence Council 2000.

22 State Department data, reported in Patrick 2002.

23 The rise in bilateral treaties reflects a post-Cold War surge in tax, investment,
and extradition agreements with countries that previously were part of the
Soviet bloc. Multilateral treaties – which most often deal with human rights
protections, international organizations, and environmental protections –
tend to be more regulatory and politically contested. Treaties submitted to
the Senate have increasingly been passed with reservations, understandings,
and conditions. This shows that the United States has more reservations about
multilateral commitments, but it provides a way for the country to join international agreements that it does not fully agree with and that it might not
otherwise join. See Schocken and Caron 2001.

24 Since 1945 the US executive has submitted 958 bilateral or multilateral treaties to the Senate. Of these treaties, 505 are bilateral and 453 are multilateral.
These do not include executive agreements, such as the North American Free
Trade Agreement and other multilateral trade agreements. There have been
approximately 11,000 executive agreements signed during the postwar
period. (Interestingly, the only complete record of these executive agreements is contained on green index cards at the State Department, presided
over by an elderly official who appears to be the only person who knows
where each is located.)

25 Boot 2002: A29.

26 The classic statement of structural realism is Waltz 1979. The legal scholar
Lassa Oppenheim argued that a balance of power among states is "an indispensable condition of the very existence of international law. . . . If the
Powers cannot keep one another in check, no rules of law will have force,
since an overwhelming State will naturally try to act according to discretion
and disobey the law" (1912: 193).

27 Economic comparisons calculated from Organisation for Economic Cooperation and Development statistics (July 1999 Web edition). Gross national product measures are figured at 1990 prices and exchange rates. For military capacity, see International Institute for Strategic Studies 1999.

28 The best description of American unipolarity is Wohlforth 1999.

29 Realists differ on the uses and importance of multilateral institutions. See Schweller and Priess 1997 and Jervis 1999.

30 Kagan 2002: 4.

31 Odell 2000.

32 Victor 2001.

33 Waltz 2000: 24.

34 Zakaria 2002: 76.

35 Brooks and Wohlforth 2002 argue that unipolar power enables the United States to act unilaterally, but they go on to say that this does not mean that unilateralism is an optimal strategy for unipolar America. Indeed, unipolarity gives the United States the ability to think about long-term security, for which they argue a multilateral – or "benevolent" – approach is best.

36 In this regard, there is a tension in the neorealist account of unipolarity. Those who argue that unilateralism is unavoidable because of overwhelming American power do so because in the absence of an effective countervailing coalition, there is no "restraint" on US foreign policy. But neorealist mechanisms of selection and competition are premised upon the need for the state to worry about relative power. If the United States does not need to care about relative power, the structural effects of anarchy are actually quite unimportant to American behavior. This suggests that domestic, ideological, and other factors are stronger determinants of US foreign policy in the current era.

37 As one journalist reports, "The Bush administration is stocked with skeptics of international treaties and multilateral organizations" (Kessler 2002: A1).

38 This split in American strategic thinking about the efficacy of arms control as it broke into the open over the failed SALT II treaty during the Carter and Reagan years is detailed in Graham 2002.

39 Fidler 2001: A6.

40 On the logic of cooperation in US–Soviet arms-control negotiations, see Weber 1992.

41 The Bush administration's rejection of the Convention on Trade in Light Arms appears to be a more straightforward deferral to the National Rifle Association.

42 Because of America's unrivaled military power, it is also true that the costs of cheating by other states have been reduced. For this reason, the explanation of shifting costs and benefits is inadequate without an appreciation of how elite ideologies and policy ideas color such calculations.

43 For example, Under-Secretary of State John Bolton, prior to joining the administration, argued that a great struggle was unfolding between what he calls Americanists and globalists. Globalists are depicted as elite activist groups who seek to strengthen "global governance" through a widening net

of agreements on environment, human rights, labor, health, and political-military affairs and whose not-so-hidden agenda is to enmesh the United States in international laws and institutions that rob the country of its sovereignty. Americanists, according to Bolton, have finally awoken and are now seizing back the country's control over its own destiny. This is a view that evinces not just a healthy skepticism of multilateral rules and agreements, but sees American resistance to the encroachment of those rules and agreements as a patriotic duty (see Bolton 2000).

44 For a general characterization of this unilateral – or neo-imperial – thinking, see Ikenberry 2002. Its grand strategic agenda is discussed in Baker 2003 and Ricks 2001.

45 Snyder 1991; Kennedy 1987; Kupchan 1994.

46 Snyder 2003.

47 Nye 2002.

48 For a discussion of international regime creation that distinguishes between imposed and consensual processes, see Young 1991.

49 Chinkin 2000; Reisman 2000.

50 Indeed, some commentators worry precisely that the American position will lead to a new principle about the use of force. Henry Kissinger said to the Senate Foreign Relations Committee: "It cannot be either the American national interest or the world's interest to develop principles that grant every nation an unfettered right of preemption against its own definition of threats to its security" (quoted in Harding 2002: 10).

51 Keohane 1990: 742.

52 Keohane 1984.

53 Keohane 1990.

54 There is an expanding line of research exploring the logic of credible commitment. For an important statement of this problem, see North and Weingast 1989.

55 Vernon 1995; Jackson 1994; Winham 1998.

56 This argument is developed in Ikenberry 2001.

57 The larger literature on hegemonic stability theory argues that the presence of a single powerful state is conducive to multilateral regime creation. The hegemonic state – by virtue of its power – is able to act on its long-term interests rather than struggle over short-term distributional gains. This allows it to identify its own national interest with the openness and stability of the larger global system. The classic statement of this thesis is Gilpin 1981. In Keohane's formulation, the theory holds that "hegemonic structures of power, dominated by a single country, are most conducive to the development of strong international regimes whose rules are relatively precise and well obeyed." Such states have the capacity to maintain regimes that they favor through the use of coercion or positive sanctions. The hegemonic state gains the ability to shape and dominate the international order, while providing a flow of benefits to smaller states that is sufficient to persuade them to acquiesce. (See Keohane 1980: 132.)

58 For a discussion of constitutional logic and international relations, see Ikenberry 1998.
59 For sophisticated arguments along these lines, see Martin 1993 and Lake 1999.
60 Ikenberry 2001: ch. 3.
61 Zoellick 1999: 5.
62 Farley and McManus 2002: A1.
63 A new investigative report by Bob Woodward (2002) shows in detail how the multilateral approach to Iraq won out in administration policy circles.
64 Wright and McManus 2002; Preston 2002; Peel 2002.
65 National Security Council 2002.
66 Schense and Washburn 2001.
67 The ICC is treaty-based, and its jurisdiction is only over citizens/subjects of signatory parties and citizens/subjects of nonstate signatories that commit crimes on the territory of signatory parties. It aims to universalize this jurisdiction.
68 Stephens 2002.
69 See surveys in McDougall 1997 and Mead 2001.
70 Huntington 1983.
71 There are, of course, political ideas and traditions in the American experience that support unilateral and isolationist policies, which flourished from the founding well into the 1930s and still exist today. But these alternatives to multilateralism, as Legro 2000 argues, were discredited in the face of World Wars I and II and opened the way to internationalist and multilateral ideas and strategies. These multilateral ideas and strategies, in turn, are given support by the deeper American rule of law and civic national traditions.
72 This distinction is made by Smith 1986.
73 Deudney and Ikenberry 1999.
74 While Woodrow Wilson sought to justify American post-war international-ism on the basis of American exceptionalism and a duty to lead the world to democratic salvation, advocates of internationalism after World War II emphasized that the United States belonged to a community of Western democracies that implied multilateral duties and loyalties; see Stephanson 1995. For the claim that this wider Western community has reinforced American internationalism and multilateral commitments, see Risse-Kappen 1995 and 1996; Hampton 1996; Nau 2002. This insight about Western com-munity has also been used to explain the rise of NATO in the Atlantic and the absence of a similar postwar multilateral security organization in East Asia; see Hemmer and Katzenstein 2002.
75 Ruggie 1996: 170.
76 On the ways in which American ethnic groups encourage foreign policy activism, see Smith 2000.
77 Bush 2001: 4.
78 Bush 1990: 3.
79 Chicago Council and German Marshall Fund 2002: 27.

80   In this sense, for the system to become less multilateral, there would need to be evidence that economic and security ties were becoming more divisible: an erosion of ties in the direction of separate regional spheres, a decline in mutually agreed-upon rules and principles of order, and a lessening of open economic and societal interaction.

References

Baker, Gerard (2003) "After Iraq, Where Will Bush Go Next?" *The Financial Times*, April 14, p. 19.

Balz, Dan (2003) "President Puts Onus Back on Iraqi Leader," *The Washington Post*, March 7, p. A1.

Bolton, John (2000) "Should We Take Global Governance Seriously?" *Chicago Journal of International Law* 1: 2: 205–22.

Boot, Max (2002) "Doctrine of the 'big enchilada.'" *The Washington Post*, October 14, p. A29.

Brooks, Stephen G., and William C. Wohlforth (2002) "American Primacy in Perspective," *Foreign Affairs* 81: 4: 20–33.

Bull, Hedley (1977) *The Anarchical Society: A Study of Order in World Politics* (London: Macmillan).

Bush, George H. W. (1990) Address before the United Nations General Assembly, October 1.

Bush, George W. (2001) Address before the United Nations General Assembly, September 12.

Chicago Council on Foreign Relations, and German Marshall Fund of the United States (2002) *A World Transformed: Foreign Policy Attitudes of the US Public after September 11*. Available at <www.worldviews.org/docs/U.S.9-11v2.pdf>. Accessed April 29, 2003.

Chinkin, Christine (2000) "The State that Acts Alone: Bully, Good Samaritan or Iconoclast?" *European Journal of International Law* 11: 1: 31–41.

Crozier, Michael (1964) *The Bureaucratic Phenomenon* (Chicago: University of Chicago Press).

Deudney, Daniel, and G. John Ikenberry (1999) "The Nature and Sources of Liberal International Order," *Review of International Studies* 25: 2: 179–96.

Elrod, Richard B. (1976) "The Concert of Europe: A Fresh Look at an International System," *World Politics* 28: 2: 159–74.

Farley, Maggie, and Doyle McManus (2002) "To Some, Real Threat is US," *The Los Angeles Times*, October 30, p. A1.

Fearon, James D. (1997) "Signaling Foreign Policy Interests: Tying Hands Versus Sinking Costs," *Journal of Conflict Resolution* 41: 1: 68–90.

Fidler, Stephen (2001) "Conservatives Determined to Carry Torch for US Missile Defense," *The Financial Times*, July 12, p. 7.

Gilpin, Robert (1981) *War and Change in World Politics* (New York: Cambridge University Press).

Goldstein, Judith L., Miles Kahler, Robert O. Keohane, and Anne-Marie Slaughter, eds. (2001) *Legalization and World Politics* (Cambridge, Mass.: MIT Press).

Graham, Thomas, Jr. (2002) *Disarmament Sketches: Three Decades of Arms Control and International Law* (Seattle: University of Washington Press).

Grieco, Joseph (1997) "Systematic Sources of Variation in Regional Institution-alization in Western Europe, East Asia, and the Americas," in Edward D. Mansfield and Helen V. Milner, eds., *The Political Economy of Regionalism* (New York: Columbia University Press), pp. 164–87.

Hampton, Mary N. (1996) *The Wilsonian Impulse: US Foreign Policy, the Alliance, and German Unification* (Westport, Conn.: Praeger).

Harding, James (2002) "Albright Laments 'rash exuberance' over Iraq," *The Financial Times*, September 27, p. 10.

Hemmer, Christopher, and Peter J. Katzenstein (2002) "Why Is There No NATO in Asia? Collective Identity, Regionalism, and the Origins of Multilateralism," *International Organization* 56: 3: 575–607.

Huntington, Samuel P. (1983) *American Politics: The Promise of Disharmony* (Cambridge, Mass.: Harvard University Press).

Ikenberry, G. John (1998) "Constitutional Politics in International Relations," *European Journal of International Relations* 4: 2: 147–77.

Ikenberry, G. John (2001) *After Victory: Institutions, Strategic Restraint, and the Rebuilding of Order after Major Wars* (Princeton: Princeton University Press).

Ikenberry, G. John (2002) "America's Imperial Ambition," *Foreign Affairs* 81: 5: 44–60.

Ikenberry, G. John (2003) "State Power and the Institutional Bargain: America's Ambivalent Economic and Security Multilateralism," in Rosemary Foot, S. Neil MacFarlane, and Michael Mastanduno, eds., *American Hegemony and International Organizations* (London: Oxford University Press), pp. 49–70.

International Institute for Strategic Studies (1999) *The Military Balance 1999–2000* (London: Oxford University Press).

Jackson, John H. (1994) "The World Trade Organization, Dispute Settlement, and Codes of Conduct," in Susan M. Collins and Barry P. Bosworth, eds., *The New GATT: Implications for the United States* (Washington DC: Brookings Institution Press), pp. 63–75.

Jervis, Robert (1999) "Realism, Neoliberalism, and Cooperation: Understanding the Debate," *International Security* 24: 1: 42–63.

Kagan, Robert (2002) "Power and Weakness," *Policy Review* 113 (June and July): 3–28.

Katzenstein, Peter J. (1997) "The Cultural Foundations of Murakami's Polymorphic Liberalism," in Kozo Yamamura, ed., *A Vision of a New Liberalism? Critical Essays on Murakami's Anticlassical Analysis* (Stanford: Stanford University Press), pp. 23–40.

Kennedy, Paul (1987) *The Rise and Fall of the Great Powers* (New York: Random House).

Keohane, Robert O. (1980) "The Theory of Hegemonic Stability and Changes in International Economic Regimes, 1967–1977," in Ole R. Holsti, Randolph M. Siverson, and Alexander L. George, eds., *Change in the International System* (Boulder, Colo.: Westview Press), pp. 131–62.

Keohane, Robert O. (1984) *After Hegemony: Cooperation and Discord in the World Political Economy* (Princeton: Princeton University Press).

Keohane, Robert O. (1986) "Reciprocity in International Relations," *International Organization* 40: 1: 1–27.

Keohane, Robert O. (1990) "Multilateralism: An Agenda for Research," *International Journal* 45: 4: 731–64.

Kessler, Glenn (2002) "Reaffirming a Policy of Preemption," *The Washington Post*, September 13, p. A1.

Koromenos, Barbara, Charles Lipson, and Duncan Snidal (2001) "The Rational Design of International Institutions," *International Organization* 55: 4: 761–800.

Krauthammer, Charles (2001) "The New Unilateralism," *The Washington Post*, June 8, p. A29.

Kupchan, Charles A. (1994) *The Vulnerability of Empire* (Ithaca, NY: Cornell University Press).

Lake, David A. (1999) *Entangling Relations: American Foreign Policy in Its Century* (Princeton: Princeton University Press).

Leffler, Melvyn P. (1992) *A Preponderance of Power: National Security, the Truman Administration, and the Cold War* (Stanford: Stanford University Press).

Legro, Jeffrey (2000) "Whence American Internationalism," *International Organization* 54: 2: 253–89.

Martin, Lisa L. (1993) "The Rational State Choice of Multilateralism," in John Gerard Ruggie, ed., *Multilateralism Matters: The Theory and Praxis of an Institutional Form* (New York: Columbia University Press), pp. 91–122.

McDougall, Walter A. (1997) *Promised Land, Crusader State: The American Encounter with the World since 1776* (Boston: Houghton Mifflin).

Mead, Walter Russell (2001) *Special Providence: American Foreign Policy and How It Changed the World* (New York: Knopf).

National Intelligence Council (2000) "Global Trends 2015: A Dialogue About the Future with Nongovernment Experts," available at <www.fas.org/irp/cia/product/globaltrends2015/index.html>. Accessed May 16, 2003.

National Security Council (2002) "The National Security Strategy of the United States of America," (Washington, DC: Office of the President), September 17.

Nau, Henry R. (2002) *At Home Abroad: Identity and Power in American Foreign Policy* (Ithaca, NY: Cornell University Press).

North, Douglass, and Barry Weingast (1989) "Constitutions and Commitment: The Evolution of Institution Governing Public Choice in Seventeenth-Century England," *Journal of Economic History* 49: 4: 803–32.

Nye, Joseph S., Jr. (2002) *The Paradox of American Power: Why the World's Only Superpower Can't Go It Alone* (New York: Oxford University Press).

Odell, John S. (2000) *Negotiating the World Economy* (Ithaca, NY: Cornell University Press).

Oppenheim, Lassa (1912) *International Law*, 2nd edn. (London: Longmans, Green, and Company).

Patrick, Stewart (2002) "Multilateralism and Its Discontents: The Causes and Consequences of US Ambivalence," in Stewart Patrick and Shepard Forman, eds., *Multilateralism and US Foreign Policy: Ambivalent Engagement* (Boulder, Colo.: Lynne Rienner Publishers), pp. 1–44.

Peel, Quentin (2002) "Bush Starts to Look for Allies," *The Financial Times*, October 9, p. 19.

Philpott, Daniel (2001) *Revolutions in Sovereignty: How Ideas Shaped Modern International Relations* (Princeton: Princeton University Press).

Pollard, Robert A. (1985) *Economic Security and the Origins of the Cold War, 1945–1950* (New York: Columbia University Press).

Preston, Julia (2002) "Bush's Step Toward the UN Met by Warm Welcome," *The New York Times*, September 13, p. A11.

Purdum, Todd S. (2002) "Embattled, Scrutinized, Powell Soldiers on," *The New York Times*, July 25, p. A1.

Reisman, W. Michael (2000) "Unilateral Action and the Transformation of the World Constitutive Process: The Special Problem of Humanitarian Intervention," *European Journal of International Law* 11: 1: 3–18.

Reus-Smit, Christian (1997) "The Constitutional Structure of International Society and the Nature of Fundamental Institutions," *International Organization* 51: 4: 555–89.

Ricks, Thomas E. (2001) "Empire or Not? A Quiet Debate Over US Role," *The Washington Post*, August 21, p. A1.

Risse-Kappen, Thomas (1995) *Cooperation among Democracies: The European Influence on US Foreign Policy* (Princeton: Princeton University Press).

Risse-Kappen, Thomas (1996) "Collective Identity in a Democratic Community: The Case of NATO," in Peter J. Katzenstein, ed., *The Culture of National Security: Norms and Identity in World Politics* (New York: Columbia University Press), pp. 357–99.

Ruggie, John Gerard (1993) "Multilateralism: The Anatomy of an Institution," in John Gerard Ruggie, ed., *Multilateralism Matters: The Theory and Praxis of an Institutional Form* (New York: Columbia University Press), pp. 3–47.

Ruggie, John Gerard (1996) *Winning the Peace: American and World Order in the New Era* (New York: Columbia University Press).

Schense, Jennifer, and John L. Washburn (2001) "The United States and the International Criminal Court," *The International Lawyer* 35 (Summer): 614–22.

Schlesinger, Arthur M., Jr. (2000) "Unilateralism in Historical Perspective," in Gwyn Prins, ed., *Understanding Unilateralism in American Foreign Relations* (London: The Royal Institute of International Affairs), pp. 18–29.

Schocken, Celina M., and David Caron (2001) "Trends in US Treatymaking Practice: 1945–2000," unpublished paper, University of California, Berkeley.

Schroeder, Paul W. (1994) *The Transformation of European Politics, 1763–1848* (Oxford: Oxford University Press).

Schweller, Randall L., and David Priess (1997) "A Tale of Two Realisms: Expanding the Institutions Debate," *Mershon International Studies Review* 41: 1: 1–32.

Smith, Anthony D. (1986) *The Ethnic Origins of Nations* (Oxford: Blackwell).

Smith, Tony (2000) *Foreign Attachments: The Power of Ethnic Groups in the Making of American Foreign Policy* (Cambridge, Mass.: Harvard University Press).

Snyder, Jack (1991) *Myths of Empire: Domestic Politics and International Ambition* (Ithaca, NY: Cornell University Press).

Snyder, Jack (2003) "Imperial Temptations," *The National Interest* (Spring): 29–40.

Stephanson, Anders (1995) *Manifest Destiny: American Expansionism and the Empire of Right* (New York: Hill and Wang).

Stephens, Philip (2002) "American Breaks the Global Ties," *The Financial Times*, July 5, p. 19.

Van Oudenaren, John (2003) "What is 'multilateral'?" *Policy Review* 117 (February and March): 33–47.

Vernon, Raymond (1995) "The World Trade Organization: A New Stage in International Trade and Development," *Harvard International Law Journal* 36 (Spring): 329–40.

Victor, David G. (2001) *The Collapse of the Kyoto Protocol and the Struggle to Slow Global Warming* (Princeton: Princeton University Press).

Waltz, Kenneth N. (1979) *Theory of International Politics* (Reading, Mass.: Addison-Wesley).

Waltz, Kenneth N. (2000) "Structural Realism after the Cold War," *International Security* 25: 1: 5–41.

Weber, Steve (1992) *Cooperation and Discord in US–Soviet Arms Control* (Princeton: Princeton University Press).

Weber, Steve (1993) "Shaping the Postwar Balance of Power: Multilateralism in NATO," in John Gerard Ruggie, ed., *Multilateralism Matters: The Theory and Praxis of an Institutional Form* (New York: Columbia University Press), pp. 233–92.

Winham, Gilbert R. (1998) "The World Trade Organization: Institution-building in the Multilateral Trade System," *World Economy* 21: 3: 349–68.

Wohlforth, William (1999) "The Stability of a Unipolar World," *International Security* 24: 1: 5–41.

Woodward, Bob (2002) "A Struggle for the President's Heart and Mind," *The Washington Post*, November 17, p. A1.

Wright, Robin, and Doyle McManus (2002) "Bush Veers From Unilateral Course with Appeal to UN," *The Los Angeles Times*, September 13, p. A1.

Young, Oran (1991) "Political Leadership and Regime Formation: On the Development of Institution in International Society," *International Organization* 45: 3: 281–308.

Zakaria, Fareed (2002) "Our Way: The Trouble with Being the World's Only Superpower," *The New Yorker*, October 14, pp. 72–81.

Zoellick, Robert B. (1999) "The United States," in Robert B. Zoellick, Peter D. Sutherland, and Hisashi Owada, eds., *21st Century Strategies of the Trilateral Countries: In Concert or Conflict?* (New York: The Trilateral Commission), pp. 1–25.

Index

Abbas II 77
accessibility 95–6, 128–30, 131–2, 156, 159–60, 203
accommodation strategy 198
accountability 129, 156, 191, 203
Acheson, Dean 25, 32, 34, 39, 153, 202, 205
Adenauer, Konrad 37
advertising 103
Afghanistan 11, 214, 222, 236
After Victory (Ikenberry) 2
Ahmed Arabi (Arabi Pasha) 76
Albright, Madeleine 10
alliances
  ad hoc counter-hegemonic 91
  as pacts of restraint 122, 202–3, 215
  postwar 6, 10, 66–72, 150, 203–4, 251
  US–UK on terrorism 210
Allied Council for Japan 70
American hegemony
  and civic identity 163–4
  decline 3, 21, 24, 80, 99
  and "empire by invitation" 22, 35–9, 94, 155–6, 190
  getting it right 10, 186–96, 200
  global backlash 187, 224–6, 227–8

liberal characteristics or "stakeholder" 10, 146, 156–61, 186–96
nature of 22, 89, 133, 157–60, 165, 203
origins of 3–4, 21–50
penetrated and reciprocal aspects of 6, 89, 93–6, 131–2, 133, 149, 159–60
and public opinion 200, 233–4, 242, 259, 269
reluctant 157–8, 165
resistance to 164, 193, 214–15, 224–6, 233
American power
  acceptability of 95–6, 189–92, 227–8
  and capitalist democracy 8, 143–71
  geography and historical staging 154–6
  limits of postwar 25–7, 35, 40, 43
  mis-measure of 234–5
  robustness and durability of 146–65, 203
  safeguards against excessive 209–10
American system 198–9
  political foundations of the 201–4

Index